"INVICTA"

WITH THE FIRST BATTALION THE
QUEEN'S OWN ROYAL WEST KENT
REGIMENT IN THE GREAT WAR

THE PRESENTATION OF COLOURS, DOVER, AUGUST 6TH, 1909

"INVICTA"

WITH THE FIRST BATTALION THE QUEEN'S OWN ROYAL WEST KENT REGIMENT IN THE GREAT WAR

BY

MAJOR C. V. MOLONY

London

NISBET & CO. LTD.

22 BERNERS STREET W.1

First published in 1923

Printed & bound by Antony Rowe Ltd, Eastbourne

PREFACE

THIS book, for the most part compiled from the war diary and accounts of eye-witnesses, by Major C. V. Molony, a former Officer of the 1st Battalion The Queen's Own Royal West Kent Regiment, and now issued by those serving with it, is intended to chronicle, with as much detail as possible, the History of the 1st Battalion during the war of 1914-1918; in the hope that it will be valued both by past and present members, as a reminder of the Battalion's magnificent record and as a tribute to those who fought and died for it.

A debt of gratitude is due to Major C. V. Molony for his indispensable help, to Lieut. F. Russell who made the final arrangements for its publication, to Brigadier-General A. H. Hussey for permission to reproduce certain maps, and to Messrs Nisbet & Co., the publishers, for their valuable advice and assistance.

H. D. B.-D.

" QUO FAS ET GLORIA DUCUNT "

CONTENTS

LIST OF ILLUSTRATIONS

Portraits

Photographs

LIST OF MAPS

"INVICTA"

WITH THE FIRST BATTALION THE QUEEN'S OWN ROYAL WEST KENT REGIMENT IN THE GREAT WAR

CHAPTER I

FROM MOBILISATION TO MONS

MOBILISATION.—The 1st Battalion The Queen's Own Royal West Kent Regiment was quartered in Richmond Barracks, Dublin, when it received orders to mobilise on 4th August 1914. It had been commanded by Lieut.-Col. A. Martyn since the autumn of 1912, and it formed part of the 13th Brigade. The other battalions forming this were the 2nd Bn. King's Scottish Borderers, the 2nd Bn. Duke of Wellington's West Riding Regiment, and the 2nd Bn. King's Own Yorkshire Light Infantry. Brigadier-General Cuthbert had recently succeeded the late Major-General Thompson Capper in command of the Brigade.

Except that it had taken part in the little Adarega Campaign from Aden in 1901, the Battalion had not been on active service since the operations on the Indian Frontier in 1897. However, it was in fine order, well disciplined, well trained, and good at musketry. Fortunate in the possession of a populous recruiting district and a good name among the recruit-supplying classes, the Regiment had, for many years, experienced no difficulty in keeping its ranks filled from its own area.

The men were nearly all men of Kent. As soon as they enlisted, recruits began to receive instruction in the history of their Regiment, and, while at the depot at Maidstone, were frequently taken to see the old Colours and numerous memorials in All Saints' Church. Therefore, by the time they joined the Battalions they were well on the way towards that pride which, when combined with the confidence in their leaders and their weapons that the right sort of training instils, is so essential to the highest efficiency.

Mobilisation proceeded smoothly according to the Battalion Scheme based on Regulations, though it was somewhat hampered by the necessity for finding guards for important points in and about Dublin. The men of the Army Reserve, as they came over from Maidstone, were exercised as far as time would allow in marching, drill and musketry, in order to remove the rust occasioned by their more or less prolonged absence from the service ; supplementary equipment was issued and horses and harness to complete the transport were drawn. Since a Battalion on the Home Establishment is numerically weaker than its war strength, and is largely composed of partially trained recruits and of men under 19 years of age, who, at that time, were not considered eligible for active service, all four companies had to be largely reconstructed. The recruits, men under age, and those medically unfit were eliminated, their places being taken and the companies brought up to war strength by Reservists. Of men medically unfit there were but four ! As an order was received to detail two officers to proceed to the depot to assist in forming the 6th (Service) Battalion, Capt. R. Lynch White and 2/Lieut. W. R. A. Dawson did not leave Dublin with the unit.

The Voyage.—Mobilisation was complete and the Battalion in all respects ready for the field by the evening of 8th August. It had been supposed that the move would take place on the 9th, but it was not until 9.30 a.m. on Thursday, 13th August, that the Battalion actually embarked at the Alexandra Basin in the s.s. " Gloucestershire " of the Bibby Line. Embarking strength was 26 officers and 1015 other ranks.

The names of the Officers were as follows :

Lieut.-Colonel A. Martyn	Commanding Officer.
Major P. M. Buckle, D.S.O.	2nd in Command.
Lieut. G. B. Legard.	Adjutant.
Lieut. H. G. Rogers	Quartermaster.
Lieut. D. J. Johnston	Machine Gun Officer.
Lieut. W. Newton .	Transport Officer.
Lieut. W. P. Croker, R.A.M.C. .	Medical Officer.

" A " Company :

Captain G. D. Lister	Officer Commanding.
Captain G. F. Keenlyside	2nd in Command.
2/Lieut. S. K. Gore .	No. 1 Platoon Cmdr.
Lieut. Wilberforce Bell	No. 2 ,,
2/Lieut. A. A. E. Chitty .	No. 3 ,,
Lieut. C. K. Anderson	No. 4 ,,

" B " Company :

Major C. G. Pack Beresford	Officer Commanding.
Captain W. C. O. Phillips	2nd in Command.
Lieut. F. Fisher	No. 5 Platoon Cmdr.
Lieut. D. C. C. Sewell	No. 6 ,,
2/Lieut. M. F. Broadwood	No. 8 ,,

" C " Company :

Major P. Hastings .	Officer Commanding.
Lieut. W. V. Palmer	2nd in Command.
Lieut. C. A. M. Holloway.	No. 9 Platoon Cmdr.
Lieut. W. K. Ames .	No. 11 ,,
Lieut. J. H. Whitehouse .	No. 12 ,,

" D " Company :

Capt. R. G. M. Tulloch	. . .	Officer Commanding.
Capt. H. D. Buchanan Dunlop	.	2nd in Command.
Lieut. H. B. H. White	. . .	No. 13 Platoon Cmdr.
Lieut. N. J. P. K. M'Clelland	.	No. 16 ,,

Sergt.-Major H. S. Doe was Battalion Sergeant-Major.

Brigade Headquarters, the K.O.S.B.'s and the Duke of Wellington's were accommodated in the same ship. The ladies of Dublin presented every man with a packet of refreshments, an attention that was very much appreciated.

The " Gloucestershire " sailed at 2.20 a.m. on the 14th. Accommodation on board was very limited, but luckily the weather was fine. There was much speculation as to the destination, which had been kept secret. Havre was the favourite guess and this turned out to be correct. The ship came alongside the quay there at 2.30 p.m. on the 15th. Rain was coming down in torrents, but there were huge sheds close by in which the men could take shelter as soon as they disembarked. Most of them occupied the intervening time with singing. It was still raining heavily when, at 6 a.m. next morning, the Battalion marched to a Rest Camp about 5½ miles from the docks. In the afternoon the weather cleared, and Lieut.-Colonel Martyn took the opportunity to read to his men the address from His Majesty the King. The inhabitants of Havre flocked to see the British troops and it was an amusing afternoon for the men. The French girls were particularly anxious to obtain cap and shoulder badges as " souvenirs." This, as some of the men remarked, was the only " English " word the French people seemed to know !

At 2.30 p.m. on the 17th the weather improved, and

Lieut.   Capt.   Lieut.   Lieut.   Lieut.   Lieut.   Lieut.   Lieut.&Q.-M.   Lieut.
W. V. Palmer B. Johnstone Barnes W. K. Ames D. J. Johnston M. F. Broadwood H. G. Rogers Ogle

Capt.   Capt. H. D.   Capt.   Major   Lieut.-Col.   Lieut.&Adjt.   Major   Capt. G. F.   Capt.
Lynch White B.-Dunlop G. D. Lister P. M. Robinson A. Martyn G. B. Legard P. Hastings Keenlyside J. C. Parker

GROUP OF OFFICERS AT DUBLIN, 1913

[To face p. 4

the Battalion marched to Havre railway station and entrained. One enormously long train took the whole Battalion with its transport. Officers were accommodated in ordinary carriages ; the men in cattle trucks fitted with benches—forty men to a truck. The train left before 9 a.m. and, passing through Rouen and Amiens, arrived at Landrecies about midnight. All along the route the French people showed their enthusiastic gratitude to their Allies for coming to their assistance, and at every station pressed fruit, flowers and cigarettes on officers and men alike. Detraining at Landrecies, the Battalion went into comfortable billets at La Basse Maroilles, two miles from the station, on a small tributary of the Sambre. Here it remained until the 21st whilst the Army was concentrating. The 19th and 20th were spent in route-marching and training. On the afternoon of the 20th the Divisional Commander, Sir Charles Fergusson, visited Maroilles and made a very stirring speech to the Battalion, giving much valuable advice.

The Phase of the Battle of Mons.—The 13th Brigade, together with the 14th and 15th, formed Major-General Sir Charles Fergusson's 5th Division of the 2nd Army Corps, which was now under Sir Horace Smith-Dorrien, successor to Sir James Grierson, who died suddenly on the 17th August. The brunt of the Battle of Mons, now fast approaching, fell on the 2nd Army Corps.

The short account of the events leading up to the battle which follows, has been drawn from Lord Ernest Hamilton's " First Seven Divisions."

The two Army Corps of the British Army were brought up to prolong to the left the line of French resistance to the German advance on Paris. It had been originally intended to hold a line running from Charleroi

B

through Binche to Mons, but, the French having fallen back beyond the line of prolongation, Charleroi was already in German hands and the plan had to be abandoned. The actual position occupied was therefore fixed by necessity rather than choice. The First Corps was posted along the Beaumont-Mons road. The Second lined the canal between Mons and Condé, forming an angle of 45 degrees with the First.

The canal position was strong except just north of Mons, where a loop two miles long formed a salient to the north. This loop constituted so serious a defect in his position that Sir H. Smith-Dorrien had prepared a more defensible line in the rear which ran through Frameries, Pasturage, Wasmes and Boussu. This was not only a better position, but it had the further advantage of flattening out the angle at the junction of the two Corps. The canal was to be held only to gain time, the real stand being made on the line in rear. The latter was never occupied as a whole because of an unexpected order, from Sir John French, to retire in conformity with the French movements on the British right.

The first clash between British and German arms was an assault on the weak part of the canal, the loop, held by the 3rd Division. The attack soon spread to the straight part of the canal held by the 5th Division, of which The Queen's Own was the right battalion in the line. But though the German onslaught developed first against the loop, one company of the Battalion was engaged early in the day, as shall be related. Indeed, Sir A. Conan Doyle remarks, " The day began by some losses to the West Kent Regiment, who were probably, apart from cavalry patrols, the first troops to suffer in the Great War."

The March to Mons.—To return to the doings of the Battalion : On 21st August, the two Army Corps being now nearly complete, the 13th Brigade began its march northwards, leaving Maroilles at 6.30 a.m. It was a hot, muggy day and the march of nearly 17 miles to Houdain (one mile north of Bavai) was a trying one. However, the men stuck to it well and only a few failed to keep up, though some of the Reservists had hardly recovered their marching legs. The companies went into billets for the night. On the 22nd the march was resumed, the Battalion being in the Advanced Guard, whilst " C " and " D " Companies under Major Buckle formed the Vanguard. The Belgian Frontier was crossed after about three miles. On reaching Dour at 9 a.m. Brigadier-General Cuthbert gave verbal orders for the occupation of the line of the canal. " C " and " D " Companies were posted on the bridges north and northeast of St Ghislain with " A " and " B " Companies in reserve near St Ghislain. All the afternoon and evening until dark was spent in entrenching, loopholing, barricading, etc. There were many rumours of Uhlans with guns having been seen some miles to the north. " D " Company's position on the night of the 22nd marked the right of the 5th Division and was adjoined by the 3rd Division.

On Sunday, 23rd August, the work of fortification was resumed as soon as daylight appeared. At 8 a.m. " A " Coy., under Capt. Lister, was sent across the canal to support reconnoitring cavalry and cyclists. Capt. Lister's own account of the action in which his company became engaged is here given.

Capt. Lister's narrative.—" On the night of 22nd-23rd Aug. 1914 ' A ' and ' B ' Companies were in billets at Hornu. At 5.30 a.m. on the 23rd I was told by the

Adjutant that I had to be at the bridge over the canal at
8 a.m. with my company.   I was informed that at that
hour the 5th Divisional Mounted Troops ('A' Squadron
19th Hussars and the 5th Divisional Cyclist Company)
were to cross the canal to make a reconnaissance, and
that my company was to go with these troops and take
up a position approximately at the cross roads south of
the village of Tertre, with the object of covering the
retirement of the mounted troops if necessary.

" I arrived at the bridge with my company at about
7.50 a.m.   The only information I received of the enemy
was that a few Uhlans had been seen the previous day
north of the canal.

" The Divisional Mounted Troops under Major Parsons
(19th Hussars) arrived about 8.15 a.m. and we at once
crossed the canal.   Shortly afterwards there were a few
shots fired at us from a north-easterly direction.

" The mounted troops went forward and I halted my
company as ordered at the cross roads, south of Tertre.
Then, in company with Capt. Keenlyside, I personally
reconnoitred the ground to the front and decided to
dispose of my company as follows :—

" No. 1 Platoon under 2/Lieut. Gore at A (see sketch).

" No. 2 Platoon under Lieut. Wilberforce Bell at B.

" No. 4 Platoon under Lieut. Anderson at C.

" No 3. Platoon under 2/Lieut. Chitty was kept in
reserve, just behind No. 2 Platoon at B.

" The platoon commanders commenced at once to
improve existing cover and No. 2 to loophole the garden
walls, etc., of a small farm-house at B.

" No. 1 Platoon had a fair field of fire of about 250
yards, whilst Nos. 2 and 4 had a better one of about
450 yards.   The line of retreat to the canal was very
difficult, as the ground was intercepted with numerous

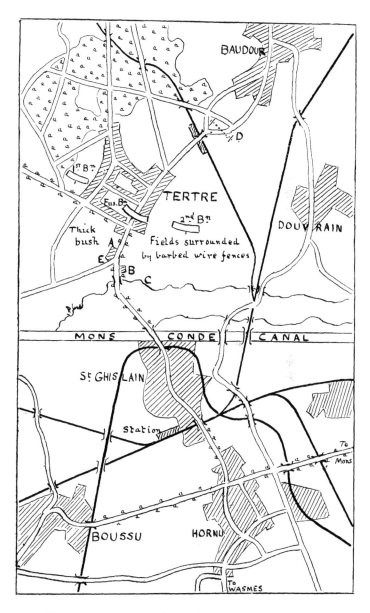

MAP TO ILLUSTRATE CAPTAIN LISTER'S NARRATIVE

represents a Battalion of the 12th Brandenberg Grenadier Regiment

[*To face p.* 8

deep dykes and barbed wire. As far as time permitted
I had this wire cut.

" The lines of retreat, which I ordered, were arranged
with the view to avoid the masking of the fire of the main
body in position along the canal.

" These preparations were scarcely complete when I
saw four cyclists with an officer coming at full speed
down the road from Tertre.   On arriving at our position,
they flung themselves down by me, and the officer in
charge stated that the remainder of his detachment had
been blown to pieces by the enemy's artillery fire.

" I told him to send a cyclist back at once to the canal
with this information.

" Within five minutes I saw the enemy's infantry
debouching from Tertre in large numbers.   I counted
on the east side of the road some 400-500 men.

" Fire was at once opened upon them and it could be
seen that the enemy was suffering considerable loss.
After a short time he returned the fire heavily.

" I sent a report of this to Headquarters at the canal
bridge, at the same time asking if any news had been
heard of the Divisional Cavalry.   This was answered in
the negative.

" Shortly after this I received by cyclist a memo.
from Major Parsons (Officer Commanding Divisional
Mounted Troops) asking me to cover his retirement.
There was no indication from whence the message had
been written, and so I considered that the only way in
which I could do this would be to hold on to my position
as long as possible. This I decided to do.

" By this time a battery of the enemy's artillery had
come into action at D (on sketch), and another body
of enemy troops, which proved to be a machine-gun
company, came into action straight to our front.

" All this time numbers of the enemy had been deploying east and west of the Tertre-Hornu Road. Hence I decided to send half a platoon (No. 3) under 2/Lieut. Chitty to reinforce No. 1 Platoon, which appeared to be somewhat exposed at A.

" I sent back another report to the canal, and asked once more if any news had been heard of the Divisional Cavalry. I again received an answer in the negative, but was told I had better commence to retire if things were getting too hot.

" I decided to retire and sent an order to No. 1 Platoon to commence the retirement.

" Just at this moment, I perceived that No. 4 Platoon at C had already commenced to retire. It did so in good order in a S.E. direction, but it had apparently suffered some loss. It was impossible at that moment to stop this retirement, so I then extended the half platoon I had in reserve at B along a some-what deep and very boggy dyke to replace No. 4 Platoon.

" The platoon sergeant of No. 4 came to me almost immediately afterwards and informed me that Lieut. Anderson had been killed, and he had been told that we had retired. He apparently realised that his retirement had been premature.

" A message now reached me from a small connecting post that I had established at E that No. 1 Platoon had got successfully away.

" I then crossed to the west side of the road in order to collect the men on that side, and thereby endeavour to take up a position to cover the retirement of the centre (No. 2 Platoon).

" I saw the advancing German infantry some hundred and fifty yards away and also about twenty men, probably of No. 4 Platoon, slowly retiring in file along the western side of the road.

" I at once realised that, unless they either scattered or crossed to the deep ditch on the east side of the road, they must be annihilated. So I went out into the field to attract their attention and to issue instructions, but I was, unfortunately, wounded through the right shoulder and fell close to the road. I was unable to move and so could do nothing further.

" Two or three men doubled past me and offered to carry me back, but I refused to allow them to do so as it was almost certain to mean sacrificing their lives.

" Shortly after this I became unconscious and remember nothing more until I was aroused by a German, who gave me a drink and bandaged me up as best he could.

" Since the action I have ascertained that in my immediate front the Germans had three battalions of the Brandenburg Grenadiers, one battery of Artillery and one machine-gun company.

" From information since received it appears that some 90 men out of 200 got back to the main position on the canal.

" The enemy's losses, according to their own account, were very heavy and included Major Praeger, who commanded the Fusilier Battalion.

" Finally, the officers, N.C.O.'s and men of the company comported themselves well under difficult circumstances, and although the premature withdrawal of No. 4 Platoon was an error, it did not seriously affect the situation."

The following extract from the diary of Major Hastings, commanding " C " Company, gives a good

account of the action fought by the main body of the
Battalion in position on the canal.

Major Hastings' Diary.—" Sunday, 23rd August.
Continued entrenching and barricading. As soon as
it was light the Divisional Cavalry (19th Hussars) and
Cyclists went through our barricade. Shortly afterwards Lister's company followed as a support, and
went out towards Tertre. At 11.30 a.m. we heard gun
fire and saw smoke in front of us. Shortly afterwards
we saw ' A ' Company being driven back by artillery
and machine-gun fire, and many men were falling.
Eventually the greater part of ' A ' Company passed
through our post having lost Lister, Anderson, and
nearly one hundred men. Chitty was wounded ;
Keenlyside and Gore came in safely. The attack was
then turned on to our defences and we were shelled
fairly continuously until it was dark. A few infantry
attacks were made on us but, when fired on from our
position, the enemy got under the cover of a ridge and
passed along from east to west towards Pommerœul.
All houses near us were shelled heavily, especially the
train depot held by Whitehouse, a subaltern of ' C.'
We were reinforced by Sergt. Fittall with the whole
or part of a platoon of ' B ' (? ' D ' Company [1])
Company, and he was put into a trench on the
east side of the road. Whitehouse had originally been ' earmarked ' to hold the bridge itself and
had prepared the position. Owing, however, to the
trend of events, he was then sent up to prepare the
train depot for defence and, as no one had arrived to
hold it, he was ordered to stay there. We got up some

[1] Major Hastings thought Sergt. Fittall's platoon belonged to " B "
Company, for later he says that he thought the platoon had been withdrawn
by Beresford.

meat during the day, but scarcely any of the men would eat.   We also had some tea in degchies after dark.

" After dark the German infantry came in quite close, but did not open fire upon us.   The enemy positions varied from 150 to 500 yards from us.   Fisher, a subaltern of ' B,' was sent with his platoon to strengthen the left of Ames' (of ' C ' Company) position.   Part of ' B ' Company also helped to man the Battalion Head-quarter buildings and part were there in reserve.   We had eight men wounded in ' C ' Company by shells and a good many others were slightly wounded.   During the day many aeroplanes went over, both German and French or British.   The Germans fired about twenty rounds at one, but the shells appeared to burst far behind it."

" D " Company on the right held the railway bridge which passed over the canal just north of St Ghislain. This company had two platoons defending the bridge under Capt. Dunlop, while the other platoons were entrenched a bit to the left front.

The platoon holding the railway bridge dug a trench across the line about 50 yards in front of the bridge, with a communication trench back to the bridge. Trenches were also dug on the flank of the railway embankment and the slopes of the embankment cleared of trees, brushwood, etc.

The trench on the line itself was camouflaged by con-cealing it with cinders, and the rails were also covered, so as not to disclose the position of the trench, whilst a conspicuous dummy trench was made on the end of the bridge itself.

When the enemy shelled the position, he did most accurate shooting at the dummy trench and no one in the real trenches was touched by his shell fire, though

Corporal Rogers was shot through the heart by rifle fire, while observing from the trench on the railway line.

These two platoons remained at the bridge throughout the day, holding the trenches with a few men. The remainder were under the bridge.

The two machine guns of the Duke of Wellington's Regiment were in position about 50 yards west of the bridge. The enemy apparently located them, as he got a direct hit on their emplacement, severely wounding Lieut. Ozanne, the Duke's Machine Gun Officer.

When the two bandsmen, who were with Capt. Dunlop's party as stretcher bearers, ran out to the emplacement to tend to the wounded of the Duke's they found no casualties other than Lieut. Ozanne.

Capt. Dunlop received a shrapnel wound in the head and Sergt. Sterry a nasty one in the leg. The latter was afterwards left behind in St Ghislain when the Battalion withdrew. He became a prisoner of war. Owing to the Field Ambulances not having joined the fighting troops, it was impossible to clear the wounded and they had to be left in charge of the Belgians.

Battle Experiences.—The experiences of the other companies were much the same. From noon till dark —eight hours—the Battalion was subjected to a heavy shelling from about 30 German guns. Six enemy batteries were in full view firing over open sights at a range of 1800 yards. The only British battery available in this sector of the line was soon put out of action, and thereafter the fire was concentrated on the infantry defences. Fortunately there was a grove of trees in front of the defensive position, through the trunks and branches of which the men could see to fire, but which screened the trenches and the defended walls from the view of the Germans. Consequently their artillery never found the exact position and hence their shell fire, trying though it was, did considerable damage to the buildings, but comparatively little to the men.

The German infantry suffered considerable loss from our rifle fire during their advance, and although they succeeded in working up to within about 300 yards of our position by nightfall, they never really attacked as if they meant it. This was due either to the fact that the portion of front held by the Battalion was not their objective, or because they had had all the fighting they desired in their morning's argument with " A " Company. As we shall see directly, there are ample grounds for believing that the latter reason may explain their comparatively unenterprising behaviour during the afternoon. In any case, that part of the line was never in the slightest danger.

The spirit of the men in this, their first fight, was all that could be wished. Lieut.-Colonel Martyn observes : " All ranks worked with the greatest courage and intelligence throughout the day's fighting and, as it was the opening fight of the War and they were attacked by five times their number and many guns, I consider their behaviour was beyond all praise."

Some fine acts of devotion to duty by the Battalion stretcher bearers were witnessed during this first day's fighting. One of the most notable of these was the action of Pte. Donovan of " C " Company, who, when Lieut. Wilberforce-Bell called for a volunteer to assist him in bringing in a badly wounded man of " A " Company (Pte. Bradley), who had been left out in front when " A " Company retired, went forward with great gallantry with that officer and effected the bringing in of this wounded man. For this act Pte. Donovan was afterwards awarded the D.C.M.

What seemed to impress the rank and file, almost
more than the unpleasantness of the German shell fire,
was the very low standard, compared with their own, of
the German rifle fire. " The Germans couldn't hit a
haystack," said one private. A lance-corporal remarked, " The Germans came across the valley in front
of us in thousands, but their rifle fire as they advanced
was absolutely rotten, while the only damage inflicted
on us was wrought by the big guns which covered their
advance."

It is a wonderful stroke of luck that we have a good,
reliable account of The Queen's Own share in the battle
as seen through German eyes. *The Times Literary
Supplement* published a review on the book of a German
novelist which throws a new and very welcome light on
the efficiency of the resistance put up by " A " Company,
and therein justifies the suspicion that the reason there
was no serious infantry attack in the afternoon, may
have been due to the fact that the German infantry had
had the heart knocked out of them in the morning.

Here it is :—

Capt. Bloem's narrative.—Walter Bloem, the well-
known German writer, author of three excellent novels
on the Franco-Prussian War and manager of the
Hoftheatre, Stuttgart, was, in 1914, forty-six years of
age. He was at that time about to relinquish his
managership and enjoy himself travelling with his
family for a couple of years, when war broke in on his
happiness. Within a few days of freedom he was called
to the colours and, as a Captain of the Reserve, found
himself in command of a company in the 1st Bn. of
the 12th Brandenburg Grenadier Regiment (III Corps).
His book is a most remarkable one. It is not a novel,
though at times one is reminded of the pages of ' La

Débâcle ' and ' Le Desastré,' but a truthful, vivid and
first-hand account, told with much literary skill and
dramatic effect, of what an actual combatant in Von
Kluck's Army saw and felt from the moment that the
war cloud arises until the author falls wounded, before
our Second Army Corps near Missy on the Aisne.

As a military work the book is of high value, as it
tells us with evident truthfulness many details, which
we have long desired to know, of Von Kluck's great flank
march down to the Marne and of his historic retirement,
and much of interest as regards our own men.

" The first serious engagement of this Regiment, the
12th Brandenburg Grenadiers, is with the British."

The Regiment marched down to the Condé Canal
towards St Ghislain, and, all unconscious, the author
tells a story that must ever redound to the high military
qualities and training of the old army and to the credit
of the Queen's Own Royal West Kent Regiment in
particular. The 12th Grenadiers are halted in Baudour,
north of the canal.

" Hussar patrols trot by and report that for 80 kms.
(50 miles) to the front all is clear of the enemy. Field
kitchens are brought up and we halt for a comfortable
midday rest. The meal was not finished before blood-
stained hussars gallop in and report the enemy near at
hand in the next village ! All is confusion for a while ;
then the Captains are summoned to the Battalion
Commander who says : ' Maps out, gentlemen. The
village Tertre in front of us is occupied by the enemy,
strength not yet known. The regiment is attacking,
supported by three batteries,' etc. The Brandenburgers
deploy and advance by rushes, fired at by an always
invisible foe and losing men every time they rise. The

British fire gradually seems to die down, the company gets to within 150 yards and the order passes : ' Now for a general rush of 30 yards, then fix bayonets and storm the houses.' " Captain Bloem continues : " The enemy seems to have waited for the moment of a general assault. He had artfully enticed us to close range in order to deal with us more surely and thoroughly. A hellish fire broke loose and in thick swathes the deadly leaden fire was pumped on our heads, breasts and knees. Wherever I looked, to the right and left, nothing but dead, and blood-streaming, sobbing, writhing wounded." The unfortunate remnant is glued to the ground. More fire, apparently from their own people, is poured into them, until at last night comes and they creep back half a mile knowing that they are beaten. Capt. Bloem has lost all his five officers and half the men of his company. He meets his Battalion Commander, who lays his hands on his shoulders and, with shaking voice, says : " My dear Bloem, you are my sole and only support. . . . You are the only company commander left in the Battalion. . . . The Battalion is a mere wreck—my proud, beautiful Battalion." So it was with the Regiment—' shot down, smashed up, a handful only left ' ; and the full consciousness of defeat soaks in : " Heavy defeat, why not admit it ? Our first battle is a heavy, unheard of heavy defeat, and against the English, the English we laughed at."

The poor man's despair might have been even more overwhelming had he known that the ' enemy, strength unknown,' that knocked out 3000 Brandenburg Grenadiers—it is almost bathos—was one company of the 1st Bn. The Queen's Own Royal West Kent Regiment, with the sole help of a few men of a cavalry squadron and of a cyclist company, not 300 all told. The odds

of Agincourt once more, ten to one—truly the men of
Kent have not degenerated in 500 years. A nice
problem the fight will be for the German professors to
explain, who cannot yet understand the English victory
in 1415, except on the supposition that Henry V. had
superior numbers.

Next morning, to the utter astonishment of the
Germans, they hear the explosions of the canal bridges
being blown up. " It is quite impossible. The English
—destroy the bridges ! Sheer lunacy ! It must be
something else." Eventually they advance with caution,
for " Curse them, they seem to understand war, these
English. We find convincing signs of this everywhere.
Marvellous how they have converted every house, every
wall into a fortress . . . and have finally slipped away
without waiting for our bayonets and our butt ends."
Brave words the day after the battle, but over-night the
Colonel of the Brandenburgers had said, " If the English
have the slightest suspicion of our condition and make
a counter-attack, they will completely do us in." The
Regiment (The Brandenburg Grenadiers), though in
the advance guard quite lost touch with us (The British).
" The enemy was off—the signs of a hasty retreat, but
not of a disorganised flight, are to be seen everywhere—
disabled motor cars, burnt supplies, but not a single
weapon or article of equipment." Later on Capt. Bloem
again notices that there are no signs of disorder.

Another account of the battle by the same writer
published in *Die Wocke* in 1916 differs considerably
from the above, and is evidently " cooked " for public
consumption. In this the author complains that the
Brandenburgers had to attack without artillery support
—an obvious misstatement. He also remarks upon the
deadly machine-gun fire of the English. At one period

" we were only exposed to machine guns, but there were many, which shot excellently and were absolutely invisible." Though this may have been written in good faith, Capt. Bloem is almost certainly mistaking rapid rifle fire for that of machine guns. At that time the British Army, compared with the Germans, had very few of the latter weapons.

Neither of the two machine guns belonging to the Battalion was with " A " Company. The truth is that very few German officers then had any conception of the capabilities of the rifle in British hands. Since the South African War an immense advance in musketry training had been made, and the quick and neat manipulation of the bolt of the rifle had received as much attention as accurate shooting. This had entailed much hard work, and British Infantry in general, and The Queen's Own Regiment in particular, should be very grateful to Capt. Bloem for his testimony to the result of their labours.

CHAPTER II

AS has been remarked, Sir H. Smith-Dorrien had never intended to hold the line of the canal for long, and the 3rd Division in the Mons loop having suffered heavily, he decided to withdraw to the more defensible position to the south during the night.

Throughout the hours of daylight of the 23rd the enemy had been crossing the road bridge next to the St Ghislain Railway bridge on the east, and towards evening began to fire into the back of " D " Company's position at the railway bridge. Their position was rapidly becoming untenable.

The order to retire on Wasmes reached the Battalion at about 7 p.m. on the 23rd. This retirement is perhaps best described by Capt. Dunlop's account of " D " Company's experiences of that night ; experiences which were common to the other companies of the Battalion.

Capt. Dunlop's Account.—" When it got dark Tulloch came up to my position on the railway bridge, and we arranged our plan for holding it during the night. The enemy was quite close up to us, and so we had asked for and received a company of the Duke of Wellington's Regiment to assist in holding the position.

" I went along to Battalion Headquarters to get my wound dressed. Here I met the C.O., who told me about ' A ' Company, and Lister being wounded. While talking to him a message arrived ordering the

c

Battalion to withdraw during the night. The C.O. told me to let Tulloch know, and that the signal for blowing up the bridges (there were about six bridges or locks on the Battalion front) would be the blowing up of the centre bridge, where Battalion Headquarters were, and that this could not take place before midnight.

" The Medical Officer was not at Battalion Headquarters, so I went back to Tulloch and we arranged about the withdrawal.

" All picks, shovels, stretchers, spare ammunition, etc., were sent back to the transport. A few men were detailed to pick the road, to induce the enemy to think we were entrenching.

" By 12 midnight we withdrew all the men across the canal, while we held the near side of the bridge and lock on our front, each with one platoon. Lieut. M'Clelland was in command of the railway bridge party, while I had charge of the platoon at the lock. In this position we watched for over an hour, momentarily expecting the enemy to appear suddenly out of the darkness to rush the bridges.

" Apparently, however, his patrols were not active, for nothing happened. About 1.30 a.m. the centre bridge went up in the air. A few minutes afterwards the Sappers with us fired their charges, and all along the front explosion after explosion occurred.

" Directly our bridges went up, and having made sure they were demolished, we hurried back to the Square in St Ghislain, where we found the Battalion formed up waiting for us."

The Withdrawal from St Ghislain.—As will be seen, the withdrawal was not an easy operation because the Germans were close in front, and many ruined buildings

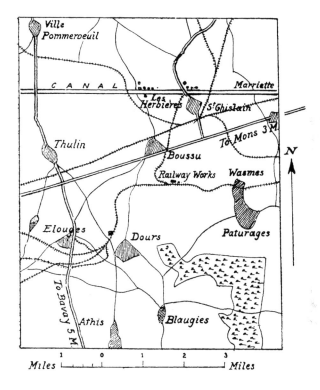

Ville Pommerœuil

C A N A L

Marriette

Les Herbieres

St Ghislain

Thulin

To Mons 3 M.

N

Boussu

Railway Works

Wasmes

Elouges

Dours

Paturages

To Bavay 5 M.

Athis

Blaugies

Miles   1   0   1   2   3   Miles

MONS

[To face p. 22

had to be passed in the dark before the bridges were reached. The operation throughout was quite successfully accomplished, the companies withdrawing section after section, until only a few men were left in position. The Germans made two half-hearted attacks during this operation, but they were easily beaten off.

About 1 a.m. on the 24th Lieut. Wilberforce Bell and twelve men were ordered to cross the canal and to hold their bridge until the last. Should the bridge be blown up before they could get away, they were to swim the canal.

They encountered two German patrols, which they beat off successfully, and finally crossed the bridge about 1.30 a.m. immediately prior to it being blown up.

By 4 a.m. the Battalion was formed up in the Market Square at Wasmes, having passed through the Duke of Wellington's Regiment, who were holding the outskirts of the village.

In the meantime, however, at about 2 a.m. the Commander of the 2nd Army Corps received the totally unexpected and exceedingly unwelcome order to retire on Bavai. Now, as all dispositions had been made on the assumption that the new line south of the canal would be held, the order to fall back involved a very difficult operation. The immense transport accompanying a modern army had to be got away, and this necessitated strong rear-guards to hold back the enemy until the transport was clear. The withdrawal was in general successfully performed, but at the expense of heavy casualties and much suffering to the troops who, separated from their transport, were deprived of their rations.

Wasmes.—Soon after the Battalion arrived in Wasmes the Germans began to shell the place heavily, but by keeping close up to the buildings on the least exposed side of the Square, it escaped casualties.

At about 10 a.m. a German infantry attack began to develop, and " A," " B " and " C " Companies were sent to various points to assist the Duke of Wellington's. " B " Company, in taking up its position, came under close rifle and machine-gun fire, losing about thirty-five men. Major Pack Beresford (Commanding), Capt. Phillips (2nd in Command), and 2/Lieut. Broadwood were killed, and Lieut. Sewell was mortally wounded. The German infantry came on with a confidence that suggested that they thought the place had been evacuated. They advanced through the narrow streets in thick masses. The various parties of The Queen's Own and of the three other battalions in the town received them with the close fire of both rifle and machine guns. This occurred again and again, and the German losses must have been enormous.

At 1 p.m., having sufficiently held up the German advance, the troops in Wasmes were withdrawn and the 13th Brigade was directed on St Waast La Vallée. It was a very trying march of about fourteen miles. The weather was still very sultry, and though the men had been hotly engaged for over twenty-four hours, they had had no food. All were much exhausted by the time St Waast La Vallée was reached, but even then there was no water, and no supplies of any kind were available.

Major Hastings' diary contains an interesting account of the happenings of the 24th August, and the following extract is taken therefrom :—

Major Hastings' Diary.—" Monday, 24th August. (St Ghislain.) Companies ordered to withdraw across main bridge into St Ghislain, ' C ' Company to withdraw last. I sent to warn the four platoons, keeping Sergt. Gilbey's

platoon on the barricade and in the big building to the
last.   Just before we were going a very heavy fire was
opened from Sergt. Fittal's trench, and there appeared to
be firing from a small wood in front of him.   I withheld,
and after about five minutes it stopped.   Soon afterwards I heard that Ames' platoon had crossed the bridge,
and I then withdrew Sergt. Gilby's platoon.   As soon as we
were across the bridge it was blown up.   I had received
orders to withdraw my own company, but the post
allotted to me was held by parts of several companies.

" Hence Sergt. Fittal's platoon was left in the trench,
as I was under the impression that they had been withdrawn by Beresford.[1]

" They eventually got away at 4 a.m., and made
their way back over the top part of the bridge which,
fortunately, had not been destroyed.   Four men were
wounded whilst getting away.

" The Column marched away about 2 a.m. to Wasmes,
where we halted in the Square.   We passed through the
' Duke's ' and other regiments holding a line above
Wasmes, and firing commenced as we were passing them.
Whilst we were in the Square the guns began to shell it,
but we got under cover of the houses.   The regiments
above us suffered heavy losses, and the Duke of Wellington's lost several officers.   Beresford, who was sent up
to support them, was killed, together with Phillips and
Broadwood ; Sewell was severely wounded.   Several
N.C.O.'s and men were killed and wounded, including
Sergt.-Major Saunders.   ' C ' Company was sent by
the General to a place close to the road, and on the left
of it when facing the enemy.   The railway station was
on the other side of the road.   ' D ' Company was
afterwards sent out to our left, and beyond it were the

[1] See footnote, p. 12.

K.O.Y.L.I., etc. On our right, across the road, were some Bedfords, etc. Fisher, with ' B ' Company, eventually withdrew to our lines, and a number of the ' Duke's ' and others passed through our line. The General sent me a verbal message by Sergt. Stroud that I was to form the rear-guard and cover the retirement of the Brigade. I waited for over an hour, then as everyone appeared to have retired and as I had received no orders, and the Bedfords on our right were being turned, I sent a message to Tulloch (Commanding ' D ' Company) to say I was retiring. We then went slowly back. All this time the German guns had been shelling the batteries behind us, and it was very interesting to watch the shells bursting well beyond our position. Very few infantry bullets came near us.

" The weather was very hot indeed.

" All the losses appeared to have taken place north of the big Squares. I had heard that our baggage had been sent to Athis and, as other troops appeared to be going that way, we retired via Petit Wasmes, Blaugies, to Athis. Here there was a big block, and I sent forward to find our bivouac, and then rested the Company as they had had practically no rest for 36 hours and no food for 24. I then heard that Athis was dangerous and that the whole Division was going back to Bavai.

" At this moment some German infantry appeared in a field close at hand and we prepared to attack them Some Bedfords came up at this moment and frightened the enemy scouts away. ' C ' Company then formed an ambush to catch any Uhlans who might follow up the retirement. None came, so ' C ' Company formed part of an improvised rear-guard of Bedfords and West Kents. Eventually the Divisional Cavalry came out and covered our retirement on Houdain. Here there was a great collection of troops, and we were told that the 13th Brigade was going to St Waast des Bavai. We arrived there just before dark, nearly dead from fatigue and want of food. We found the regiment and then bivouacked. We heard that the Cavalry Division had been having a very bad time during the afternoon."

The Retreat.—At 3.20 a.m. on the 25th the retreat was resumed. The Battalion was with the main body of the 5th Division and was not engaged, though once it was sent back to support the rear-guard, which was fighting on and off all day. The day was again very hot and the men were still without food. They stuck to it very well, however. Here it might be remarked that throughout the retirement from St Ghislain to Le Cateau the men were without rations. Their last dinner was on the 23rd, and it was not until the evening of the 25th that emergency rations were allowed to be used, and even then only one between four men! The poor inhabitants did all they could to mitigate the men's sufferings with substantial offerings of bread, fruit and water ; this in spite of the fact that the army was retiring and abandoning the district to the Germans. The route of the retirement lay along the western edge of the Forêt de Mormal, whose tall and dense trees kept off any breeze there might have been. A bivouac some two miles south-west of Le Cateau was reached by the evening.

The Commander-in-Chief had apparently hoped to concentrate his army on a line south of the Mormal Forest, but the 1st Corps moving east of the Forest was much pressed by the enemy and was forced to fight a series of rear-guard actions. Its movements were so hampered thereby that when on the evening of the 25th the 2nd Corps, together with the newly arrived 4th Division, were concentrated west of Le Cateau, both the Divisions of the 1st Corps were still beyond supporting distance. The Commander-in-Chief was obliged to fix on a position west of St Quentin, some twenty miles farther south, for the reunion of his Army Corps. By the evening it had become clear to Sir H. Smith-Dorrien that the pressure of the Germans on his exhausted infantry had become so severe that he could no longer continue his retreat without relieving it. It must be remembered that the Germans moved their advanced infantry in motor lorries. There was but one possible expedient—to turn and fight alone. He was forced to take this desperate measure, fully understanding that he could expect no assistance whatsoever from the 1st Corps, and being well aware that his three divisions (two of them very tired and depleted) would have to face the onslaught of at least seven German Divisions backed by an overwhelming preponderance of artillery.

Le Cateau.—The right of Sir H. Smith-Dorrien's line at the Battle of Le Cateau was held by the 5th Division, of which the 13th was the centre Brigade. The K.O.Y.L.I.'s and the K.O.S.B.'s were in the line, on the right and left respectively, with the Duke's and West Kents in support; the first named with their right resting on a point just east of the Roumont Road.

The main German thrust was directed against the right and right centre, but the Battalion, being in support, did not suffer very seriously. It was behind the K.O.Y.L.I. some two miles S.W. of Le Cateau. The position was occupied soon after daybreak on the 26th, the Battalion entrenching itself in two lines in the corn-fields, where the corn had nearly all been cut and stood in stooks, about 600 yards behind the first line positions.

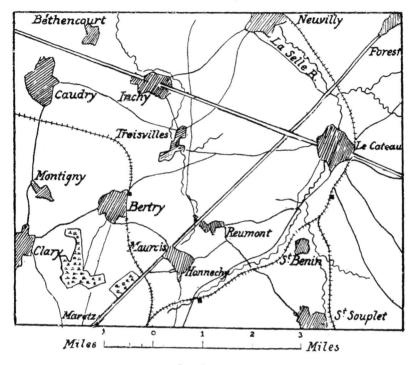

Béthencourt

Neuvilly

La Selle R.

Forest

Caudry

Inchy

Troisvilles

Le Cateau

Montigny

Bertry

Reumont

Clary

Maurcis

St Benin

Honnechy

Maretz

St Souplet

Miles

0   1   2   3

Miles

LE CATEAU

To face p. 28

As the German attack developed, the battalions holding
the first line suffered heavily both from shell and rifle
fire. By about 3 p.m. the enemy had succeeded in
working round the right flank to a position from which
he could enfilade the forward battalions of the 13th
Brigade. A retirement was then ordered. The Queen's
Own, remaining until the other battalions of the Brigade
had moved to the rear, retired in extended lines of half
battalions. Taking up a succession of fire positions,
they held up the German infantry until the rest of the
Brigade was well clear. The last two companies then
formed a rear party to cover the troops moving on St
Quentin. Although under heavy shell and rifle fire
during the retirement, the men displayed the greatest
coolness in taking up their successive positions and
retiring at the right moment.

Major Hastings' diary for this period is again quoted :

Major Hastings' Diary.—" Wednesday, 26th August
(Le Cateau).—First of all we were told that the retirement was to be continued. ' C ' and ' D ' Companies
were sent off to dig fire trenches to cover the battalions
who were forming outposts. After we had started this,
all the plans were changed and we were told that the big
fight was to take place there, and that we were to hold
a long line of trenches prepared by civilian labour. In
our Brigade the firing line was held by the K.O.Y.L.I.
on the right, and the K.O.S.B. on the left. In local
reserve, we were behind the K.O.Y.L.I. and the Duke's
were rather behind us on our left. We started working
very hard making shelter trenches with entrenching
implements (all our tools had been lost at St Ghislain).

" The soil, fortunately, was very favourable, and we
obtained some big picks but no shovels. The men used
the entrenching implements, mess tins and their hands,

with the result that we had a very fair lot of trenches
before the guns began.

" ' C ' Company's trenches were behind a crest, and
' A ' Company's could be seen about 50 or 70 yards
ahead of us. ' D ' Company was on our right. We
could see nothing to our left, but had an excellent view
to the right and the right front. At first the guns
began searching the slopes behind us, and we watched
the limbers of the batteries being quietly moved about to
avoid the shells. They suffered a little. Most of our
guns appeared to be in front of us, but I could only see
one battery which was on a spur to our right front.
A 60-pounder battery appeared to be in rear of us, and
also, I think, a Howitzer battery. The main line of
infantry trenches appeared to have been about 500
yards in front of ' A ' Company, but I never saw them.
I heard they were very badly made by civilian labour,
much too wide and shallow. All the enemy guns were
firing as hard as they could, and the noise was terrific.
Sometimes they searched the ground we occupied, but
they did not hit a man, as we kept well down at the
bottom of the trenches. Sometimes we got a spell of
machine-gun fire, but it was no doubt aimed at something in front. The noise was like a whip being swished
backwards and forwards. Fortunately we appeared to
escape most of the Howitzer fire, which burst beyond
us whilst trying to get the 60-pounders. The ordinary
shrapnel from guns did not get into our trenches, but
splinters and bullets fell all around us. During the lulls
I was able to observe what was happening on our right.
Across the main road I saw a number of wounded men,
probably gunners, running or crawling back. Of these
many were wounded again during the journey. The
gun wagons and limbers were very quiet and frequently

changed their position, sometimes coming close behind us.

"I also saw a party of a regiment coming back. Presently other men of the same corps (I should think two companies) were brought forward to take their places and later some of these were driven back. Sometimes during a lull I walked round our trenches to see the men. I also visited the C.O. who was on our left, and Tulloch ('D' Company) who was on our right. In any part of the line one could stand up and not be seen from the front. Part of the time I read the *Daily Mail* and, being very tired, also went to sleep. The Company Sergeant-Major, M'Intosh, and one man were in the short trench with me. After what seemed hours to me, we saw the limbers galloping forward to try and get the guns back. One battery galloped past our trench within a few yards. The Captain was leading and shouting 'Come on, boys,' at the top of his voice. Another lot went forward to the battery to our right, and another past the left of our trenches, but I did not see the others. After a bit they came back, but it was a sad sight. Very few returned and these had the greatest difficulty in moving the horses. I saw one gun from our right front coming back at a slow walk, dragged by four horses. The two drivers were flogging for their lives, and shells were bursting all over them. A few gunners were hanging on to the limbers and others were straggling back wounded. I think that was the only gun that came back from that battery, but there may have been two. Of the lot who passed close to us I think two guns came back, and they were going at a good pace. There was a good deal of fire, but I could not keep down as it was so exciting. It was impossible to see what happened to the battery which passed on the

left of our position. To our right front I could see a
dismal wreck of guns and limbers where the battery
on the spur had been. Several wounded gunners came
into ' C ' Company's trenches, one having three wounds
in one leg. We could do very little but give them water,
as I could not find our doctor who had been in a trench
just behind us. I then saw large bodies of German
infantry appearing on our right front, but they were
invisible except with field glasses. Many of the infantry
on our right across the road kept retiring, and it looked
as if the spur would shortly be occupied by the enemy,
and that we would be outflanked. Then the K.O.Y.L.I.
came back through our lines, they had suffered terrible
losses in their trenches and had lost most of their
officers. Some of their men joined my company. ' A '
Company then passed through our lines, and shortly
afterwards the C.O. ordered me to retire. We made
short retirements and were most fortunate in escaping
shells. There were several slight wounds including
Ames and Whitehouse, but I did not hear of anything
serious. We had the Colonel and Buckle and Legard
with us, and the men went back steadily in splendid
order.

" We stopped for almost half an hour in one position
and got a good deal of shell fire, but luckily we found
some small trenches dug there. A few men behind us
appeared to be in a position, and we thought they were
coming forward, but, after firing over our heads for a bit
they retired. Buckle went to the left to see the General.
Eventually we retired right back on the road behind
the village of Reumont. Again we were fortunate in
escaping shells. All the afternoon we had reports of
French Armies coming up on our right and left, but they
never came. Then followed a long and very tiring

march past Maretz near Premont, to Estrées. There
was a hopeless block of transport, guns and infantry
extending for miles. It rained lightly the whole
evening and everyone was nearly dead with fatigue,
lack of sleep and want of food. Tulloch had been
hit in the head, but insisted on walking most of
the way.

" Every wagon was full of wounded or men who could
not march. We got a bivouac about 10 p.m. and then
both men and officers had some tea and bread, and lay
down anywhere (mostly in the mud) and slept."

Before proceeding with Major Hastings' diary for the
27th, it would be only just to relate briefly " D "
Company's adventures on the 26th.

An eye witness remarks :

" The Companies retired in good order from the first
to the second position, and although this movement was
carried out under shell, machine gun and rifle fire, the
lines of men were preserved just as if the manœuvre
were being executed on the barracks square at home.

" Capt. Tulloch, C.S.M. Hutchings, and a number of
men were wounded in the second position.

" In the retirement of ' D ' Company from the second
position much gallantry was displayed by various men
of the Company, in assisting the wounded back, and if
any one could be particularly mentioned in this respect,
it would be Sergt. M'Cormick, who displayed great
gallantry throughout the retirement."

Major Hastings' diary continued :—

" Thursday, 27th August (Estrées).—We moved
about 1 a.m., after three hours' rest, and then had a
very long wait before we could start, owing to the mass

of transport. We marched through St Quentin and Ham, spending the night at a farm near Ollezy. The men were very tired. We were accommodated four or five in tiny rooms, but luckily I had a bed to lie on. We had one alarm during the night.

" Friday, 28th August (Ollezy).—We left between 3 and 4 a.m., and marched to the main Paris road near Berlencourt. The whole Divisional Ammunition Column, together with some motor lorries, were told off to carry ' lame ducks.' We eventually reached La Pommeraye and bivouacked and obtained some food.

" Saturday, 29th August (La Pommeraye).—We had a much needed rest the whole day in our bivouac. In the evening orders were received to march off at 7.40 p.m. to some billets five miles away. After marching a few miles we got fresh orders to bivouac on the road. Several hours were spent marching these few miles, and the long halts were very tiring. We heard a good deal of gun fire in the early part of the day."

The Retreat.—At La Pommeraye, four miles S.E. of Noyon, the most critical period of the retreat came to an end. The British Army had succeeded in extricating itself from a very dangerous position ; a feat that the Germans certainly did not believe could be accomplished. On this day of rest all the Divisions were once more in touch with each other, and the opportunity was seized to sort out and reorganise the units. Although the retreat was to be continued for some days yet, the Army was, from that moment, in a condition to turn on its pursuers when required.

On the 30th August the 5th Division crossed the Aisne, the Battalion reaching its bivouac at Jaulzy, ten

miles E. of Compiegne, at 2.45 p.m.   The weather was
again very hot and sultry.

On the 31st, still in broiling weather, the march was
resumed, beginning with a long and steep ascent out of
the Aisne Valley.   The Division was billeted that night
at Crépy.   The Battalion was ordered to form part of
the outpost line.   " B " Company was on the right,
in touch with the Duke of Wellington's ; " A " was in
the centre, and " C " on the left, with " D " Company
in support.

Crépy.—1st September.—At 5 a.m. the German
cavalry and infantry, the latter having been brought up
in motor lorries, beigan to " feel " and test the outpost
line.   At 9.30 a.m. the enemy attacked.   At 10.15 a.m.
General Cuthbert ordered the outposts to withdraw.
" A " and " D " Companies with the machine-gun section
were closely pressed during the withdrawal, but reached
Crépy without much loss.   " C " Company, on the other
hand, had a very exposed piece of ground to cross and
suffered severely in consequence.   Among others, the
Company lost its Commander, Major Hastings, whose
diary has been so valuable in recording the opening
events of the campaign, and 2/Lieut. Ames ; both of
whom were killed.   The order to retire did not reach
" B " Company until 1 p.m., up to which time the
Company held on to its position, and then successfully
withdrew.   On completion of the withdrawal, the
Battalion followed the route of the Division and
billeted at Silly le Long, two miles S.W. of
Nanteuil.

End of the Retreat.—2nd September.—" C " and
" D " Companies were rear-guard to part of the Division.
On arrival at Cuisy, six miles N.W. of Meaux, the
Battalion took up a covering position a mile north of

that place, and at 6 p.m. it was relieved and went into billets.

3rd September.—The Division crossed the Marne. The Battalion, being in the main column, was not engaged. It went into billets at Coulommes, five miles S.E. of Meaux, at about 3 p.m. The weather was still very hot.

4th September.—The Division rested until 11 a.m., when the Battalion marched to Tournan, five miles S. of the centre of a line joining Paris and Coulommieres. Tournan was reached at 9 a.m. next day—the 5th. Here the Battalion bivouacked on a stubble field about a mile to the south of the town.

This day the Battalion received its first reinforcements of 84 N.C.O.'s and men under Lieut. Vicat. This body had been mobilised in Dublin with the Battalion, and reached France about a week after it. Lieut. Palmer, who had been employed on Staff work on the railways, rejoined at the same time.

CHAPTER III

THE MARNE AND THE AISNE

GENERAL SITUATION.—Von Kluck, commanding the German right, swerved away from his advance on Paris to assist the Armies in the centre, on the sound principle that an army's objective must be its enemy's main force rather than a town, however important that town may be. Von Kluck, however, must have failed to realise the actual situation, and miscalculated the powers for offence of the Allied troops in his own front. In wheeling to his left, he exposed his flank to the French 6th Army, in the neighbourhood of Roye. This army at once brought up its left, threatening to encircle Von Kluck's right. At the same time the British Army, with the French 5th Army on its right, faced about and began to press his front. Part of Von Kluck's miscalculation may have been that he considered that Sir John French's troops had been so hammered as to be a negligible force. If so, he must have been most unpleasantly undeceived. He quickly found himself in a dangerous position, and was forced to retire precipitately northwards.

The diary of Lieut. Palmer, who assumed command of " D " Company, will be employed for the narrative of the Battalion's advance ; any amplifications thereof being interpolated in brackets.

Lieut. Palmer's Diary.—" 6th September.—The first day of our advance against the Germans. 4 a.m. left

D

Tournan for Villeneuve (as part of the advanced guard to the Division ; ' A ' and ' B ' Companies, under Major Buckle, were vanguard), and took up outpost positions. ' D ' Company was in support in a thick wood. Left hurriedly at 2 p.m. to start pursuit of Germans. Marched to Dammartin (on the Grand Morin, south of Crécy), without incident.

" 7th September.—5 a.m., marched to Boissy le Chatel through Coulommieres (at head of main column of Division). Every village had been turned inside out by the Germans, and empty bottles were as thick as peas. Bivouacked for night.

" 8th September.—Marched at 4 a.m. (in the advanced guard) for Saacy, but just north of Doué a German rear-guard was reported in position at St Cyr (on the Petit Morin). The Brigade was ordered to attack. ' D ' Company was in support, and in a very short time we were close to a battery which was being heavily shelled. However we escaped damage (though some men of ' C ' Company were wounded by this fire). Enemy soon retired and we advanced through St Cyr ; no enemy against us, but every village pillaged. That night bivouacked near Noisement.

" 9th September.—Stood to arms at 4 a.m., and marched at about 7 a.m. to Saacy, and from there the Battalion and the K.O.Y.L.I. were sent round the left flank to try and find a German battery, which could not be located by the Flying Corps. Near Montebard ' D ' Company was sent to hold wood on our right against Germans reported there, but found nothing. Germans abandoned their guns. Bivouacked, but moved at 2 a.m.

" 10th September.—At 2 a.m. we started a night advance against Montreuil. March was unopposed, but very wet. Had a meal in village and continued march

[*Lambert Weston & Son*

BRIGADIER-GENERAL A. MARTYN, C.B., C.M.G.

(Who commanded the Battalion at Mons)

[*To face p.* 38

through Gandelu to Chezy, and bivouacked. (Many signs of the hurried German retirement were evident on this march : dead men and horses, abandoned arms and equipment, hastily evacuated bivouac grounds, etc. A reinforcement consisting of Lieut. Moulton-Barrett, Lieut. Furber, 2/Lieut. Russell and 185 N.C.O.'s and men joined at Chezy.)

" 11th September.—Marched about 7 a.m., Brigade forming the advanced guard to 5th Division. Marched through Dammard and St Remy to Hartennes (8 miles S. of Soissons), about 15 miles and, as it had been raining in torrents, we billeted there and I got fairly dry sleeping in front of a fire. On arriving at our billets we were told the Brigade had marched five miles more than was intended, but we were allowed to remain there.

" 12th September.—Marched at 5 a.m., again as advanced guard, through Chacrise, Serches to Ciry. Drenching rain all day. In Ciry we met a Cavalry Brigade which had been doing great work. After waiting in Ciry about an hour, we were told there was no room to billet there, so marched back to Serches, about five miles away. Dog-tired and wet through. Again managed to get fairly dry sleeping in front of a fire. ' D ' Company was billeted in one large farmyard, the owner of which was much worried about his pet rabbits, that he seemed to value highly.

" 13th September.—A bad day for us. Marched at 4 a.m. to attack and cross the bridge at Missy-sur-Aisne. On reaching Sermoise, ' B ' and ' C ' Companies were sent forward to occupy woods on either side of the road leading to the bridge, ' D ' Company being detailed to attack if the bridge were intact. ' A ' Company was in support. ' B ' Company at once came under fire from infantry and machine guns, and Capt.

Fisher (commanding the Company) and Lieut. Vicat
were both killed within a very short time. There were
also a good many other casualties in ' B ' Company.
The bridge was found to be destroyed and so we remained in Sermoise all day. Late in the afternoon ' D '
Company relieved ' B ' in the wood on right (east) of
bridge, but without coming under fire. At 12 midnight
' D ' Company was withdrawn, given tea on the river
bank, and then sent across the river on small rafts and
a boat ; only four men being able to go on each at a
time. ' A ' and ' C ' Companies had previously crossed
the river and were holding positions to cover the bridge."

Lieut. Palmer's diary is here interrupted in order to
amplify the history of the crossing of the Aisne.
Missy-sur-Aisne.—On the evening of the 12th Sept.
Lieut.-Colonel Martyn with his Battalion was ordered
to force the crossing of the Aisne at Missy on the following day or night. He was informed that the bridge was
believed to be still intact. As, however, the inhabitants
consistently stated that the French had destroyed it
during their retreat and that it had not been repaired,
he doubted if it were intact. Accordingly, that night
he sent a patrol under Lieut. Moulton-Barrett to try
to make certain. The patrol succeeded in getting to
within 150 yards of the bridge, but, as both banks of
the river were occupied by the Germans, they could get
no further and were forced to abandon the attempt,
losing one sergeant—killed. On the morning of 13th,
Colonel Martyn moved the Battalion down to Sermoise,
three quarters of a mile south of the Bridge, supported
by the K.O.S.B. " B " and " C " Companies were then
ordered to move forward and take up fire positions to
cover the attack of " D " Company, about 200 yards from

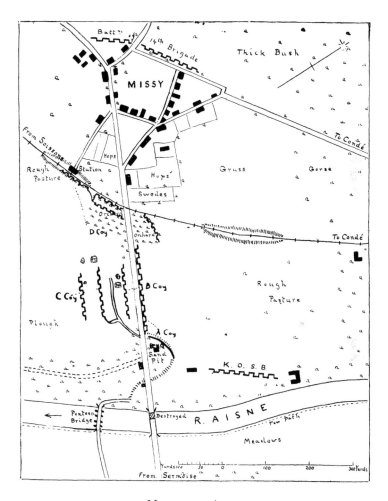

MISSY SUR AISNE

To face p. 40

the bridge ; " B " on the right and " C " on the left of the road.

The order of the advance was as follows :—

6 and 8 Platoons under 2/Lieut. Russell, supported by 5 and 7 Platoons under Lieut. Vicat.

Capt. Fisher took Lance-Cpl. Atkins and went on ahead to reconnoitre the line of advance, but he was killed as soon as he came in sight of the bridge.   Lance-Cpl. Atkins had a very narrow escape.

The Company (" B ") came under heavy rifle and machine-gun fire from the far bank, but in spite of this the advance was continued. Platoons supported each other by fire and eventually 6 and 8 Platoons reached the river bank, losing Lieut. Vicat and Sergt. Burr (both of No. 6), as well as a number of men. Both platoons and " C " Company opened a heavy fire on the opposite bank, whilst the remainder of " B " Company succeeded in pushing a small party (under Sergt. Hylands) up to the river bank, to reconnoitre and ascertain if the river were fordable. The patrol reported that it was impossible to cross, the bridge being blown up and the river about 40 yards wide and very deep. It was manifestly impossible to cross such a river by daylight, otherwise than by boats or rafts. The platoons of " B " Company remained all day in their positions, but towards afternoon were withdrawn and relieved by " D " Company ; " C " Company remaining in its fire position until dark. The fire positions of " B " (subsequently " D ") and " C " Companies commanded both banks of the river. During the stay on the river bank a German aeroplane passed overhead, dropping a lot of little steel darts which, happily, did no damage.

After dark had set in, a small boat, without oars, was

found on the south bank and some sleepers were brought from a railway lin ɛ a quarter of a mile away, with which a small raft was constructed. No rope was available so barbed wire was used to lash the raft and to tow the boat and raft to and fro across the river. Neither boat nor raft could accommodate more than four or five men at a time. The Germans gave no sign until about forty men were across. Then a patrol of five men came down to within about 200 yards of the river; three were killed, and the other two badly wounded. Sergt. Banfield with two men went out and prevented the enemy recovering their wounded during the night.

Later in the evening the Germans twice attacked, but were easily beaten off by the covering party. Presently a section of Royal Engineers arrived from Sermoise with rope and other materials, and constructed a larger raft. Before daylight both The Queen's Own and the K.O.S.B. had crossed, and were entrenched on the northern side of the Aisne. Capt. W. H. Johnston and Lieut. Flint of the 59th Field Company, R.E., were awarded the V.C. and D.S.O. respectively for their gallant work here.

On the 14th the Battalion advanced and took up a position between the damaged bridge and Missy, which it was destined to hold till the end of the month. The transport was kept to the south of the river at Sermoise, rations, etc., being brought up every night across a pontoon bridge constructed by the R.E. The weather was cold and, for the first week, very wet. The men were never dry and often had to sleep in trenches full of water. This was mainly due to the fact that water was struck a foot below ground level, and so most of the line had to be constructed of breastworks, the men living mainly under the improvised cover of ground sheets supported by a framework of branches. Nevertheless, they kept surprisingly healthy. Many casualties were suffered, as the trenches were on low ground and were continuously sniped by the Germans in the heights above, in addition to being under incessant high explosive howitzer fire. During the first week in this locality many men were hit by snipers, but this evil was largely overcome later, when the trenches were improved, adequate communication trenches dug and the positions screened from view with branches, etc.

During the stay of the Battalion on the Aisne, the men, *if* they did not know it before, learned the art of " scrounging." The rations, at this period, consisted mainly of bully beef, and the men used to scrounge in the neighbouring gardens for vegetables, with the result that they had a stew in their canteens in lieu of cold bully. The M. and V. ration was issued for the first time. Cigarettes and tobacco were very scarce, but again the ingenuity of Tommy prevailed. He smoked dried tea leaves in his pipe or, if more fastidious, rolled them in the paper from the M. and V. ration tins, and so made his cigarettes.

It was whilst in this locality that the men who had been lost in the Retreat began to come back. It was no uncommon occurrence for the platoon sergeants, when " dishing out " tea at night, to hear a man (who had been reported missing some weeks back) say, " I'm in mess to-night, Sergeant," and on looking round he would find one of his old original platoon back from the blue.

Lieut. Palmer's diary is here continued from the point at which it was broken off.

Lieut. Palmer's Diary.—" September 14th. Raining. ' A ' and ' C ' Companies still holding the same positions with K.O.S.B. on their right, ' B ' and ' D ' Companies being in support. The latter were in a small wood where ricochets were unpleasantly thick. Lieut. Wilberforce-Bell of ' A ' Company was dangerously wounded, but his life was saved by the K.O.S.B.'s doctor, who was close at hand. After dark the Battalion moved forward towards the village of Missy and entrenched along the side of the road. ' A,' ' B ' and ' D ' Companies were in the firing line, with ' C ' Company in support. It was raining most of the night. After digging down about two feet we came to water, so the trenches were not at all comfortable.

" 15th September.—About 10 a.m., when Lieut. White and I were having some bully beef, the German guns started shelling the village of Missy just on our left. After firing about six shells they put four all round us, one landing plumb in the middle of our trenches. The concussion was terrific ; mud and bits of trees fell on us in showers. Several men were partially buried but only three were slightly wounded. One man was blown up into an apple tree, 30 yards behind the trench, where he hung head downwards, grunting, until helped out of his precarious position, suffering only from slight concussion. We were soon at work digging a new trench, the old one being badly wrecked. The hole made by the explosion was enormous, and it is probable that the shell was an 11-inch one. Except for the snipers, peace reigned for the rest of the day.

" 16th September.—Improving trenches, sleeping and eating. No shells to-day, but the enemy snipers keep busy and are almost always successful in bagging one or two. But we defeat them by putting up screens of branches, so that they cannot see us. Rain nearly all day.

" 17th September.—Still working on trenches and getting more comfortable. At 2.30 p.m. the shelling started again, but did little damage. Capt. Bonsor (3rd Battalion) arrived and took command of ' D ' Company. Capt. Beeman and 2/Lieuts. Williams, Kerr and Tinne joined at the same time. Still raining.

" 18th September.—Shelling started about 10.30 a.m., but very few came near ' D ' Company. One landed on the road near the Headquarter trenches, and blew the back part of the machine guns' limbered wagon to bits, killing three horses and putting Lieut. Johnson out of action. Capt. Tulloch returned from home and took over his old Company (' D ').

" 19th September.—No shells till late in the afternoon. Just as I was going down to Headquarters the shells began flying over, and one, which landed on the road, killed Sergts. Fitzgerald, Barden and Warnett, all of ' B ' Company. They were valuable N.C.O.'s, and so a great loss. Raining nearly all day.

" 20th September.—Started some more trenches to strengthen our position, also some wire entanglements. We could hear heavy firing all day on our right and left. In the evening the Germans bombarded the village of Missy, about 200 yards on our left, and wrecked many houses and also the small railway station. The East Surrey Regiment held the village, but did not suffer much. Borrowed a razor and had first shave since the 5th—a rather painful operation. Still raining.

" 21st September.—Fairly fine day but some showers. Managed to get a change of boots, mine being worn through and full of mud and water. Village shelled again, and houses set on fire, but we were untouched. Snipers busy all day. Stood to arms after dark, expecting to move, but nothing happened.

" 22nd September.—Fine. Shelling started about 8 a.m., and village was heavily bombarded for about an hour. Every day we do a bit more to strengthen our position. We can only work during darkness, and so from 5 p.m. till 5 a.m. everybody is hard at it.

" 23rd September.—Fine but very foggy. At about 9 a.m. I was sent with Sergt. Smith and six men to reconnoitre the village of Condé, about three miles to the east of our position. I was particularly instructed to find out if the village were held by Germans. I got to within a mile of the village through thick woods, but then had to crawl about 500 yards through very thick grass. A German patrol of three men came close to us, but when we fired at them, they fled, shouting. We then reached the bank of the River Aisne, which was very open, so we had to move along a watery ditch with thick rushes over our heads. The river bank seemed deserted and also the first houses of the village, so when we came to a place about 100 yards from the bridge, I went into a farm to talk to the inhabitants, and was promptly fired on from a big house just across the river. One of my men ran in to tell me that the Germans were firing from the windows. I told him to bolt back. This he did and had a very close escape, as bullets struck the ground between his feet. I left the farm through a side window and was fired at, so got down behind a small bank, crawled as hard as I could for about 200 yards, and then ran. I found my patrol waiting for me, and we all got back safely to the Battalion at 5 p.m., and were able to make a useful report. We found that our trenches had been shelled hard all the afternoon, and a few men had been killed. Very tired and hungry. Had a good sleep till 2 a.m.

" 24th September.—Lieut. Harding and 2/Lieut.

Pownall arrived and joined the Battalion. The former
was posted to ' D ' Company together with forty-seven
men. Very intermittent shelling commenced in the
morning and went on, with interruptions, till about
4 p.m. Capt. Bonsor and Lieut. White suffered from
cold and wet. The former was subsequently sent home.

" 25th September.—Still adding to Company's defence work. No shelling all day. Heard that a big
German gun in Condé Fort had been knocked out by our
heavy guns.

" 26th September.—No shelling all day. Rumours
of enemy having crossed river at Condé in large numbers
proved to be false. Only small parties crossed in
rowing boats. Battalion stood to arms and extra
patrols were sent out, as an attack was expected at dusk.

" 27th September.—Shelling started about 10 a.m.,
while L.-Cpl. Eldridge was cutting my hair, and
a heavy bombardment took place. At 2 p.m. the
shelling decreased, but at 3 p.m. it again increased and
shrapnel was poured on the village. The day finished
with terrific salvos at 5.30 p.m. Quiet night.

" 28th September.—Shelling commenced at 8.30 a.m.,
but was not violent ; the guns seemed a long way off.
Intermittent shelling all day, but no damage done.
Though two of these shells (5·9's) were direct hits on the
haystack behind which ' B ' Company (Moulton-Barrett)
had its Company Headquarters, and the haystack
rocked visibly each time, luckily both shells failed to
explode. Added one more small piece of trench and
completed a very formidable obstacle.

" 29th September.—Shelling started at 5.30 a.m. at
' C ' Company, whose trenches seemed to be very accurately ranged on, as they got all the shells. The
officer's dug-out was twice demolished. Fairly heavy

bombardment all day, so had to keep to trenches all the time.

"30th September.—Shelling started about 8.30 a.m. again at ' C ' Company. Heavy bombardment later in the day.

"1st October.—Very peaceful day, no shells. At 7 p.m. we were told Lancashire Fusiliers were going to relieve us at night and we were going to rest and refit for a week. At 8 p.m. I was sent to reconnoitre track to pontoon bridge, and had a beastly walk of five miles."

Retrospect.—As the end of September marks the close of a definite phase of the campaign, it is a good time to take stock and to see how the Battalion had come through the War up till then.

I.—Officers.

The Battalion started the campaign with 27 officers. Seven, namely, the Commanding Officer, Senior Major, Adjutant, Machine Gun Officer, Transport Officer, Quartermaster and Medical Officer (attached), were Headquarter officers. Of the remaining twenty, six were with " A " Company, five with " B," five with " C " and four with " D."

The Headquarter officers were still all available except Lieut. Johnson, the Machine Gun Officer, who was hurt by a shell on 18th September and sent to England the following day.

" A " Company had lost : Capt. Lister (Commanding), wounded and prisoner ; Lieut. Anderson, killed ; 2/Lieut. Chitty, wounded and prisoner—all at Mons ; and Lieut. Wilberforce-Bell, wounded near Missy on 14th September.

Four officers out of six.

" B " Company had lost : Major Pack Beresford (Commanding), killed ; Capt. Phillips (2nd in Command), killed ; 2/Lieut. Broadwood, killed ; and Lieut. Sewell, mortally wounded at Wasmes. Capt. Fisher, who had succeeded to the command, and Lieut. Vicat were killed at Missy Bridge on 13th September.

This accounts for all the original five officers and one in addition.

" C " Company had lost : Major Hastings (Commanding), and 2/Lieut. Ames, both killed at Crépy on 1st September.

Two out of five.

" D " Company had lost : Capt. Buchanan-Dunlop (2nd in Command), wounded at Mons. Capt. Tulloch (Commanding), wounded at Le Cateau, but had returned from England during September.

Thus the total officer casualties from 23rd August to 30th September were : 9 killed, 2 wounded and prisoners of war, 4 wounded—15 in all. Of these, 14 had started the campaign with the Battalion. There remained 13 of the original officers and 10 others, namely, 2 captains and 8 subalterns, who had joined in September, and were still present on 30th. The Battalion left the Aisne with 23 officers.

The commanders of the companies were now :—

" A "—Capt. Keenlyside, who had served from the start.

" B "—Lieut. Moulton-Barrett, 2nd Bn., who was serving at the depot when the War began.

" C "—Capt. Grant, 2nd Bn., who was serving at the depot when the War began.

" D "—Capt. Tulloch, wounded but returned.

Lieut. Palmer took command of the machine gun section.

II.—OTHER RANKS.

The losses in action among W.O.'s, N.C.O.'s and men amounted to about 390. Of these, 31 were killed and 96 wounded in the trenches near Missy. It is impossible now to allocate the rest of the casualties to the various engagements.

With regard to the first fortnight, when the Army was falling back under circumstances which often rendered it impossible to bring away the seriously wounded, or to account for men who were not to be found, many reported as " wounded and missing " were really killed, whilst still more reported as " missing " were either killed or badly wounded. No one can now differentiate between those who disappeared because they were hit, those who got temporarily lost—that is, could not find their own battalion—as was the case with a few in all units, and those who simply collapsed under the physical strain, and so fell into the hands of the enemy.

Besides the battle losses, a few men were sent to hospital : the wet trenches on the Aisne accounted for nearly all these.

The Battalion had been reinforced by 84 N.C.O.'s and men on 5th September, 185 on 10th, 176 on 23rd, or 445 in all. They were nearly all men of The Queen's Own Army Reserve, but included a few returned wounded, and stragglers from The Retreat. The Battalion left the Aisne with a total strength of 986— within a few of the numbers it had when the campaign commenced.

CHAPTER IV

GENERAL SITUATION.—In the latter part of September began that curious extension of the contending lines towards the north-west, as the leaders on each side came to realise that a frontal attack on a prepared position was almost hopeless, and that the only chance of reaching a rapid decision was to outflank the opponent. Both French and Germans were trying desperately to effect this on the only open flank, towards the Channel ports, with the result that the engaged lines seemed to grow outwards daily towards the coast of the North Sea. The Germans had a great preponderance of fresh forces available for this purpose, whilst in addition, they were expecting the immediate fall of Antwerp. This event alone, would release about 90,000 men at a point conveniently situated to outflank the Allies' left.

When the deadlock on the Aisne became evident, Sir John French obtained Marshal Joffre's concurrence to transfer the British Army to Flanders. This movement, in addition to the manifest convenience of shortening the line of communication with England, brought the 7th Division—which was landing at Zeebrugge and Ostend to assist the Belgians—into line with the rest of the British Army.

The Move to Flanders.—The IInd Corps was the first to move, the 13th Brigade evacuating its trenches on the night of 1st-2nd October. At 1.20 a.m. on the 2nd, the Battalion handed over its trenches to the Lancashire

Fusiliers, of the 4th Division ; and, crossing the Aisne by the pontoon bridge, marched to Couvrelles (near Braisne). This place was reached, by hard marching, just after daybreak. Next night the march was continued to Maast et Violaine (six miles S.W. of Braisne). Here the Battalion was billeted in big caves, and the men were specially warned to keep under cover during the day, in order to escape aeroplane observation. Another night's march brought the Battalion to Hartennes, where it had billeted on the 11th September. It was here that the men were paid out, it is believed, for the second time since leaving Ireland. Hartennes was a memorable place to the officers also, for it was here that they slept in their valises—the first time for many weeks. The next day, the 4th, was Sunday, and Divine Service was held. Up till now it had been believed that the Brigade had been moved out of the trenches merely for a rest, but, when orders for a night's march of 17 miles westwards were received, the officers, at least, began to suspect that the Army was to operate on the left of the French. This march brought the Battalion to Largny (three miles W. of Villers). The road was good, the weather fine, and there was a full moon ; but the march was a fatiguing one owing to constant checks, due, probably, to the route crossing lines of communication of French troops.

Concerning this march Lieut. Kerr remarks : " Owing to the constant checks on the route, this march lasted from 6.30 p.m. until 5 a.m. Many of the men went to sleep as they marched and just fell down at the halts. My platoon was doing baggage guard and I remember that twice I went to sleep and walked into the horse of the C.O. of the K.O.Y.L.I., who were immediately in rear of us."

" Fresnoy was reached by a short march of 8 miles on the 6th, and at 7 next morning the Brigade started for Pont St Maxence, where it was to entrain. The Brigadier, Gen. Hickie, who had succeeded General Cuthbert, marched in the ranks of the Battalion for some way and yarned with the men. The men were all very bucked over it, and talked about it for a long time after.

" The route of this march crossed the line of retreat which the Battalion had traversed on 31st August. Pont St Maxence was reached at 3 p.m., but it was found that the Battalion could not entrain before 7 p.m. Even then there was no room on the train for 300 men. These, together with the transport, had to be left behind to follow next day. Once again Lieut. Kerr's remarks are interesting to note. He says : ' Nineteen days in the wet trenches on the Aisne had caused everybody's boots to shrink and crack, and so it was a very painful march to Pont St Maxence. It often used to take half an hour to get one's boots on before parade. Moulton-Barrett had sprained the tendon at the back of his heel and hobbled along with one boot cut down like a shoe, whilst I remember seeing one man of the K.O.S.B. with puttees wound round his feet in lieu of boots.'

" Our destination was still kept secret, but at 5.30 a.m. on the 8th the Battalion detrained at Abbeville, in the vicinity of which town all the 5th Division was concentrating.

"The French left flank now extended to the neighbourhood of Béthune, and the urgency of the situation in that region necessitated an immediate advance of the IInd Corps, both to assist our Allies and also to cover the concentration northwards of the Ist and IIIrd Corps.

E

The 13th Brigade began its march towards Béthune on the same day that it detrained, the 8th October, the Battalion commencing its march at 6 p.m. The 300 men left at Pont St Maxence only arrived half an hour before the Battalion marched off. Many troops were on the move and the road was frequently blocked. Therefore, although the distance was only about 10 miles to Gueschart (S. of the River Authie), the Battalion did not arrive until nearly midday on the 9th. After numerous contradictory orders had been received, the Battalion marched at 11 p.m. eight miles northeastward to Haravesne, where it arrived at 3 a.m. on the 10th. From now onwards the journey was to be continued in motor lorries, but those for the use of our unit were not ready until 11 p.m. that night, so we bivouacked by the road-side for the whole of the day. The lorries took the men to Valhuon (15 miles S.W. of Béthune) where the last party arrived at 5 a.m. on the 11th. The transport reached the same locality by route of march."

General Situation.—The Allied Commanders intended to use the British Army to outflank the right of the main German forces which were stretching in a N.E. to S.W. direction across Northern France. The neighbourhood of Béthune, where the British right linked up with the French left, was to be the pivot of a great turning movement. Much advance was not required in this region where the 13th Brigade was operating, nor would it have been possible, as the German forces here were known to be too strong. The greatest movement was to be on the other flank, the left, where the Germans thinned out. It was hoped that the British Army might swing round like a mighty door, from facing N.E. to facing S.E., on its hinge at Béthune. This hope was

not destined to be realised, firstly because of the fall
of Antwerp on the 8th October, and still more, because
of the quite unexpected strength of the fresh forces
that the Germans succeeded in concentrating on their
right flank.   When the movement was finally checked,
on the 19th October, the British Army stretched in a
jagged line from Givenchy (between Béthune and La
Bassée) on the right, with its centre in advance of
Armentières, and its left near Paschendaele.

In this position the British Army had subsequently
to withstand the furious counter attacks of the Germans,
who, with greatly superior forces and an overwhelming
preponderance of artillery, strove with all their might
to batter their way through the thinly held British line,
and so to win to the Channel ports.   After events have
shown how serious a disaster to us their success would
have been.   The wonderful resistance of Sir John
French's forces with, on occasions, notable French
assistance, frustrated the German aim, but it may be said
almost to have cost the sacrifice of the Old British
Regular Army.   The old units remained of course, but
their ranks were no longer filled with pre-war regular
soldiers, of whom but few survived after this great
battle.

Operations near Béthune.—On 11th October the 13th
Brigade, under Brigadier-General Hickie, left Valhuon
at 8 a.m. as reserve to the IInd Corps.   The Battalion
reached Drouvin (4 miles S. of Béthune) at about 6 p.m.
and billeted there.   At 9 a.m. on the 12th it marched
to Beuvry (2 miles S.E. of Béthune).   Here the Brigade
received at 3 p.m. orders to advance in a S.E. direction
against the enemy, who was in position between La
Bassée and Vermelles.   The Queen's Own was on the
right of the Brigade, the Duke of Wellington's in the

centre, and the K.O.S.B. on the left, with the K.O.Y.L.I. in reserve. After passing Annequin the enemy was found to be holding his position in force, and the Brigade entrenched in advance of the road between Givenchy and Noyelles.

The Battalion was on the left of the French in this operation, which was the first attack on Vermelles. It was understood that the French also were attacking at 3 p.m., but they did not do so, and the Battalion appeared to attack alone. No headway could be made and we had no artillery support. Major Buckle and Lieut. Legard walked up and down behind the supports smoking cigarettes. During the day the Battalion suffered over fifty casualties, among whom was Sergt. Hylands (now C.S.M.), who was wounded, in the early part of the day, near the slag heaps. These losses were caused principally by an enfilading rifle and shell fire from the village of Vermelles.

The 13th was occupied in strengthening the trenches. The guns on either side were busy, but their fire was mostly directed against each other, and the infantry was not seriously harassed. The French, on our right, subsequently attempted an advance against Vermelles, but could make no progress. Lieut.-Col. Martyn took over the command of the Brigade on this day, as Brigadier-General Hickie had to go on sick leave. The command of the Battalion then devolved on Major Buckle. The 14th passed as the previous day, without much incident. After dark that evening The Queen's Own was relieved in its trenches by a French battalion. The companies assembled at Annequin after the relief and marched to billets at Quesnoy (a mile N. of the railway between Béthune and La Bassée).

On the morning of the 15th the Battalion moved N.

MAJOR P. M. BUCKLE, D.S.O.
Killed while commanding the Battalion at Neuve Chapelle)

To face p. 56

in support of the 14th Brigade, and on the 16th The Queen's Own and the K.O.Y.L.I. came under the orders of the G.O.C. 3rd Division, and marched to Richebourg St Vaast. Whilst here, " B " Company's officers were billeted in the Mayor's house. During the morning of the 17th the Mayor's wife came back to her house and made an awful fuss because a window had been broken. It was probably her last visit to her house for four years, and if she has again seen it she will have been lucky if one stone is left upon another. The two battalions remained in billets at Richebourg until 2 p.m. on the 17th, when they were sent to Neuve Chapelle in support of the 7th Brigade.

Before daybreak on the 18th the Battalion relieved the 3rd Worcestershire Regt. in trenches facing Illies. The position had only been occupied since the previous evening, but the Worcesters had entrenched as far as possible. The trenches were improved during the day. The Battalion was now under the orders of the G.O.C. 7th Brigade, and had the South Lancashires on its right and the Wiltshires on its left. Illies was very strongly occupied, and no advance was attempted. There was a good deal of shelling during the day and some casualties were suffered, including Lieut. Kerr, who was wounded while reconnoitring towards Illies.

On the 19th the situation remained unchanged, but further casualties were sustained from shell fire. The night was very wet. Before dawn on the 20th the Battalion was relieved by the Worcesters, and went into billets near Bois de Biez. At 1 p.m., however, it was called out again to support the South Lancashires who had been heavily attacked near Lorgies. It took up a line behind that Regiment and, after dark, two companies moved up to reinforce it. At dusk on the 21st the

other two companies also advanced to the front line.
The trenches had been much wrecked by shell fire.
The Battalion remained in this position throughout the
22nd. A German attack was expected at any moment,
but none came, and that part of the line was not heavily
shelled. Capt. Grant, commanding " C " Company, was
wounded by a sniper this day. On the 23rd, when it
got dark, a German patrol approached a haystack just
in front of our position. One of our patrols fired on it
and hit several, one of whom was apparently carrying
petrol, as, when he started to run away, his clothes
broke into flames and he ran screaming until eventually
he fell dead. Soon after midnight on the 23rd-24th,
the Battalion was ordered to withdraw and to take up
a more retired position near Neuve Chapelle. This was
disheartening to all ranks, as they had worked hard to
strengthen the position they had gained. The retirement
was in accordance with Sir H. Smith-Dorrien's occupation of the most defensible line to be found in the vicinity
of the points already reached, it being now realised that
further advance was impossible. Moreover, the ever
growing strength of the enemy was compelling the
IInd Corps to change its attitude from attack to defence.

Neuve Chapelle.—The history of the days spent in the
Neuve Chapelle trenches is related by five survivors.
The plan is supplied by Capt. Palmer, and his diary for
the 23rd is first quoted. He was then a Lieutenant and
commanded the machine-gun section.

Lieut. Palmer's Diary. — (1) " October 23rd.—
Reached what was supposed to be a prepared position
near Neuve Chapelle about 4 a.m. and found one good
piece of trench, the rest being very poor and only half
finished. Put the machine guns on the left of the

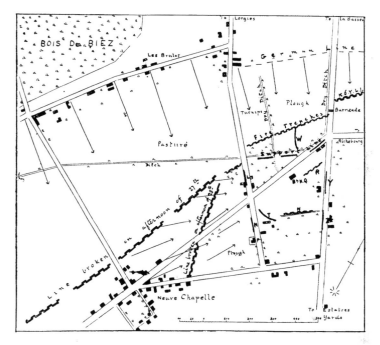

NEUVE CHAPELLE

EXPLANATION

The Queen's Own positions are in red.

On 26th October two platoons each of D, B, and A Companies, in that order from right to left, occupied the fire trenches with their other two platoons in support. A had a platoon on the left of the Lorgies Road. C was in reserve at R.

On 27th Companies were in the same position, except that C had relieved D, which latter Company had suffered particularly heavily. The right-hand support trench having been obliterated, the two support platoons of C remained at R, while D moved into a new reserve position at N.

When the line beyond the left gave on the 27th, the platoon of A to the left of the Lorgies Road and the support platoons of that Company took post at L, while the reserve Company D lined the road at M. The enemy, having reached P, which had been the Bn. First Aid Post, D took a new line at T.

On the 28th when the Germans again broke the line on the left, penetrating as far as Bn. H.Qs., 'A' Company fell back and held the road at Y, while 'D' Company prolonged the line to the left at ZZ. The left of 'B' Company being refused and occupying position W.

C.S.M. Penny was killed on the road at Y, and Lieut. Gore, commanding 'A' Company, at ZZ.

[To face p. 58

Battalion trenches with ' A ' Company, and had opposite us a village, with road running from it towards us, about 350 yards away. The cottages on this side of the village were burnt to prevent Germans getting snipers into them. We could hear Germans firing at our old position, but houses behind us were very soon shelled and set on fire. Three German aeroplanes passed over us early. Enemy started arriving in village in front of us about 2.30 p.m. and we opened fire whenever we saw him. Machine guns soon attracted attention and our guns and sandbags were frequently hit, showers of mud being thrown over us. It was very unpleasant looking over top of parapet as several bullets passed remarkably close to my head, whilst one scorched the top of Pte. Nelson's cap as he was working a gun. Enemy's fire ceased about 5 p.m. and after dark he brought up three searchlights and played them all over us. From the sound of voices, Germans were apparently digging, and loop-holing walls of cottages. No disturbance in front of us at night, but there was heavy firing on our left and right. ' B ' Company in the morning found that they had killed twelve Germans, who had been digging close in front of us."

(This account is continued subsequently on page 68.)

An account by Capt. R. M. G. Tulloch, D.S.O., Commanding " D " Company, who was first wounded at Le Cateau, and again in this battle.

Captain Tulloch's Narrative.—(2) " The story opens on the 24th of October, when the Battalion held a position S.W. of Neuve Chapelle, forming part of a defensive line held by the IInd Corps. Previous to the 24th the Battalion had been continuously fighting, marching and entrenching for ten days or more in face of a steadily increasing German force, so that by the 24th we had had a considerable amount of fighting in the neighbourhood of Béthune.   Returning now to the operations on, and subsequent to the 24th October, the position held by the Battalion was 450 yards in extent, and formed part of a continuous line of trenches running roughly N.E. and S.W.   Owing to the broad front held by the Battalion, it was necessary to detail three companies for the firing line.   These had each approximately two platoons in the firing line, and two platoons in supporting trenches some 100 or 150 yards in rear.   Prior to the 24th, the Germans had been pushing up towards our position and entrenching themselves at about 500-800 yards from it.   From the 24th onwards, they made repeated attacks both on the line held by us, and on the positions held by the battalions on either flank.   On our right were the K.O.Y.L.I., who held their position splendidly and, by a certain amount of cross fire, aided materially in the defence of the right portion of our line ; but on our left we were not so fortunate, as the battalions on this flank were eventually driven back.

" I will now go into the details of what happened to my own company on the right of our line on the 24th-26th, as the attack on it was typical of the German attack on the rest of the line held by the Battalion.   The area covered by my firing, support, and communication trenches was approximately 150 yards square, and into this area the Germans turned the fire of several 6-in. howitzers, commonly called ' Black Marias,' as well as three or four field guns, in addition to rifle and machine-gun fire.   The shrapnel and machine-gun fire we could compete with, as our fire trenches, and especially the supports in dug-outs in a broad ditch some fifteen feet wide by eight feet deep, were proof against such fire.

But we could not compete with the fire of the 6-in. howitzers, as their shells descend at a very steep angle and wreck everything they strike, making a hole in soft soil some 6 feet deep by 8 feet across. During the afternoon of the 24th the Germans put some sixty ' Black Marias ' into that area 150 yards square, which is referred to above, and, after dusk, opened with shrapnel into the line of the fire trench, so as to prevent us either repairing any damage done to the fire trench, or bringing up supports. Little damage, however, was done that day though some buildings and a wood just behind the support line were badly wrecked ; the road being rendered quite impassable for vehicles owing to the shell holes. That night the Germans attacked the companies to our left, but left us alone, which we regretted, as we badly wanted to get our own back and to repay the shelling we had had to endure during the afternoon.

" The next day (25th) the same thing was repeated, only the shelling was somewhat worse. Either through spies or aeroplanes, probably the former, the enemy located our support trench, putting ten or twelve shells right into it and completely wrecking not only our dugouts, but also the ditch itself. Luckily the men had been shifted to a safer spot just before, otherwise our casualties would have been extremely heavy. I have never seen such a mess as they made of that ditch ; broken timbers, branches torn from overhanging trees, gaping holes in the ground ; in fact, not a yard of level surface anywhere. All that remained of a solid wooden bridge, under which the Company Headquarters had been, was one jagged beam pointing skywards. That night the enemy repeated his shelling of our position with shrapnel for about two hours, but made no attack.

During these two days my Company had lost twenty men killed and wounded, which was not excessive, considering the amount of shell and rifle fire experienced. During this period the Germans had, by night, dug another line of trenches some 150 yards nearer our line.

" The 26th was the day on which the enemy had determined to launch a real attack, and the shelling this day was the worst I have ever experienced, while the amount of ammunition used by the enemy must have been enormous. Beginning about 7 a.m. the Germans shelled slowly, but methodically, the area behind our support trenches, where reserves were thought to be, and then, soon after midday, fire was concentrated on the vicinity of the fire and support trenches. Considering the small area shot at, the fire was terrific ; no sooner was the debris clear from the explosion of one shell than the next was heard arriving, and at one time I reckoned that they were falling at the rate of 100 an hour. Everything was wrecked, the support trench was rendered impassable as well as the communication trench, so that to reach the fire trench we had to double across 150 yards of open ground. Here the heavy fire helped us, as the smoke and debris from the bursting shells were so thick that men were often able to reach the fire trench unperceived by the machine guns, which were trained on, and fired at, the area behind the fire trench, in order to prevent supports coming up.

" About 2 p.m., owing to several 6-in. shells having burst actually in the fire trench, wrecking parts of the trench and burying men alive under the debris, it was very necessary to send up extra men with shovels to clear the debris. Ten men volunteered for this job, and, armed with two shovels each, raced for the fire trench. Luckily only one was hit, and then the job of digging out the entombed men began. It was no easy job as, owing to the parapet being wrecked, and to heavy machine-gun and rifle fire, to say nothing of 6-in. shells which were falling within a few yards of the trench, it was impossible to stand up to dig. As it was, three of the volunteer diggers were hit to my knowledge, and more may have been. Anyway we dug out two men alive, which was great satisfaction. As the Germans were not coming on, the fire trench was left weakly held in order to avoid losses and, as soon as dusk fell, extra men were pushed up in twos and threes to try and get across the fire-swept area from the support to the fire trench. But, in spite of the darkness, many were hit. Then started the worst shrapnel shelling I have ever experienced. At one time they were bursting at the rate of ten a minute, and the dirt from the parapet was continually knocked all over the men. The only thing was to crouch under cover and trust that the shelling would stop to allow of men looking out before the actual infantry attack took place. This is actually what happened. For myself, thinking that I ought to take a peep to the front into the night, I incautiously put my head above the parapet, when a shell, bursting almost in my face, knocked me over and rendered me useless for the rest of the fight.

" Earlier in the afternoon, a shelling, similar to that which my Company had endured, had been too much for the regiment on our left and it had vacated several of its trenches, leaving our left flank dangerously exposed. A platoon from our Reserve Company was sent to cover this flank, but reinforcements coming up from elsewhere relieved the situation.

" To return to my own Company's experiences : the attack developed about two hours after I was knocked

over and, in spite of the loss of all its officers (Beeman
and Harding having become casualties before dark),
and the loss of over fifty men, the remainder of the
Company held their ground and met the Germans with
rifle fire and the bayonet.   Personally, I was immensely
proud of the way in which my Company worked, and
consider that no infantry could have done more.   In
this Major Buckle cordially agreed, and spoke to the
Company, praising them for their resolute and soldierly
behaviour.

" This ends my part of the story.   From what I have
since heard, not only did the Regiment gain great credit
for its resolute action in holding the position, but, when
the line was broken on our left subsequent to the 26th,
the action of the Regiment saved that part of the line from
a very serious situation.   We have to deplore the loss of
many brave comrades, but at the same time one cannot
help being thrilled with pride at the noble way in which
all ranks answered to the call of duty."

An account by Capt. E. T. Moulton-Barrett who was
then commanding " B " Company :—
Capt. Moulton-Barrett's Narrative.—(3) " To continue
Tulloch's narrative and to say what I know of the
situation during the heavy fighting commencing on
October 24th I must first remark that when a trench is
referred to, a trench containing one platoon is implied.

" The night of October 24th was very dark, and,
at about 8 p.m., heavy firing was going on from
the Company's left trench, which had some high wire
entanglement about 25 feet in front of it.   It was said
that some of the enemy were endeavouring to cut the
wire, while some others were throwing up a rough trench
about 60 feet away.   This was ' pooh-poohed ' by a

section of the occupants of the trench, but at dawn on October 25th it was found that the firing was justified, as three dead Germans were found at the entanglement, and, a short distance in front, was some newly thrown up earth.

" Major Buckle came into the trench and asked for a volunteer to go forward and see if there were any Germans behind the parapet. Without any hesitation L.-Cpl. Wright of ' B ' Company went over the parapet and made a reconnaissance. On his return he stated that there were ' no live Germans, but a dozen dead ones ! ' On the evening of the same day Sergt. Bishop took out a party to fill in this new trench. He had a covering party consisting of L.-Cpl. Wright and three men, whilst twelve men accompanied him with shovels. This was accomplished with no firing. On the morning of the 26th it was apparent that some of the enemy must have crawled forward, as enough earth to hide two men had been thrown up, but on this occasion they were not heard.

" During the night 25th-26th some firing was heard coming from the direction of ' B ' Company's right trench. In the morning about fifteen of the enemy lay dead 50 feet away from the trench.

" Towards the evening of the 26th we were being subjected to a very heavy shrapnel bombardment in the support trenches, similar to that described by Tulloch.

" October 27th.—Up to 2 p.m. all had been comparatively quiet, when suddenly a hail of bullets was showered on ' A ' and ' B ' Companies' support trenches, and some other British troops, having fallen back apparently from the line which they held, were seen coming through our lines. Thereupon the supports were taken out of their trenches and moved to a position about 50 yards away, lining a road at right angles to the general line of our trenches, in order to cover our left, which was now exposed. Some crawled forward, but it was impossible to get very far owing to the heavy fire of the enemy which they were under during the whole period of their advance to the new position. On arrival at the road, the enemy could be seen collecting in masses about 250 yards from us. We opened fire and they did not advance.

" It is difficult to state the Germans' actions, movement by movement, but it is clear that they wished to get round to the back of our fire trenches ; but, owing to the determined manner in which our men held the road, with odds roughly four to one against them, the enemy were frustrated in their attempts. Great credit was due to Company Sergeant-Major Penny on this day for the cool manner in which he behaved, walking about smoking a cigarette in an entirely collected manner. His action proved a great steadier to the men in this critical situation, since at that time there was a gap of at least 400 yards on the left of our line of trenches.

" Now, as the enemy saw that the road was denied them, they decided to extend their right and so overlap our flank, but further down the road ' D ' Company, who were then in reserve, conformed to our movements and so extended our line. This was still insufficient, and the Germans got into a village (Neuve Chapelle) on our left flank, having thus completely broken through the British front line. Dusk was beginning to fall and, owing to a request on our part for reinforcements, we learned that the 9th Bhopal Infantry were coming to our help. In the meantime there was a small incident worth recording. On one occasion a couple of men appeared round a house and when challenged, replied,

COMPANY SERGEANT-MAJOR W. PENNY

(Killed at Neuve Chapelle)

[*To face p.* 66

' We are English,' which was greeted by a volley from our men, as such a reply deserved, as it is a well-known trick of the enemy to reply to a challenge in English. Just before the 9th Bhopal Infantry came up we could hear the Germans collecting preparatory to a charge, calling out ' Deutsche hier,' but on the arrival of the Indian troops they withdrew. That night we had to readjust our line temporarily. The 9th Bhopal Infantry prolonged our left, bending the line back from our left flank, as the trenches formerly held by British troops were now occupied by Germans.

" The following conversation was overheard by an officer of the 9th B.I. whilst passing behind one of our trenches :—

" Pte. A. ' Hallo, who's that passing behind the trench ? '

" Pte. B. ' That ? Why, that's an officer.'

" Pte. A. ' But we ain't got no officers left.'

" Pte. B. ' That's a British officer of the Indian troops.'

" Pte. A. ' Thank Heaven ! I'm glad to know there are still some officers about.'

" On October 28th we were told that a combined force of British, French, and Indian troops were going to make an attack, and retake the trenches lost the previous day. Consequently our artillery started shelling Neuve Chapelle very heavily. But, in the meantime, the enemy were also shelling our trenches preparatory to an attack. They were beginning to develop their attack. When the Allies discovered this they devoted their efforts to attempting to shell the hostile infantry. But, unfortunately, their shots fell short and we in the fire trenches were subjected to both shrapnel and heavy artillery fire from friend and foe. About 2.45 p.m. the

German attack having developed more quickly than our own, they were enabled to push a force of about 400 men through the gap, which had yet to be filled. From our point of view, in the fire trenches, it was impossible to do anything beyond getting two men to fire over the left traverse of the left trench. Shortly after this we had a number of shots in our backs, but these ceased in about fifteen minutes. I myself was in the fire trenches and consequently can give no actual account of what went on in the support and reserve trenches. But at dusk I took a small party to visit the headquarter and reserve trenches, and found that the Germans had been there, but had departed.

" Thus ended five days of very severe fighting, and the Regiment had managed to hold the line allotted to it without once having been compelled to withdraw ; although at times the enemy had completely turned our flank and was behind us."

The further account by Capt. W. V. Palmer, who, on Capt. Tulloch becoming a casualty, took over command of " D " Company :—

Capt. Palmer's Narrative continued. — (4) " The accounts of the fighting between the 24th and 28th October, written by Tulloch and Moulton-Barrett, describe what took place in the firing-line trenches held by the Battalion. My narrative only deals with what occurred behind the firing-line on the 27th and 28th, as on both days I was in the headquarter and reserve trenches.

" October 27th. — About 2 p.m. messages came to Headquarters that the Germans had broken through the battalions on our left, and were enfilading our trenches. This soon became very apparent to us, for the 200 yards of plough which separated the reserves from Headquarters, were swept by a very heavy rifle fire from the left. The Commanding Officer at once ordered me to get the reserve company, ' D ' (about 80 strong), into a position to meet this flank movement. This could best be carried out by lining a road about 50 yards from the reserve trenches, which ran parallel to the enemy's advance. Unfortunately, in the noise, the order went wrong and only about 20 men lined the road, the remainder moving to another position. However, our numbers were slightly increased by some officers and men of the regiment which had been on our left, and these undertook to protect my left flank by holding a farm building about 100 yards down the road. As soon as we had lined the road, we could see the Germans about 500 yards away moving across our front to the left, and apparently using the vacated trenches to enable them to do so ; while, at the same time, they brought a heavy and accurate fire to bear on us. As the Germans continued to move round on my left, I went down the road towards the farm to ascertain if they were moving round behind us, and was promptly fired at by a party which had worked up to the farm unseen. What happened to the troops holding the farm I cannot say, but they disappeared and accordingly my left had to be thrown back still further, and the Battalion was now facing the enemy in three directions : front, left flank and left rear. Shortly after this, in the darkness, we heard shouts in a foreign language very close behind us. A large body of troops loomed out of the darkness, who, to our great relief, proved to be Indian Infantry coming to support us.

" October 28th.—The orders for the day were as follows :—

F

" 'The trenches which had been vacated on the 27th were to be retaken, and the village of Neuve Chapelle occupied. At 11 a.m. a general bombardment of the enemy's position would be undertaken by our Brigade of guns, assisted by nine French batteries, and at 11.15 a.m. the line would commence its advance.'

" As the Battalion had not vacated its trenches on the 27th it had no advance to make, but the advance was to be supported by our fire. However, soon after 12 noon, ' B ' and ' C ' Companies reported that the Germans were attacking in front of their trenches. This attack apparently developed all along the line, for, soon after 2 o'clock, the enemy again broke through on our left flank and once more we were heavily enfiladed. While endeavouring to get what remained of ' D ' Company out of the reserve trenches, I caught an enfilade bullet which broke my leg and left me in an open field. This field was seemingly the target for the artillery and infantry of both sides, for it was swept by a very heavy fire for a considerable period. From my position I could see little of what was going on, but there was rifle fire on both sides of us, so I imagined our companies had been compelled to withdraw, especially as, at about 5 p.m., a party of Germans came to within 100 yards of me from the direction of our firing line. However, at 9 p.m. I was picked up by a patrol from ' C ' Company, who, to my intense delight, told me that the Battalion had never moved from its trenches."

Account by Lieut. H. B. H. White, D.S.O. :—

Lieut. White's Narrative.—(5) " About 7 p.m. on the night of October 28th, Capt. Moulton-Barrett, who was wounded in the head, came to me and said that 2/Lieut. Russell and I were the only officers left and, owing to the retirement of the regiment on our left, the Germans had broken through the line and thus we were in danger on that flank and also on the left rear, about a quarter of a mile off. ' C ' Company was then on the right of the firing line and ' B ' Company on the left. ' A ' and ' D ' Companies, who were in support, had no officers with them. I was in command of ' C ' Company and 2/Lieut. Russell of ' B ' Company. Captain Moulton-Barrett then had to leave owing to his wound, and I communicated the situation to the Headquarters of the 7th Brigade. The strength of the two companies in the firing line was about 200, each company having one platoon in support. The Yorkshire Light Infantry were still holding their trenches on our right, which made that flank safe.

" Having posted the night sentries, I went to find a staff officer and, after some trouble, found the Staff Captain of the Brigade. He informed me that about ninety men of ' A ' and ' D ' Companies were coming up to support me ; that the Duke of Cornwall's were advancing to support the Yorkshire Light Infantry on our right, and two companies of the Bedfords and one of the Cheshires were advancing on our left. At about 11 o'clock, after a conference between Major Allason (commanding the Bedford Company), the Staff Captain and myself, it was decided that ' C ' Company should hold its trenches, but that ' B ' Company should be thrown back almost at right angles to ' C ' Company, facing the village which the Germans now occupied. The two companies of the Bedfords and the one of the Cheshires prolonged to the left.

" At about 11.30 p.m. ' B ' Company, in spite of a most arduous day, dug fresh trenches and were warmly complimented thereon by the Staff Captain at a later date.

" The remnants of ' A ' and ' D ' Companies, roughly
a 100 strong, came up about midnight under Acting
Sergeant-Majors Mockford and Duffield respectively.
I then detailed a fatigue party from them to go and
draw rations and teas, the remainder assisting ' B '
Company to dig their trenches.

" By dawn on the 29th these trenches were completed ;
' B ' and ' C ' Companies being in the firing line, with
' A ' and ' D ' Companies in support in a ditch behind
' B ' Company, which had been improved and converted
into a support trench.

" Throughout the day we were under hot shell and
machine-gun fire ; otherwise the day was uneventful.
At 2 a.m. on October 30th, the Seaforth Highlanders
relieved us, and we marched back to Touret."

An interesting account is given by Sergt. (now
Regimental Sergeant-Major) Stroud, D.C.M., who was
present throughout the fighting at Neuve Chapelle :—

Sergt. Stroud's Narrative.—(6) " On the night of
24th-25th October near Neuve Chapelle, my Company
(' C '), was ordered into the firing line. At first we had
two platoons here and two in support, but afterwards the
whole company was put into the firing line, as our
frontage was rather long. The officers present were :
Lieut. White, Company Commander ; Lieut. Whitehouse, No. 12 Platoon, and Lieut. Holloway, No. 9
Platoon. At dawn we stood to arms, and at daylight
found we had quite a respectable trench, with a barbed
wire entanglement in front.

" During the morning we sent out a patrol to set fire
to a village just in front of our position, but this patrol
was fired upon by an enemy patrol, and so was unable
to achieve its object. The N.C.O. in charge, Corpl.

REGIMENTAL SERGEANT-MAJOR M. STROUD, D.C.M.

[*To face p.* 72

Verrall, received three bullets through his emergency ration of bully beef, en route. About 10 a.m. we began to see Germans in large numbers moving across our front, in single file, behind a hedge. We opened fire by sections at about 1000 yards, but, owing to the hedge, could not observe our fire. During the afternoon we saw the enemy entering a house with two machine guns on stretchers. At first we thought they were wounded men, but, as afterwards we saw ammunition boxes being taken in, information was sent back to the Artillery, who dealt with them effectively.

" We were relieved during the next night by ' B ' Company, when the whole of ' C ' Company went into Reserve. During the remainder of the night we were busy getting up rations, etc., for the companies in the line, and also making some overhead cover for our trench.

" There was a white house just in front of our trench, on which the Germans managed to get a direct hit, causing the house to vanish completely. Only a very few minutes before, a large number of men had been against the side of this house making tea, but Major Buckle had ordered them away just in time.

" Several wounded men from the firing line came into our trench for dressing, and told us they were having a rather bad time forward. All day we were kept under arms, expecting the Germans to attack. What with the effect of the shell on the house just in front and ' Black Marias ' beginning to fall about us, some of the men began to show signs of restlessness. Whereupon Major Buckle walked over to them and, standing on the top of the trench, gave some good advice, saying : ' Remember you belong to The Queen's Own ! ' We were all very much impressed by Major Buckle's words, and felt rather ashamed of ourselves, as he stood on the top calmly talking to us with shells bursting all round, and we were crouching as near the bottom as we could. His wonderful example had a great effect in steadying the men.

" Later, my platoon was ordered to get up S.A.A., and we managed to replenish each company with ammunition, besides leaving 36 boxes at B.H.Q.

" At dawn on October 27th we stood to and, at stand down, were ordered to keep under cover as much as possible the whole day. We were not bothered much, but they were evidently still having a bad time forward, for wounded men who came back told us of the situation. Towards evening things began to liven up and the Germans opened a heavy bombardment, back areas receiving special attention.

" During the bombardment the O.C. Company had to visit Bn.H.Q., and, on his return, gave orders that we were to occupy the support line, the supports having been sent into the firing line. We were now subjected to a very heavy shrapnel fire, the worst I had yet experienced, and, to reach the support line, we had to go through it. We simply ducked our heads and made a dash for it ; strange to say only one man was hit, and he was hit in the heel.

" We occupied the support line and were then told to await orders. These were not long in coming. My platoon (12) and No. 9 were ordered into the firing line to relieve the remnants of ' D ' Company. At this time there was great confusion, as a few Germans had broken through the line ; it became impossible to issue orders as everyone was so excited.

" In order to get to our position, under as much cover as possible, we had to go through a gully under the road.

This was a very unpleasant job, as it was half filled with filthy smelling mud. From the gully we had to climb a steep bank to get on to the road and, as the recent rain had made these banks very slippery, it was a tricky job to reach the top. No. 9 Platoon, who were following in our rear, did not go under the gully, but reached the road by another route and this caused some confusion as, when some Germans suddenly dashed up the road, the two platoons were almost facing one another. When firing started, my platoon tried to take up a position on the side of the road, but, owing to the slippery nature of the sides of the ditch, the majority immediately slipped to the bottom of this ditch. Eventually we got the men lying across the road, but it took some time to get the platoons together, as the night was very dark.

" I was ordered to go and take over the trenches with what men we had round us, and my Platoon Commander said he would follow later with the remainder. I was lucky and struck the part of the trench which was occupied by the senior N.C.O., Corpl. Hammond. He was very cheerful, although he looked very bad, and when I told him I had come to relieve his company, he said : ' Well, you have only these to relieve,' pointing to about seven men around him. One of the men, Pte. Harris, even then did not want to go. Before Corpl. Hammond left, he informed me that the enemy was digging a trench about eighty yards away, and that it had been impossible to stop this with fire, for as fast as the Germans fell, others came and carried on with the digging.

" About this time Major Buckle came to our trench and asked who was in command. I told him that I was, until my Platoon Commander arrived. He asked for a volunteer to reconnoitre the trench in front of us, to see if it were occupied. I volunteered to go, but at first Major Buckle would not allow me to do so. Afterwards, however, I was given the necessary instructions and was allowed to go, but had to take two men with me, who were to stay at the wire and inspect it whilst I continued to the trench. Major Buckle said he would await my return.

" I took about three-quarters of an hour to do my job and, on my return, the Major was very pleased, but not more so than I. Among other things, I reported that a German patrol of six was approaching by a ditch, which led to our trench. Major Buckle said : ' Right, we will wait for them to come up,' and, revolver in hand, he and Corpl. Verrall awaited their approach. He accounted for the six of them and was very pleased, it being his first chance of killing Huns.

" After this I was sent by Major Buckle with a message to the Brigadier. The purport of this message was to ask for reinforcements, as he was expecting an attack by the enemy, who was occupying strongly the trench eighty yards from our front line. On arrival at B.H.Q. I was made quite a fuss of by the General, who was very pleased with the stand made by the Battalion. After asking me a host of questions, the General handed me his message for Major Buckle, wishing me the best of luck. The General's reply was to the effect that there were no reinforcements, but he expected, during the night, one officer and forty other ranks whom he would arrange to place in a favourable position, so that they could assist should the attack develop.

" Major Buckle was rather disappointed, but he told me to take over command, as he had had to send my Platoon Commander away sick. He said the situation

was very serious and that we had a wonderful opportunity of making a name for the Regiment. Every man
must fight to the last, and under no circumstances was
anyone to leave the line. ' D ' Company had lost a lot
of lives in holding the trench, and ' C ' Company must
follow their example and also hold it. Ammunition,
etc., would be sent up from the rear. Then Major
Buckle shook me by the hand.

  " I got back to my Platoon feeling very tired, but
had scarcely entered the trench when a sentry gave the
alarm, and everyone started firing. It took a considerable time to stop this firing, but, when it had ceased
we went out and found a German officer lying on our
few strands of wire, riddled with bullets. He was
wearing rubber gloves and had wire cutters in his hands.
We searched him, and found dozens of photographs of
himself in his wallet, and I relieved him of his field
glasses, which were a very fine pair and subsequently
came in very handy. Except for spasmodic bursts of
fire, nothing happened during the night.

  " Before dawn on the 28th, Lieut. White, commanding
' C ' Company, took over command of the firing line,
and C.S.M. Crossley was left in command of the support.
As soon as Lieut. White arrived in the trench, he
ordered a standing patrol to be sent to a clump of trees,
just in front of our trench. Soon a man came back
from this patrol and reported that there were a lot of
German wounded in the vicinity of their post. I was
sent back with the man and saw about twenty German
officers lying dead and wounded in one group. It
appeared they had been holding a conference, and were
suddenly caught by our fire. As the post was presently
withdrawn, we were unable to get any identifications.

  " An hour before dawn, preparations were made for

the expected German attack, but to our surprise, nothing happened. When daylight appeared, we were surprised at the number of German dead and wounded lying in front of our trench, and if only the men of ' D ' Company could have seen them, they would have been gratified. Here was a splendid opportunity for souvenir hunters, and it was not long before No. 9 Platoon had thirty-six German helmets lined behind their trench, Private (Onion) Hill being responsible for the majority of them.

It was a very pitiful sight to see so many German wounded lying out in front and, as no help was rendered them, we made several attempts to bring them in. However, the enemy fired on us, killing two of our men, whilst doing this work, so we had to desist and were compelled to watch them struggling to reach their own line. Corpl. Verrall made several journeys out, taking water for these wounded.

" During the day the Germans shelled heavily, but, owing to faulty direction, the shells fell about 50 yards to our right flank, where there were no trenches. Whilst this shelling was proceeding, the Germans commenced an attack and we were able to give them a hot reception. Each time the enemy made a rush, a machine gun traversed our parapet with very accurate fire. This kept our heads down and caused many casualties. Eventually, however, it was put out of action by a fine piece of fire direction on the parts of Ptes. Rabbit, Simpson, Bennet and Sage.

" We could not understand the object of the Germans in this operation, as they got to within 100 yards of our trenches, but made no further advance and yet kept sending up more lines from the rear. Either we must have inflicted very heavy losses on them, or their trench

must have been crowded out. They apparently, however, broke through on our flank. During these attacks
the Germans were led by officers armed with sword and
revolver, but a noticeable feature was that the men
wore no equipment.

" Soon after this we heard that Major Buckle had
been killed, and efforts were made to prevent this
sad news passing down the line, owing to the effect it
might have on the men. The news leaked through
somehow, but there was so much happening about this
time, that one had no time to think, and so very few
realised the great loss.

" We could now see the Germans at our old Battalion
Headquarters. They opened the mail bags and took
away parcels, and also fired into the boxes of S.A.A.
that were stacked there. Also we could see them marching prisoners away. By this time the Germans had
got to the rear of our trench and were firing on us. A
young soldier turned to fire back, but was told by one
of more experience : ' You don't do that here, look to
your front and let those in the rear deal with them.'
Subsequently, however, it became necessary to detail
men to watch our rear.

" We, in the front line, were now cut off and could get
no information ; though we kept sending messages out
by runners, they never seemed to get through. At this
stage Lieut. Holloway said he would try and get through,
but the next we heard was that he had been shot through
both legs. News was now received that Capt. Battersby
had been killed ; he had taken over command when
Major Buckle was killed, and had only been with the
Battalion one day.

" An order was then passed down the line for all
correspondence to be destroyed and all identification

marks to be removed, as it was thought we should assuredly be captured. There was then a very amusing incident. When we first came into these trenches, the men's boots were very bad, whilst Pte. Duke had hardly any at all. During one of Major Buckle's tours round the line, he told the man that he ought to take a pair from a dead German (they carried a spare pair in their packs). Having plenty from which to select, Pte Duke soon found a pair to fit and then threw his old pair away. Henceforward he was always singing the praises of the German boot—' How comfortable they were, etc.,' and ' Why didn't the British Government have boots like them, etc.' However, when the above order was passed round the line, Pte. Duke was told that if he were taken prisoner with a pair of German boots on, he would certainly be shot. He suddenly discovered that German boots were far from comfortable ; that they gave him a sore heel, etc., and at once commenced a frantic search for his old discarded boots, which, to his great relief, he at last found.

" At dusk Capt. Moulton-Barrett (Commander of ' B ' Company, which was holding the trenches on our left), had a chat with Lieut. White. Capt. Moulton-Barrett had just been bandaged as he had been wounded in the head. Corpl. Cronk and I overheard the conversation, which was anything but cheering.

" Shortly afterwards Capt. Moulton-Barrett had to leave owing to his wounds, thus leaving 2/Lieut. Russell in command of ' B ' Company. Lieut. White now became Battalion Commander and went back to endeavour to establish a headquarters, leaving me in command of the firing line of ' C ' Company. He established his headquarters in our support line. During the night rations were sent up and these were an absolute godsend; though one man could not refrain from the universal grouse because the bread 'ran' four to one loaf.

" That night, I happened to be looking through my German glasses and saw the enemy advancing towards our trenches, by short rushes of about ten yards. The night was very clear and, with the aid of the glasses, I could see them quite plainly. I gave orders for every one to stand to and load their rifles, instructing them not to fire until I gave the order. I allowed the Germans to get very close, and then gave the order just as they got up to start one of their rushes. We managed to stop that attack.

" Soon after this Pte. Richards, who had been sent to the rear with a message, came back and reported that a party of the enemy were in a house directly behind our trench. Some men were sent to ascertain if this were true when, suddenly, fire was opened and it was some time before it could be stopped. It happened that Indian troops were now occupying the house and Pte. Richards, hearing them talking, and seeing their turbans, which looked like German helmets in the dark, came to the conclusion that they were Germans.

" The remainder of the night was very quiet, and we took this opportunity of burying our dead and getting up S.A.A. and water. At dawn, we saw the result of our little shoot during the night; Germans were lying dead everywhere. During the day all was quiet, I think the enemy had had enough during the night. Pte. White was killed this day by a sniper. He had jumped out of his trench to hand in a dead man's pay book, and, returning along the back of the trench, was just going to hand me the book, when a sniper got him through the side. Pte. Sage and Drummer Noble were also killed by snipers.

" Much to our surprise we were shortly relieved by a battalion of Seaforth Highlanders. The major who commanded the company who had to take over our sector of the trench told me he was not going to let me go until I had explained everything to him, and, to ensure this, he held me by the coat sleeve. Eventually I joined my Company and we commenced our march to billets, legging it as hard as we could in order to get out of the place as soon as possible. We were met by a staff officer who could not do enough for us.

" About daybreak we arrived in a field where we met the transport, who gave us quite a reception. Hot tea and rum were issued and I was given some brandy by the officer's mess corporal. In a short while everyone was asleep, for we had had little rest since the 19th. One thing which struck me was the difference between the faces of the men of the transport and those who had just come from the trenches. The faces of the latter were ghastly.

" Thus ended the Battle of Neuve Chapelle as far as we were concerned. We marched next day to Merville, where the Battalion was billeted in a school. Every man had done such wonderful work that it is difficult to single out any individuals, but I think Corpls. Cronk and Fisher, also Ptes. Rabbit, Simpson and ' Onion ' Hill deserve special mention."

Remarks on Neuve Chapelle.—It will be seen from the above accounts that the Battalion achieved a very glorious feat of arms. Be it remembered that the Battalion had been fighting, marching and digging since the 12th October, suffering continuous losses ; that then, with no respite, it was called upon, throughout five long days and nights, to endure the high explosive

shell fire, the shrapnel, machine-gun and rifle fire described by survivors ; that it twice, on two successive
days, extricated itself from a situation of deadly danger
and, at the same time, staved off violent attacks on its
own proper front.   Then the full wonder of the exploit
will appear.   The quick decision that took the only
possible way to save the situation when the flank was
turned, was fine ; the repulse of each German assault
was in itself splendid ; but the real marvel lies in the
steadfastness which could carry human beings through
so long continued a trial, without breaking their power
to endure.

It is difficult to write with the modest restraint shown
by participators.   It would have been so   easy—so
very easy—to fall back, and so excusable.   None could
have blamed them if, attacked in flank and rear, they
had, as a unit, withdrawn from a position which, had
not The Queen's Own proved the contrary, would have
been accepted by all as impossible.   They were told
to stay and, desperate and nearly officerless, stay they
did.   One young soldier, almost a boy, observing men
of other units trickling to the rear, began to look over
his shoulder.   In another instant he might have been
gone, but an old private seized him none too tenderly
by the ear, shouting : " None of that, my lad ! We
don't do that in The Queen's Own."

The Fifth Division in the Great War, commenting on
this exploit, says :

" Exposed to terrific shelling, with their left flank
uncovered, the West Kents immortalised themselves by
repulsing the German attack and holding their own ;
they lost most of their officers and were sadly reduced in
numbers, but they stuck to their trenches and were
finally brought out of action by two subalterns, one

with two years' and the other with six months' service."

Reviewing this operation, it will be seen that fourteen officers went into action. On the 26th Capt. Keenlyside was mortally wounded ; Capt. Beeman and 2/Lieut. Harding were killed, and Capt. Tulloch, D.S.O., was wounded.

On the 27th Major Buckle, D.S.O., was killed whilst trying to restore the line beyond the Battalion's flank. Capt. Legard, the Adjutant, was killed at the same time : 2/Lieuts. Holloway and Williams were wounded.

On the 28th Capt. Battersby and Lieut. Gore were killed ; Capt. Moulton-Barrett and Lieut. Palmer were wounded.

The two officers who survived to bring the Battalion out of action were Lieut. White and 2/Lieut. Russell. Both received the D.S.O.

The casualties among other ranks seem nowhere to be recorded, but Capt. Dunlop, who joined the Battalion a few days after, and made out the casualty returns, estimated the number as approximately 450.

Major Buckle was a great loss to the Battalion, and his death was much felt at the time by all ranks. He never seemed to consider his own safety, but walked about encouraging the men. On one occasion he, with Sergt. Stroud and a few men, repelled the advance of a German patrol. It was, in a large measure, due to his example that others were able to endure the ordeal which they were called upon to go through.

Regimental Sergeant-Major H. S. Doe was promoted to 2/Lieut. soon after Neuve Chapelle. It is believed that he declined a commission unless it was in his own Regiment. 2/Lieut. Doe, one of the first recipients of the Military Cross, was given a platoon of " A "

Company, which platoon soon became a model one.

The conduct of the Battalion was highly praised by leaders, and appreciated by other fellow soldiers. A telegram from the IInd Corps Staff to the 13th Brigade read : " Please express to West Kents admiration of the 3rd and 5th Divisions for their gallant conduct during the last ten days' fighting. They have borne the brunt in several critical situations and have never given ground except by order. We much regret their heavy losses. Please communicate to West Kents when you have an opportunity."

General Forestier Walker telegraphed to the 5th Division on the 30th October : " By permission of the G.O.C. the Corps, the Chief Staff Officer of the IInd Corps wishes to express his admiration of the gallant conduct of The West Kent Regiment during the last few days of severe fighting." The splendid spirit displayed by the Regiment fully upheld the traditions of 100 years ago, when his grandfather, Colonel Walker, had the honour to command it at Vimiera.

On the 8th November Gen. Sir H. Smith-Dorrien, commanding the IInd Corps, addressed the Battalion as follows : " Officers and Men of The Royal West Kent Regiment : For a long time I have been wanting to address you, but in this strenuous war it has been quite impossible to catch certain battalions. I have found it impossible to get to you owing to your being in the trenches and to the trend of events.

" My reason for coming to address you is that I want you to understand that we, who are behind, appreciate your splendid services.

" I much regret that yesterday your gallant Colonel (Col. Martyn) was wounded, but I am very glad to say

G

that it is not a bad wound, although he may be laid up for a considerable time and we must lose his services for the present. I can only tell you that the Field-Marshal Commanding-in-Chief realises how splendidly the Regiment has done, and your Colonel is about to be made a Brigadier-General. That is a direct compliment to you.

" I am perfectly certain there is not another battalion that has made such a name for itself as The Royal West Kents. Everybody is talking about you. They say : ' Give them a job, they will do it ; they never leave the trenches. It is perfectly certain they will stick it out.'

" One point I want to refer to : no matter how gallant the work that has been performed or how splendid the stands that have been made, you hear nothing about it. I will just briefly explain why. We are fighting the most serious war that has ever taken place, against highly trained armies and highly trained staffs. If we were to publish that The Royal West Kent Regiment had made a gallant stand, or had done a certain thing at a certain place, the enemy would at once say : ' The Royal West Kent Regt. ! That is the —— Bde., that is the —— Div., that is the —— Army Corps,' and thus locate us at once. It is absolutely necessary to keep everything important from getting into the papers—the gallant deeds, how performed, and what such and such a regiment has done. That is why our men have to go on performing these deeds without their relations at home knowing anything about them. I hope you will understand.

" It is very galling for you to go on as you do, day after day, and your folks at home not to know. But I have records of performances of battalions and, when the time comes, these will be published. They will be handed down in the records of the Regiment, and in no records will be recorded better deeds than those of this Battalion.

" I have received from the Brigadier-General, commanding your Brigade, appreciation of the gallant conduct of Lieut. White and the other young officer (2/Lieut. Russell) who is not on parade to-day. The way these two young officers handled the Regiment after all your other officers had fallen, how they stuck to it and how, eventually when the time came, they brought the Regiment out of it. I have brought their names to the notice of the Field-Marshal Commanding-in-Chief, and sincerely hope they will receive the reward they so richly deserve.

" I will not detain you as I want you to enjoy your rest. Heaven knows you have not had much since you have been in this country !

" I do congratulate the Regiment on the magnificent work it has done. I thank you most heartily for your support to the IInd Corps, which I have the honour to command ; I regret your heavy losses—your great losses among the officers—and such magnificent officers too !

" We are going to win, and we shall win as long as we have the help of battalions such as yours. I am always thinking of you, men, and asking different officers what I can do for you. I can never forget your magnificent Regiment.

" I told the Commander-in-Chief yesterday that, day after day, I had been trying to address you, in fact, I have been out here three times. He said ' That is a magnificent regiment.'

" That is enough, good luck to you all."

A few weeks later Field-Marshal Sir John French inspected the Battalion, and took the opportunity to address them. He said :—

" Major Robinson, Officers, Warrant Officers, Non-Commissioned Officers, and Men of the 1st Battalion The Royal West Kent Regiment : I have received the most gratifying reports of you from the Army Corps Commander and the Divisional and Brigade Commanders. Sir Horace Smith-Dorrien has always expressed his appreciation of your admirable work, and I myself have wished to do the same before this, but up to now I have not had the opportunity ; the reason you will well understand, as this is your first rest. Wherever there has been fighting you have been in the thick of it, and, wherever you have fought, you have fought splendidly.

" No Regiment has won for itself a more enviable reputation than you have. Deeply do I deplore your losses, your heavy losses of splendid officers and gallant non-commissioned officers and men ; but I know that the spirit of the Regiment is not impaired and that, whatever you are called on to do in the future, you will accomplish in the same unflinching manner as you have done in the past."

Historians have shown much admiration for the Neuve Chapelle exploit. Lord Ernest Hamilton, in " The First Seven Divisions," after recounting how battalions of the 7th and 8th Brigades were forced from their ground on the 27th, continues : " The position of The Royal West Kents was now most precarious, as they had the enemy on three sides of them, and it seemed inevitable that they must follow the example of the several regiments on their left, who had been successively forced to give way.

Such, however, was not their opinion, and, undismayed by the apparent hopelessness of their position, they promptly set about preparing a defence which proved to be one of the most remarkable of the campaign."

He records the death of Major Buckle (C.O.), killed whilst trying to re-establish the position beyond the left flank ; of Capt. Legard, the Adjutant, and the assumption of control by Company Sergeant-Majors Penny and Crossley, after all the officers of their companies had fallen. He describes how The Queen's Own took up a new line " under a murderous fire," which enabled them to hang on till nightfall. On the 28th, after the retirement of the troops who had momentarily re-established the situation on the left, he says : " The position of The Royal West Kents was now as bad as ever and, once more, half the Battalion had to face about to its left flank and rear." He mentions the deaths of Capt. Battersby and Lieut. Gore and the wounding of Lieut.[1] Moulton-Barrett, leaving 2/Lieuts. White [1] and Russell the sole surviving officers, and then goes on to observe :—

" The remarkable position had by this time developed that practically the whole of Neuve Chapelle was in the hands of the enemy, with the exception of the little south-east corner by the La Bassée road, which was still stubbornly held by the undefeated [2] Royal West Kents. On the other side of the La Bassée road, and in the angle which that road makes with the Richebourg road, the K.O.Y.L.I. were still standing firm with the East Surrey beyond them, but these last two regiments were not so hardly pressed, the main attack being always on the eastern side of the main La Bassée road."

[1] These ranks are quoted from Lord Hamilton's " The First Seven Divisions."

[2] The motto borne on the cap badge of the Regiment is " Invicta."

Finally, in his summary of these operations, he remarks: "The heroes of the three days' fighting were of course The Royal West Kents, who immortalised themselves by a performance which, in many ways, must be unique."

Two incidents are chosen to show that other soldiers understood and appreciated the conduct of the Regiment.

The Commanding Officer of an Indian Regiment told Colonel Martyn: "Every day I hold up the example of your Regiment to my men as what a regiment should be."

In Flanders nearly two years later, the second in command of a newly arrived Service Battalion of the Regiment held a conversation with one of the company quartermaster-sergeants :—

"How on earth, Quartermaster-Sergeant, do the men manage to lose their cap badges at such a wicked rate ? "

"Very sorry, sir-; it's all because of us being next to the Australians."

"How do you mean ? "

"Well, sir, the Australians give our men five shillings apiece for their cap badges."

"Five shillings apiece for an article worth three halfpence ! "

"That doesn't matter, sir. What they want is to get from a battalion actually on service the cap badge of the Neuve Chapelle Regiment."

CHAPTER V

ROUND ABOUT NEUVE EGLISE.—The Battalion left the Neuve Chapelle trenches in the early morning of October 30th, on relief by a battalion of the Indian Division, and the remains of the unit were billeted at Merville. Next day they marched to Coutre Croix. Here, on the 1st November, Lieut.-Colonel Martyn resumed command, the 13th Brigade having been temporarily broken up. It must have been a very sad return for him. Of the battalion he had left only eighteen days before but a remnant remained. Not one of the brother officers who had helped him to train his men in peace time was there to welcome him. His one consolation must have been in the thought of how magnificently events had proved the value of his and their labours.

On the 1st November the Battalion was attached to the 15th Brigade and marched to Dranoutre. Throughout the 2nd the Battalion was held ready to move at a moment's notice. Capt. Buchanan-Dunlop, who was wounded at Mons, rejoined that day. About noon on the 3rd The Queen's Own, the K.O.S.B., and the K.O.Y.L.I., all under the command of Lieut.-Colonel Martyn, were sent to occupy trenches at Neuve Eglise with orders to hold them till the last. At 3.30 p.m. The Queen's Own and the K.O.S.B. were directed on Wulverghem to support an attack by the French and our cavalry on

Messines, but on arrival were sent back to Neuve Eglise.

Lieut.-Colonel Martyn now finally left the Battalion to take command of the reconstituted 13th Brigade, leaving Capt. Buchanan-Dunlop in command. At this stage Lieut. J. E. G. Brown of our 2nd Battalion joined, as well as the following five officers of other regiments, who were attached as a temporary measure:—

Capt. Curtis,	Royal Suffolk Regt.
Capt. Corrie,	Scottish Rifles
2/Lieut. Bolitho,	Devonshire Regt.
2/Lieut. Walker,	Dorsetshire Regt.
2/Lieut. Wallace,	Border Regt.

2/Lieut. Allen of the Buffs joined next day when a draft of seventy-six arrived.

The Battalion remained in Neuve Eglise, which the enemy shelled, during the 4th, finding picquets by night. On the 5th it once more took up a position of readiness to support an attack on Messines, but was again not required. On the 7th The Queen's Own with the K.O.Y.L.I. occupied trenches near Wulverghem. They came in for a considerable amount of shelling, but escaped heavy casualties.

Lieut.-Colonel Martyn, then commanding the Brigade, was hit by a fragment of shell whilst standing with his Brigade Major near a farm, which was afterwards given the name of Martyn's Farm. This wound necessitated the Colonel's return to England. Capt. Buchanan-Dunlop's horse was hit at the same time. This horse had been Major Pack Beresford's hunter, and was sold by him to the Government. It went right through the whole war and was eventually, we believe, destroyed on account of age. It was three times wounded.

YPRES SALIENT

WULVERGHEM

[To face p. 92]

At Neuve Eglise Sir H. Smith-Dorrien addressed such men as could be collected in a hurry. A German aeroplane dropped a bomb near the men as they were assembling for Divine Service in the afternoon, but, fortunately, it exploded without causing casualties. For two days the Battalion remained at Neuve Eglise, prepared to move at a moment's notice.

Lieut. Thompson joined on the 11th, and that night the Battalion moved out in support to the K.O.Y.L.I., who were taking over trenches from the French. It was very dark and raining in torrents. The men had to take cover in ditches more than half full of water, and a few were wounded by shell fire. Next night the two battalions were relieved and returned to Neuve Eglise.

The Salient.—At 8.30 a.m. on the 13th November the Battalion left Neuve Eglise for the Ypres Salient. The orders to Capt. Dunlop were to move the Battalion through Ypres to the White Château on the Menin Road, and then to report to the 3rd Division H.Q. He was told that the Battalion would be placed in reserve.

The march was a trying one, as it rained hard and steadily all day. On arrival near Ypres the Battalion was halted to wait for darkness before passing through the town, and all transport had to be left here.

The companies went through Ypres at ten minutes' intervals, marching in single file, and it was easy to see from the results of shell fire the necessity for the precautions which had been ordered. The Battalion got safely through and reassembled east of the town, reaching the 3rd Divisional Headquarters without casualties. A good many shells fell near to the

Battalion but, probably owing to the darkness, did not fall on the main road.

On arrival at the Château where the 3rd Divisional Headquarters were situated, the Battalion was halted whilst Capt. Dunlop reported. He was told to take his unit through Zillebeke to General Lord Cavan's Headquarters, which were in a dug-out close behind the troops who were holding the front line. Here Capt. Dunlop would be met by guides of the London Scottish and would take over the front line from that Regiment.

A mounted orderly was provided by the 3rd Division to guide the Battalion to Lord Cavan's Headquarters. It was a pitch dark night, raining steadily, and, as everyone had been marching all day in heavy rain, the prospects did not appear very cheerful. As Capt. Dunlop remarked: " We were all wet through, tired out, our transport and rations seven miles in rear, and we had no knowledge when we should hear of them again. We were in unfamiliar country, none of the officers had been in the trenches before, and we had one mounted guide for the whole Battalion."

However, by going slowly, we got there somehow. Unfortunately, when passing through Zillebeke, we had some casualties from the enemy's shell fire.

On arrival at Lord Cavan's Headquarters, which were in a hole in the bank at the side of the road, guides were provided from the London Scottish and the companies were moved forward to the front line. The route lay along a road nearly knee-deep in liquid mud, and then into woods. Here there was a continual crackle of musketry fire which, to those who have not experienced it before, is rather startling to say nothing else. Every shot seemed to have been fired from a few yards away, and bullets ricochetted off trees, giving nasty wounds and accounting, perhaps, for the reports that enemy snipers were concealed in the woods in rear of our lines.

The Battalion was attached for the time to the 7th Brigade. " A," " B," and " C " Companies went into the firing-line trenches, with " D " in support in dug-outs some 250 yards behind. The trenches were very inadequate, and in some places only 30 yards from the Germans. Situated in dense woods, the trees of which had been much knocked about by shell fire, an almost impenetrable tangle had been made both in front of and behind them. This obviated any chance of a sudden rush by either side, but it made it extremely difficult to get about. The only communications between the front trenches and the support dug-outs were three rides, running directly to the front. One of these means of approach was found to be commanded by a German machine gun, and the other two by snipers. The weather throughout this period was very wet. 2/Lieut. Littleboy joined.

On the 14th the snipers accounted for about a dozen of our men and, as some were shot from behind, it became evident that the Germans had got into the tangled woods in rear of the trenches. During the 15th and 16th, although the sniping continued, it was less virulent. The trenches were greatly improved and our knowledge of the locality and situation was considerably extended. 2/Lieut. Walker made some specially useful reconnaissances and reports. The weather was still very cold and wet, and the German dead in the wood became very offensive. Both sides shelled heavily on the 17th, and 2/Lieut. Thompson, among others, was mortally wounded. In the afternoon the Germans attacked the line both on the right

and left of the Battalion's trenches. " C " Company
was able to bring a heavy fire on to the flank of a
German attack on the Cavalry who were holding the
trenches on our right, causing the enemy some heavy
losses and materially assisting in their repulse. In
this attack the Germans advanced, arm in arm, to
within a few yards of the trenches, where they were
shot down. They made no attempt to fight and, judging from their actions, must have been heavily drugged,
as they did not seem to know what they were doing.
The Kaiser was reported to be visiting the German
Army which was situated in this area, and it is presumed that this useless waste of life was arranged for
his edification.

The 18th and 19th were marked by the usual sniping,
machine-gun fire, and some shelling. In the evening
of the 19th the Battalion was relieved and marched
to dug-outs in front of Ypres, proceeding the following night to Dranoutre, where the men were billeted.
Although it was freezing hard and snow was lying
on the ground the men, when relieved, could only be
provided with accommodation for the rest of the night
in open holes, with absolutely no cover or protection
from the weather. After six days practically without
sleep they were, however, so exhausted that this
worried them very little and they were soon all sound
asleep.

Major Robinson met the Battalion as it came out
of the trenches and took over the command from Capt.
Dunlop, who then became Adjutant. At Dranoutre
the Battalion enjoyed the longest rest it had had since
the campaign started—a whole week—from 21st to
26th November.

Major Robinson, who was commanding at the depot

COLONEL P. M. ROBINSON, C.B., C.M.G.

(Commanded the Battalion in France from November 1914 to
September 1915)

[*To face p.* 96

when war broke out, had been forming the 6th (Service) Battalion in England, but was sent out to take command of the 1st Battalion. However, on arrival in the trenches, as he was the senior officer, the previous commander having just been killed by a shell blowing in his shelter, he was placed in command of a sector of trenches held by several units, one of which was the Battalion.

Major Bonham-Carter, Lieut. MacNeece, 2/Lieuts. Burbury and Sharpin joined at about the same time, together with a draft of 125 N.C.O.'s and men. Brig.-Gen. R. Wanless-O'Gowan now commanded the 13th Brigade.

Reviewing the casualties sustained by the Battalion since the 13th November, these amounted to 1 officer and 52 other ranks, of whom 14 were killed. Sniping accounted for most of the losses. One private of " B " Company, named Turnbull, accomplished magnificent work. He went out regularly in front of the trenches to look for the German snipers who were such a nuisance. He used a German rifle and got his ammunition from the snipers he shot, and other dead Germans. He always returned with trophies. Such desperately dangerous work could not continue for long, and at last he was wounded. Turnbull was awarded a D.C.M. for his work on this occasion. He had been orderly to 2/Lieut. Russell at Neuve Chapelle in October, and had done fine work during the fighting there. Having had most of his foot blown off by this wound he was never fit to rejoin again. He was a great loss to the Battalion.

The modern bullet, fired at such close range as was prevalent at this period, makes terrible wounds, and led to the report that the enemy was using soft-nosed bullets. Although the Germans may have done so, as one would expect such a thing of the Huns, it is a fact that similar wounds are made by ordinary bullets when fired at very close range.

During this period in the trenches all runners and other messengers had to work in pairs to obviate the chance of a single man being wounded and not located, perhaps, for many hours. In this area exceptional difficulties were experienced in keeping the Battalion fed and supplied. No movement was possible during daylight so cookers, supply carts, and water carts had to be brought up in the dark—usually in the rain —a distance of 7 miles over soft muddy tracks, pitted with shell holes, some of which were 2 or 3 feet deep. There was considerable risk from shell fire during the journey, especially when vehicles were halted while particularly bad shell holes had to be filled in. The return journey of 7 miles had, of course, to be completed before daylight. The Quarter-master, Capt. Rogers, however, as always, rose to the occasion, overcoming all difficulties, and the Battalion was kept regularly supplied.

Returning to the march of events : Sir John French on the 27th of November inspected the Battalion. He was most complimentary, expressing his admiration of the work done by the Battalion throughout the War.

Wulverghem.—In the evening of the 27th the Battalion went into trenches in front of Wulverghem, where it remained for seven days. There was some shelling, but the only casualties suffered were from snipers, who wounded nine men. One night during this tour in the line a very large shell burst in the house occupied by Battalion Headquarters in

Wulverghem, and although the next room to the one in which the shell burst was full of runners, signallers, etc., no one was touched. Much work was done during the nights in improving the position and especially in constructing communication trenches. Steel loopholes were issued about this time, but they were not popular, as the enemy snipers took a keen interest in them and often put a shot through the aperture. When relieved the Battalion had the satisfaction of knowing that the position was left a great deal stronger than it had been when taken over. The weather during this period was not very cold, and, on the whole, the men were fairly comfortable and certainly got off very cheaply as regards casualties.

The Battalion remained in the Wulverghem sector through the winter up to 19th February 1915. It moved regularly into the trenches for two to four days at a time, returning to rest and smarten up in Bailleul, or the neighbouring villages, for the same periods. Almost every visit to the trenches occasioned casualties, but there were no important events to mark the time. It may be called a period of dreary monotony, punctuated only by casualties ; rather a squalid existence of cold, wet, and above all, of mud.

" Trench feet " were a disagreeable feature of this period, though the Battalion suffered less than most units from this particular form of adversity. The amount of night work the companies put in, when in the line, may or may not have accounted for their comparative immunity. For, as soon as it was fairly dark, the first relief would start in with spade and shovel, making new traverses, new communication trenches, new loopholes, and, above all, repairing the parapets after their knocking about of the previous day. Work in reliefs would be continuous during the night, through rain or frost, pitch dark or bright moonlight. Rifle fire, enlivened at intervals by machine guns, would be continuous, and, as a rule, the darker it was the more noise there was. There was about the same amount of firing as on a rifle range when a meeting is in progress. Ocasionally a man would be hit by this incessant musketry, though extraordinarily seldom considering its intensity, and the fact that much of the work had to be done right out in the open.

Every few minutes a Very Light would come sailing over and make things to all appearances as bright as day. Then, unless there was cover absolutely at one's elbow, the trick was to stand stock still and the chances were that, in spite of its seeming impossible, the enemy would not spot the working party. All this work had to be done in the most slimy, clinging mud imaginable, and, as many stumbles and flounders into shell holes and other inequalities were inevitable, men would be absolutely plastered within a few minutes of commencing work.

Once relieved, however, but very few hours would elapse after quitting the trenches before hardly a trace of the squalid trench life would be left. The companies, well shaved and almost as clean as if they had never heard of Flanders' mud, would be busily engaged in exercises conducive to taking any incipient bend out of men's backs and to restoring that pitch of smartness in deportment which befits a self-respecting regiment.

When in Bailleul in rest billets there was a certain amount of occupation for the men besides their smartening up process. The companies used to be taken to the Lunatic Asylum at Bailleul to have hot baths, and these were, it is believed, the first baths that the men, who had been out from the beginning, had been able to get.

At this period, two Territorial battalions were attached to the Division for training, the 9th Battalion County of London Regiment (The Queen Victoria's Rifles) and the 6th Battalion The Cheshire Regiment and went into the trenches with the Regular battalions.

The Battalion spent Christmas at St Jans Capelle, and all ranks received a Christmas Card from Their Majesties the King and Queen; and Princess Mary's Gift of cigarettes, tobacco and a pipe. The men were undergoing inoculation against enteric on Christmas Day; Divine Service was held and the day passed quietly. The Queen's Own took no part in the " fraternising " which took place on this first Christmas of the War.

Some amusements were provided by entertainments given principally by the Queen's Westminsters and Queen Victoria's Rifles, who included many clever artistes in their ranks.

The tours of trench duty whilst near Wulverghem were as follows :—

10th-13th December. Weather very wet. 3 killed, 4 wounded.

16th-19th December. Trenches now in shocking state from heavy rain. Most communication trenches impassable, necessitating reliefs and carrying parties moving across the open. 8 killed, 15 wounded.

31st Dec.-3rd Jan. (1915). 5 killed, 14 wounded.

9th-10th and 16th-17th Jan. No casualties.

21st-23rd Jan. 5 killed, 2 wounded.

3rd-5th Feb. 4 killed, 4 wounded.

7th-9th Feb. Capt. Mills and 3 men killed, 10 wounded.

H

During these tours a number of officers joined and large drafts were received from home.

December.   Capt. Mills and 2/Lieut. Le Cocq joined on 4th ; Capt. Lynch-White and 2/Lieut. Wigan on 10th ; Lieut. Westmacott on 18th ; and 2/Lieut. Poland on 24th.

January.   2/Lieuts. Cooper and Harris arrived on 6th ; 2/Lieut. Brachen on 18th ; 2/Lieut. Curshaw on 30th ; and Capt. Molony on 31st.

February.   Lieuts. Taylor, Paton, Bradley and 2/Lieuts. Daubeny and Cobb arrived on 2nd.

Capt. Moulton-Barrett (wounded at Neuve Chapelle) joined on 3rd.

2/Lieut. Wild on 8th ; 2/Lieut. Pownall (rejoined) on 16th ; 2/Lieuts. Frost and White on 16th ; Major Joslin on 18th.

The following other rank reinforcements joined :—

December.   286 on 11th ; 50 on 18th.

January.   45 on 4th ; 75 on 12th ; 50 on 20th ; 80 on 28th.

February.   61 on 8th.

1915.

Zillebeke.—The Battalion arrived in Bailleul on the night of 9th February, with every expectation of being back in the Wulverghem trenches four or five days later, but when the period of this inactivity was extended, it was realised that something unusual was occurring. After some days of " standing-by " to move at short notice, this materialised into an order for the 13th Brigade to return to the Ypres Salient. All four battalions marched together on the 19th and reached Vlamertynghe in the evening, where the Battalion was accommodated in wooden huts. That night an officer from each company went up into the trenches which were to be taken over from the units of the 28th Division.

On the night of the 20th, the Battalion moved into the trenches in front of Zillebeke. As was usual at this period of the War in the Ypres Salient, the warfare in the Zillebeke area appeared to be of a distinctly more strenuous type than that round Wulverghem. The opposing trenches were much closer to each other, and the Hun occupants (Prussians) seemed to be considerably more aggressive. The British appliances, too, for this kind of fighting were distinctly inferior to those of the enemy at this particular period. Our artillery support was meagre and had so limited a " ration " of shells, that it only just sufficed to keep it alive at all. Besides this there was a lamentable shortage of Infantry means of " frightfulness " : bombs, rifle grenades, trench mortars and all such apparatus were very scarce. Even sand bags were difficult to obtain in sufficient quantities. Hence it was rather hard to compete with the Hun on equal terms.

The Battalion, however, at once proceeded to make life as uncertain for the enemy as possible. The men, at least, had plenty of ammunition for their rifles and a few " jam tin " bombs and rifle grenades ; with these they did their best to give as good as they got, if not a little better. The losses during the first day were few : 4 killed, 3 wounded, but on the afternoon of the 22nd, the Germans brought a big trench mortar to bear on the trenches occupied by " B " Company and the left platoon of " A." Our men had nothing but rifle grenades with which to reply and, as it was extremely difficult to locate the mortar exactly, these were not successful in silencing it. It continued to fire for over two hours, killing Lieut. Brown, 2/Lieuts. Burbury and

Frost and 18 men ; and wounding Capt. Molony and 19 men.

After dark on the 22nd, the Battalion was withdrawn to support positions, and remained there without casualties through the 23rd. On the 24th, " A " Company was summoned to reinforce the front line and lost 2 men killed and 2/Lieut. Harris and 9 men wounded. That night the Battalion returned to the front line which they held until the night of the 26th, losing one killed and two wounded. They then retired to Ypres.

On 1st March the Battalion returned to Zillebeke and went into close support. It remained in the line for ten days, being sometimes in front trenches and sometimes in support, losing during that time, 4 men killed and 2/Lieut. Curshaw and 17 men wounded. On the 10th, it moved to rest billets at Vlamertynghe, and here 2/Lieuts. Travers, Liebenrood and Craston joined with 87 men.

Unfortunately, on the 14th, 2/Lieut. White was accidentally killed whilst trying a French " safety " lighter on one of the new " jam tin " bombs, which had just been issued to the Battalion. This was the first occasion on which the Battalion had been issued with bombs, and bombing started seriously. 2/Lieut White and R.S.M. Brown were the " experts " of the Battalion (because they knew what the bombs contained ?), and during this period, whilst out of the line, all N.C.O.'s were instructed in lighting and throwing bombs. The " jam tin " bomb was not a success, and most men agreed that it was far more dangerous to ourselves than to the Huns.

It was just about this time that the Battalion Trench Mortar team came into existence under the R.S.M.,

who " found " a spare trench mortar on one of the
neighbouring dumps.

St. Eloi.—On the 14th, the Battalion left Vlamertynghe
for a position to support an attack on some trenches,
which had been lost, in the vicinity of St Eloi. The
men, in their ranks, slept on the road that night and
dug themselves in next morning.

On the 16th, some trenches about two miles south of
Ypres were occupied. Three men were killed and nine
wounded between the 16th and 18th. On the 20th, the
Battalion returned to the trenches. On the 22nd the
enemy bombed the position held by " A " Company, destroying part of their trench and inflicting casualties.
On the 23rd, the unit was again relieved, having lost
Lieut. Pownall and 11 other ranks killed and 15 wounded
and 4 missing (presumed killed). The bombing of " A "
Company accounted for most of these losses. Another
visit to the trenches, from 24th to 26th, cost a further
loss of 7 killed and 22 wounded, bombs again doing most
of the damage.

On the 26th, the Battalion went to Vlamertynghe for
a rest. It was there four days and had leisure in which
to commence the Annual Inter-Company Football Competition. 2/Lieut. Maunder joined on the 28th.

A draft of 65 was received from England on April 1st.
Next day the Battalion returned to the trenches for two
days, losing therein 6 killed and 15 wounded, among the
killed being Company Sergeant-Major File. He came
out with the Battalion in 1914 as Machine Gun Sergeant,
was wounded in September and sent down to the Base.
C.S.M. File " escaped " from the hospital ship, in which
he was being sent to England, and rejoined the Battalion
in October. He was again wounded in December, but
refused to go sick—a typical example of an old " con-

temptible " ! 2/Lieut. Short joined on the 5th, and
2/Lieut. Borland on the 6th.

The Battalion, on the 6th, returned to the trenches for
another two days, and during this tour a heavy German
shell hit Battalion Headquarters, passing through two
brick walls and a wooden door without exploding.   It
only slightly wounded a telephonist at his instrument.
The casualties for these days were 2 killed, 11 wounded.

On the 10th April the whole Brigade reassembled at
Vlamertynghe.   The men much appreciated being on
firm ground again instead of in a sea of slithery mud,
not to mention the fact of being out of range of the
enemy's guns.   During this rest, baths were available
for all.   A draft of 50 arrived on the 12th, and a further
one of 25 with 2/Lieut. Job on the 15th.

At Ouderdom on the 15th, the Battalion rehearsed,
over a taped course, its forthcoming assault on Hill 60.

On the previous day a personal reconnaissance of the
position to be occupied by the Battalion in front of
Hill 60 was made by 2/Lieuts. Payton, Cobb and
Travers.

On the evening of the 16th, The Queen's Own occupied
the trenches opposite to the famous mound.

CHAPTER VI

CAPTURE OF HILL 60.—Hill 60, which was to be the scene of one of the most desperate and sanguinary encounters of the War, was but a small artificial mound of earth hardly worthy of the term " hillock." It rose some 40 feet above the general level of the country to the S.E. of Zillebeke, in that part of the line which had recently been taken over from the French by the British Second Army.

It owed its presence there, as did both the " Caterpillar " and the " Dump," to the excavations made during the construction of a cutting through which the railroad passes from Ypres to Comines. For at a distance of some 650 yards from Zillebeke, this railway enters a cutting about 15-20 feet deep and so passes over the Zwarteleen-Zandvoorde Ridge. During the workings, the excavated earth from the cutting had been heaped on either side of the line, forming eventually several small mounds of earth.

Thus it was that the British found on their front on the west side of the railway cutting, the " Caterpillar," so termed owing to its peculiar shape ; the " Dump," a somewhat smaller heap about 350 yards N.W. of the " Caterpillar," and a further mound, or the famous " Hill 60 " as it was subsequently called, situated on the east side of the railway cutting.

Slight as was its elevation it was valuable to the Germans as an excellent observation post, from which any movement over a large sector of the British line round Zillebeke and Ypres could be detected. Early in 1915, therefore, resolutions were made to take it from the enemy and, to assist in this operation, six large mines were run under the Hill. The infantry detailed to capture and hold it were the 13th Brigade of the 5th Division.

Before dawn on the 17th April, the Battalion was established in the trenches facing the Hill. The mines were to be exploded at 7 p.m. that evening, so that the men had the whole day to contemplate their task. Rather a nervous day to live through one would have thought, but the men, if anxious, certainly did not show it. They had to keep very quiet to avoid giving the enemy an idea that anything unusual was in prospect. Those off duty smoked, chatted and occupied themselves with their rations.

The arrangements had been most carefully thought out and explained. Major Joslin was to command the attack. " C " Company under Capt. Moulton-Barrett was to storm the position, closely followed by " B " under 2/Lieut. Walker. " D " Company under Capt. Tuff was to be in support, whilst " A " under Capt. Lynch-White was to be held in reserve. Two companies of the K.O.S.B. with some R.E. were to follow closely the attack with the tools, sand bags, etc., necessary for consolidating the position.

At about 6 p.m. a small artillery duel started quite unexpectedly and, it is believed, that the Germans moved some of their men up on to their hill positions, as we were shelling their support trenches. These men were caught when the Hill went up.

Punctually at 7.5 p.m. the first of the mines was exploded under the Hill and the artillery barrage

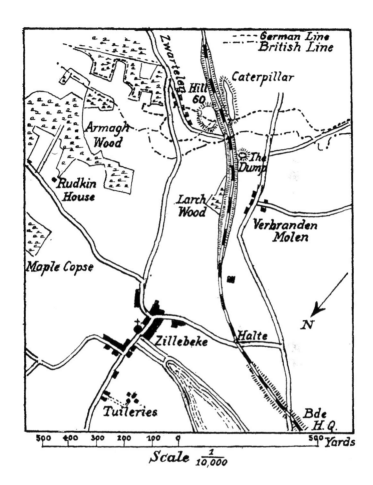

German Line
British Line

Caterpillar

Hill 60

Zwartelen

Armagh Wood

The Dump

Rudkin House

Larch Wood

Verbranden Molen

Maple Copse

Halte

Zillebeke

N

Tuileries

Bde H.Q.

500 400 300 200 100 0   500 Yards

Scale $\frac{1}{10,000}$

HILL 60

[To face p. 108

opened, whilst rapid fire was opened by the infantry and machine guns on either flank. The other mines were fired some 15 seconds later. At 7.6 p.m. " C " Company, scrambling out of their trench, rushed the position in eight separate parties. " B " Company, the machine gunners under Lieut. Westmacott, and the two carrying companies (K.O.S.B.) followed closely. Needless to say, the " Jocks " were not going to allow their mutual friends to do an attack without taking a greater part than consolidating the position. When the Hill was taken, many were using their shovels and picks quite freely on the heads of the Bosche.

So sudden had been the attack that the position was captured at the expense of only seven casualties, and even some of these were caused by the falling debris from the exploded mines. A few Germans were bayoneted, but so shattering had been the explosions that nearly all the defenders were dead or dazed. Two officers and about fifteen men of the 105th Regiment surrendered to " C " Company. One of the prisoners gave the following information :— " The British mines exploded with tremendous effect and must have killed a great many men. It was just like an earthquake and my whole platoon must have been wiped out."

The top of the Hill had been almost blown off. Several enormous craters were made, the largest being about 50 yards wide by 40 feet deep. This made it very difficult to put the hill in a state of defence in the dark. The work was immediately started however, and by 12.30 a.m. on the 18th, some sort of parapet had been constructed as well as two communication trenches. The work had to be done under an increasingly heavy shell fire ; for the Germans, rapidly recovering from their surprise, soon bombarded the hill top with all the weight of artillery at their disposal, though at first their firing was very wild. Over 50 German batteries of all calibres concentrated their fire on the trenches of the Hill, which trenches were, at the most, only 150 yards long. Not only " C " and " B " Companies at the top, but " A " and " D " in support behind the Hill, suffered heavily, and it was soon apparent that, although the actual capture had been cheaply accomplished, the holding of the position was to be a very different matter. However, the men stuck to it splendidly.

Before dawn " B " and " C " Companies were relieved by two companies of K.O.S.B. When the relief was nearly completed, a determined counter-attack was made by the enemy. The whole of " B " and " C " Companies were then off the Hill except a platoon of " B " under Lieut. Walker, who was commanding the Company, and one of " C " under 2/Lieut. Poland. These two officers at once led their platoons back to assist in the defence. Not one of the officers, N.C.O.'s, or men of these two platoons was seen alive again. Major Joslin was killed at about the same time.

The Germans, favoured by the curve of the salient and by the contour of the ground, were able to bring enfilade fire to bear from the direction of Zandvoorde, and also to lob bombs into the still incomplete trenches along the lips of the craters, causing very many casualties. " D " and later " A " Companies were brought up to assist in holding the crown of the Hill which was the target for heavy guns, howitzers, field guns, minenwerfers, and machine guns, as well as hand grenades.

The craters in many cases saved a lot of casualties,

for bombs rolled down to the bottom of them before exploding. The three craters on the left had their forward lips consolidated but we lost many casualties by rifle fire, for a man had to expose half his body to get a shot at the Bosche.

At 8.30 a.m. on the 18th, the Duke of Wellington's took over the defence, and the remains of " A " and " D " Companies and of their comrades of the K.O.S.B. were withdrawn. " D " Company was the last to be withdrawn and had the misfortune to suffer several casualties from a H.E. shell dropping in the centre of what remained of the Company, just as it was entering the town of Ypres.

It is interesting to note that it was here that the Battalion experienced gas and lachrymatory gas shelling for the first time. The shelling occurred in the early morning, just as some of the Battalion were performing their ablutions. As their eyes smarted considerably whilst washing, they all thought at first that there was something in the water. The only one who suffered was the Medical Officer (Capt. Baines), and he, only very slightly, and after the Battalion had been withdrawn.

The following account of the attack on Hill 60 is given by Sergt. Stroud, D.C.M. (of " C " Company) :—

Sergt. Stroud's narrative.—" We met with practically no resistance when we got into the German trenches, the effect of the explosions having killed or stunned the occupants. We found a German officer partially buried and some men at once began to dig him out. He rewarded them, when released, by drawing his revolver and shooting one of them. Needless to say he met his just deserts.

" When we arrived at the top of the craters, we could see the Germans bolting back across the open and down the communication trenches; the men, as is needless to say, were very sick at not being allowed to pursue them. Sergt. Fisher did great work with a machine gun, catching the Germans in their retirement and enfilading them during their journeys down the communication trenches. His action had the effect of accelerating the speed of many.

" The attack was, apparently, unexpected, as the Germans had on neither their boots nor equipment. We found an occupied dug-out undamaged, and L.-Cpl. Miller fired 9 rounds into it with the object of killing the occupants. He was unsuccessful in his endeavours, as seven Huns emerged after his musketry effort and surrendered. We then entered the dug-out and found tea ready. We ate the black bread and found the butter delicious.

" When once the platoons were established the engineers put out some wire and the digging parties got to work. We were not left tranquil for long, as the Germans, recovering from their shock, commenced to shell the Hill and very soon commenced their counter-attacks."

This action cost all the battalions engaged heavy casualties. The Queen's Own lost Major Joslin, Capt. Tuff, Lieut. Payton, 2/Lieuts. Job, Poland and Walker killed; Lieuts. Westmacott, Doe and 2/Lieuts. Borland, Liebenrood wounded; and 2/Lieut. Craston mortally wounded. The casualties among the other ranks were proportionally heavy.

At 5 p.m. on the evening of 18th April, the Battalion left the line at Hill 60 for hutments at Vlamertynghe. Some loss from shell-fire was sustained during the

(1) Capt. Lynch White
Commanded troops on Hill for
several hours during the Battle

(2) Lt. Poland
killed

(3) Lt. Craston
died of wounds

(4) Lt. Wild
wounded

(5) Lt. Maunder
wounded

(6) Lt. Hilder
wounded

(7) Lt. Liebenrood
wounded

(8) Lt. Bradley
Transport Officer, killed at Pilkem

(9) Lt. Doe
wounded

(10) Capt. Tuff
killed

GROUP OF OFFICERS TAKEN THE DAY BEFORE HILL 60

[To face p. 112

move and the Battalion made a further acquaintance with gas, luckily in a mild form.

On the march to billets the Battalion met the K.O.Y.L.I., who had been in Brigade reserve, on its way up to the line. During this unit's tour it made a splendid counter-attack, driving the Germans right off the Hill and consolidating the whole position.

The rest at Vlamertynghe lasted until the evening of 22nd, during which days both Sir C. Ferguson and Sir J. French visited the Brigade to compliment it on the Hill 60 achievement.

A draft of 20 arrived on the 20th.

Pilkem.—At 7 p.m. on April 22nd, the Battalion was on its way back to the Hill 60 position. It had gone but a short distance, when the way was blocked by French Algerian troops and other fugitives in small groups. This was occasioned by the great German gas attack on the French and Canadians north of Ypres, from Bixschoote to Langemarck. The orders for Hill 60 trenches were cancelled and the 13th Brigade spent the night in open fields to the west of Ypres.

At 9.30 next morning the Brigade was moved to a point about a mile north of Brielen, to act as a reserve to the Vth Corps. Here the men were kept under hedges, buildings, etc., to avoid detection from aircraft. At 2 p.m. orders were received for an attack on the enemy in position " somewhere near " Pilkem. This was to ease the pressure on the Canadian flank, for, owing to the French front having been broken during the gas attack, the Canadians had been forced to throw back their left wing to cover their flank. In order to effect this the 13th Brigade, in conjunction with other troops, made a counter-attack along the line of the Ypres-Pilkem Road.

Only one hour was allowed from receipt of orders to the time of attack. As a march of $2\frac{1}{2}$ miles and the passage of the Yser Canal had first to be accomplished, there was not much time to spare. The 13th Brigade had other British troops on its right and French coloured troops on its left. The K.O.S.B. and The Queen's Own, the latter on the left, were in front and the K.O.Y.L.I. and Q.V.R. in support.

Immediately on crossing the canal, the K.O.S.B. moved to the right, and The Queen's Own deployed along the canal cutting and the hollow ground to the left. The Battalion was formed in three lines with a platoon from each company leading, Capt. Moulton-Barrett commanding these advanced platoons. On the commencement of the advance, it at once became apparent that the Algerian troops were inclining inwards, and so crowding out our leading line. The supporting lines were consequently held back under cover, and only advanced a platoon at a time. As it happened, this saved many casualties. The advance was made practically without artillery support, for, owing to the difficulties of communication, the necessary artillery arrangements could not be made in time. The K.O.S.B. who had to cross some very open ground, suffered very heavily from the numerous machine guns brought forward by the enemy. Eventually the advanced lines of K.O.S.B. and of the Battalion reached a position some 300 yards from the Germans, but the situation was obscure, and it was never apparent what line exactly the enemy was holding. It soon became evident that he was strongly posted, and that it would require much greater strength and

artillery support than was then available to turn
him out.

The two battalions dug themselves in as soon as it
was dark ; the supporting lines, coming up on the left,
continuing the fire trench to the west. The Queen's
Own lost 105, including Lieut. Bradley and 2/Lieut.
Daubeny killed, and 2/Lieuts. Cobb and Maunder
wounded. Lieut. Bradley was killed some 25 yards or
so in front of his Company. He was very keen and,
owing to the shortage of officers, had recently been
taken from his appointment as Transport Officer to
command a company. The casualties would have been
very much heavier had the supporting lines advanced
as at first intended, for, owing to the inward inclination
of the French troops, the greater part of our men were
only moved up when it was getting dark. The K.O.S.B.
losses were more than double ours.

The 23rd was spent in the newly-constructed
trenches.

At 2 a.m. on the 24th, the Brigade was relieved. The
unit to relieve the Battalion was the Rifle Brigade,
whose companies were up to strength and, as a consequence, all their men could not be got into our
trenches. The Battalion was then withdrawn to the
canal. At daybreak it moved back a couple of miles
for a rest, but at 1 p.m. urgent orders to return at once
to the canal were received, as the Canadian Division was
being hard pressed. On arrival it remained in support
until dark, when it took up a position on the west of the
canal.

The whole of the 25th was spent on the canal bank,
the K.O.S.B. and The Queen's Own, both under the
command of Major Robinson, having the duty of preventing the Germans from crossing. It was reported

that the enemy had forced the canal two miles beyond our left, so that it was necessary to provide for a possible German advance down the west bank. At about 10 p.m. that night, as a new draft of 370 men under Capt. Knox with 2/Lieuts. Littleboy and Gross arrived at the canal, an unlucky high explosive shell caught the head of the column, killing two of the men and wounding several others. C.Q.M.S. Wood, who was walking at the head of the draft when the shell exploded, was badly wounded in many places. He was a great loss to his company, as his one thought had always been for the welfare and comfort of the men.

At 2 a.m. on the 26th, the Battalion proceeded to take over the front line trenches from three other units. They were hard to find, as orders and arrangements were very inexplicit. The relief was consequently not completed until after daybreak. Luckily the morning was misty or heavy casualties would have resulted, as the enemy opened with machine guns. The trenches were shallow, but, as each company brought up 50 shovels, they were much improved during the day.

In the afternoon an attack by the Lahore Division and French troops took place; part of the former passing through the Battalion's line. The French Colonial Division, before the attack, waited in our trenches. Their chief ambition in life was to get our ration marmalade in exchange for anything the men would take.

It was very evident that such an attack could not possibly succeed. The Indian Division advanced with superb gallantry, but as soon as it came under observation, when the leading wave was about level with our Battalion Headquarters, it was literally blown to pieces by 5.9 high explosive shells. The men fell by platoons

—a most sickening sight ! By the time the Division had reached the front trenches, 500 yards farther on, all the sting had been knocked out of the attack. No infantry in the world could have succeeded under the circumstances.

The Battalion's Dressing Station was situated in a farm, 400 yards behind the line, and was soon crowded with casualties from many units. The trenches were very heavily shelled and the Battalion lost many men, partly from shell fire and partly from gas.

The four following days were spent in these trenches, and more casualties were suffered from the almost incessant shell fire. On the 28th the Battalion was successful in bringing down a German aeroplane with rifle and machine-gun fire.

The Battalion was relieved after dark on the 30th, and in spite of heavy shell fire during the relief got off with only three wounded. It marched back about 2½ miles.

The total casualties from 25th-30th, were 2/Lieut. Croucher and 3 men killed ; 2/Lieut. Sharpin and 42 men wounded ; 2/Lieut. Hilder gassed, and 26 men missing. 2/Lieut. Croucher had been C.S.M. of " D " Company at Dublin. He was left behind unfit, though he tried hard to dodge the Doctor. He had only just joined as an officer and is described as becoming " at once the life and soul of his company." The " missing " were nearly all men who had been gassed and taken to French first-aid posts.

On May 1st the Battalion with the 13th Brigade moved to Vlamertynghe where, in a wood a mile north of the village, it had its first night's rest since the 21st April. During the evening of the 2nd, the Battalion returned to support positions near Brielen. Two days

I

of active preparation for a possible attack in support positions followed, the Battalion bivouacking at night.

2/Lieuts. M'Clelland and Burdett arrived with a draft on the 4th. That night the Battalion moved back to huts at Ouderdom and next day was ordered up for a renewed attempt on Hill 60.

Second Attack on Hill 60.—This Hill, having been splendidly held by battalions of the 13th and 14th Brigades for over a fortnight, was retaken by the Germans on the 5th May. They only attained their object by means of gas ; a form of attack for which, as yet, there was no defence. The holders of our trenches, The Duke of Wellington's Regiment of the 13th Brigade, remained at their posts and, when the Hun assailants arrived after the gas had passed away, they found the defenders still there. But it was a battalion of dead men and hence an easy victory for an opponent who, unable to achieve victory by fair and honourable fighting, sought to gain his ends by a means both foul and barbarous. The 15th Brigade made a grand attempt to recapture the lost position, but without success. It was therefore determined to try again and capture the Hill with the 13th Brigade in a night attack at 10 p.m. on the same day, the 5th.

The enemy had captured ground to the north of the Hill as well as the Hill itself, but exactly how much was in their possession was not clear. The K.O.S.B. were directed to assault the Hill whilst The Queen's Own, on their left, were directed against the trenches to the north of it. The night was extremely dark and the ground was much encumbered with old wire, and also cut up by old trenches and shell holes.

The attack started punctually at 10 p.m., being

preceded by a preparatory bombardment of twenty
minutes. The enemy were apparently expecting this
attack, for, as soon as our preparatory bombardment
began, they rained high explosive and shrapnel, plaster-
ing all lines of approach. What with the darkness,
the difficult ground and the general obscurity of the
situation, the attack never developed properly.

This is an instance of the sort of thing that occurred.
One platoon was directed along a road which, though
plainly marked on the map, had been quite obliterated
on the ground by heavy shell fire. Having nothing
to guide it, this platoon got too far to its right and,
when it reached trenches supposed to be held by the
enemy, found them occupied by British troops. Even
had the situation been perfectly clear, it is very doubtful
whether an attack by so small a force as two battalions
could have succeeded. Carried out as it was, in the
dark, without previous reconnaissance, over unknown
ground, upon an objective which was not clearly
defined and with the situation of our troops uncertain,
the attack had but a very remote chance of success.

On our previous attack, when the Hill was first
captured, companies had been guided into the trenches.
On this the second attack, companies had to advance
over unknown ground to attempt to recapture the
trenches into which they had been guided previously
in the dark.

Sergt. Robinson, the Battalion Signalling Sergeant,
was about the only one in the unit who had seen the
ground before in daylight, as he and his linesmen had
laid telephone wires there. During the night of the
unsuccessful attack, Sergt. Robinson performed invaluable service by going round and finding out the
positions of all companies. He did this twice during

the night, under heavy shell fire. He well deserved the D.C.M. which was afterwards awarded to him for his useful and dangerous work.

This second attack was accepted as a failure just before daylight, and the companies were ordered to occupy trenches and dug-outs for the day. They remained here under shell fire throughout the 6th. In the evening " A " and " D " Companies were withdrawn to Ypres, the other two being left out to support the K.O.Y.L.I. who attacked at dawn on the 7th. This attack was equally unsuccessful. " B " Company was relieved on the evening of 7th, and " C " on that of the 8th, when the Battalion was reassembled in Ypres.

This unsuccessful attack was only one of several. The capture of Hill 60 was attempted again and again, sometimes with much greater force, but no attack succeeded. The losses of the Battalion amounted to 110, 2/Lieut. Wild being one of the wounded.

From the 9th to the 17th May, the Battalion was billeted in and near Ypres. The town was shelled continuously, and on the 11th, part of it was set on fire. Every night strong working parties were provided to improve the defences. During this period nineteen casualties occurred, nearly all being among the working parties.

On the 15th, Capt. Parker, 2/Lieuts. Fulcher, Bullen, Richardson, Peachey and Carpenter joined. A draft of 115 had arrived on the 9th, and one of 114 on the 14th.

On the evening of the 17th, the Battalion moved to dug-outs, two miles S.W. of Ypres, where it remained for a week. Working parties up to 600 strong were furnished and these cost further casualties, fifteen men

A GROUP OF THE BATTALION'S STRETCHER BEARERS IN 1915

(1) Pte. (afterwards Corporal) George Hatch, who was recommended
for the Victoria Cross, High Wood, 1916
(2) Sergt. Rogers, the Medical Officer's assistant

A GROUP OF THE BATTALION'S SIGNALLERS IN 1915

Showing—Sergt. Robinson, 2nd figure from right sitting
Sergt. Davis, left-hand figure standing

[To face p. 120

being hit. 2/Lieuts. Fry, Cooper, Dobie, Bennett, Wacher and Sewell joined on 23rd, with a draft of twenty men.

On the 24th, Sir H. Plumer, who had succeeded Sir H. Smith-Dorrien in command of the Army Corps, inspected the Battalion.

St Eloi.—The trenches next occupied by the Battalion were those at St Eloi, which were held from 26th May till the evening of 1st June. Six men were killed and 2/Lieut. Fry and twenty men wounded during this tour. 2nd to 4th June were spent in hutments at Dickebusch, where all got baths. From the evening of the 4th, till that of the 10th, the Battalion was back in the St Eloi trenches. This tour of trench duty cost four killed and eighteen wounded. Parties of a battalion of the " Kitchener's Army," the 9th K.R.R., were at this stage attached for instruction. After three days' rest at Dickebusch, the same trenches at St Eloi were occupied for another six days. This time the losses were six men killed and twelve wounded. One day, during this tour, a message was received from the R.A. as follows : " Mother will make an effort at 9 a.m." ; this meant a 12-in. gun was about to fire— a remarkable event at that time !

On one occasion the Battalion had been relieved by the K.O.Y.L.I., the relief being complete at 1 a.m. At 1.30 the enemy exploded a big mine under the front trench, causing somewhere about 100 casualties. Had this occurred a little earlier, both battalions would have been caught.

In July three tours of duty in the St Eloi trenches were done. From the 1st to the 7th cost two killed and eight wounded. The next, from the 10th to the 16th, was marked by heavy bombardments of the position by artillery, trench mortars and rifle grenades ; the casualties being seven killed and 2/Lieut. Richardson and thirty others wounded. The final period of only two days accounted for one killed and two wounded.

The 22nd July found the Battalion at Steenvoorde, where it remained until the end of the month, training hard when the weather permitted. Sir H. Plumer visited the Battalion on the 26th, and was most complimentary.

On the 31st the Battalion left the neighbourhood of Ypres for many months.

CHAPTER VII

A T the end of July 1915 the 5th Division was transferred to the Third Army, under General Monro, and moved to the neighbourhood of Albert, where it was employed in the extension of the British line, taking over the defences in that area from the French. The Battalion entrained at Godemeads-velde on 31st and travelled via Calais, Boulogne and Amiens to Corbie, where it detrained and thence proceeded by march to Ribemont, four miles S.W. of Albert.

The Battalion now entered upon a period of comparative quiet ; very different from the time of strain which, with short intermission, it had endured for nearly a year. It was now that the unit learned to make itself much more comfortable in the trenches and, in this sector, the travelling kitchens were actually brought up into the trenches. A Battalion cookhouse was then constructed, well dug in. In this relief we took over from the French, as part of the trench stores, a cow, which provided the officers with fresh milk during their tour in this area. It had its own dug-out and was taken out to graze every evening. For in 1915 this was a " peaceful " area, in which each side was content to contain its adversary. No aggressive action on a large scale was attempted though, less than a year later, the same ground was to witness scenes of carnage almost dwarfing those of any previous engagement, even of this sanguinary war.

Carnoy.—From billets at Ribemont the Battalion moved on 3rd August to Billon Wood and Bronfay Farm, 2 to 3 miles N.E. of Bray and a couple of miles from the front line. Next day it relieved the French 293rd Regiment in the trenches at Carnoy. This is about a mile S. of Mametz ; a name shortly to become familiar to British ears. The trenches taken over were fairly good, and all were impressed by their " peacefulness," compared with those to which they had been accustomed. Of course this does not imply that life had become safe. Casualties continued to occur and the Battalion lost fourteen, including five killed and one officer, Lieut. M'Clelland, wounded during the first month. But the difference between this area and Flanders was, nevertheless, very noticeable.

It would be tedious to detail the daily doings, or even the weekly doings, of the Battalion at this period. A summary must suffice.

The tours of trench duty—always in the Carnoy Sector—usually lasted for seven or eight days, and the same periods were passed in reserve. When in the front line, the time was spent in small aggressive actions calculated to make life uncertain for the enemy, and in enhancing our own chances of safety. As regards the latter, the trenches were immensely improved. Keen rivalry existed among the companies as to which should accomplish the most and the best work, with the result that the rather shapeless trenches taken over from the French were soon got into good order. They were considerably deepened, and revetted internally with sandbags ; proper firing steps were constructed, and sump holes were made to drain both the fighting and communication trenches. This work was well repaid in the safety it provided. During one tour of

duty in October, lasting eight days, not a single man
was hit, though the enemy constantly employed trench
mortars and rifle grenades against the Battalion.

Aggressive action consisted of sniping and counter-
sniping ; bombing and counter-bombing ; shelling and
counter-shelling. " Retaliation " was a word in every-
day use. Once a battery supporting the line which
was held by the Battalion found that it had one surplus
round. Its Commander thought the Bosche might as
well have the benefit of it, so sunk the trail of a gun and
loosed it off at a distant village. The Bosche retaliated.
The British guns counter-retaliated and the affair grew
until, eventually, the whole of the Corps Artillery
became embroiled in a lively artillery duel, brought
about by one spare round and a jokelet.

Either we or the enemy were constantly retaliating.
There was no thought of abstaining from action for
fear of reprisal—at least on the British side—no " live
and let live " idea. We always made ourselves as
obnoxious to the Hun as orders and circumstances
would allow.

A peculiar fact was that the Bosche never shelled
the road leading down into Carnoy at night. Our
transport passed down this hill every night with rations,
etc., and must have been heard by the Hun. A shell
dropped anywhere on the road would have hit somebody
or something. Similarly the enemy transport in this
sector could be heard every night by us, and it was
always assumed that because we left their transport
alone they left ours.

Among the more unusual weapons used at this time
may be mentioned the 13th Brigade Catapult Battery.
This threw bombs with great accuracy to distances
up to 120 yards. An emplacement was made for it

in no-man's-land, whence it bombed the enemy's trenches. The Germans never could find out where it was. They used to get perfectly exasperated, and shell and rifle grenade the fire trench ; but they never found the catapult position.

During this period the Battalion bombing, scouting and sniping platoon, which had been started by Lt.-Col. Robinson, did great work. They were always ready and willing to take on any job, however unpleasant and dangerous. They were under the direction of the Sniping Officer.

The Battalion possessed a double-barrelled elephant gun, whose bullets could penetrate the German ironplate loopholes at a distance of 300 yards. The Sniping Officer, 2/Lieut. Quinlan, accomplished great work with this strange weapon. 2/Lieut. Quinlan also achieved great success with his famous " drain pipe " trench mortar, which was first started when we were up in The Salient. He could get four or five bombs in the air at one time, which was rather a good show, as all he had was a drain pipe with an attachment at the bottom for firing off a round. He had to reload after each bomb had been fired.

Casualties were few. From August to December the Battalion lost twelve killed and thirty-five wounded ; three officers, Capts. Parker, Russell and Lieut. M'Clelland being among the wounded. When out of the trenches the Battalion was billeted in Bray or, more often, in Billon Wood and Bronfay Farm mentioned before. Billon and Bronfay, although hardly two miles from the German front line, were fairly safe, being situated in a hollow. Air bombs were more dangerous than anything else.

Besides the usual smartening-up process, there was

a great deal to do. Working parties for improving the position and for carrying stores were large and numerous. Much training was got through, special attention being given to anti-gas measures, every man passing through a poison-gas chamber. There was a steady stream of officers and N.C.O.'s to and from various schools of instruction in the back areas. Leave to England had become a recognised institution, and as many officers and men as possible were allowed to go in rotation.

Amusements were not forgotten, football and boxing being indulged in with enthusiasm. As regards football, the Battalion was unlucky in never having an opportunity to enter anything like a representative team for the Divisional League. It devoted itself instead to an Inter-Company League, which was easily won by " C " Company. A very successful boxing competition, in which both officers and men took part, was held at Bronfay Farm. The finals had to be decided on a Sunday, because the Battalion was for the front line next day. At Evening Service the Chaplain used the boxing ring as a pulpit, after which the finals were fought off.

Another amusement, until the French people objected to our riding over their crops, was " The Battalion Hunt." Officers, mounted on horses from the transport lines, chased coveys of partridges and hares, until they couldn't fly or run any farther, when they " killed."

Once a rat hunt on a grand scale was organised at Bronfay. After an action lasting an hour or so, the enemy's casualties were found to number over 530. The corpses were laid out for inspection and, as this was probably a record, the " Battle " and its result were recorded in the War Diary.

Bathing in the Canal at Bray was a great attraction, practically every man having at least one bathe each time the Battalion was in rest.

At Bray a concert party, who afterwards became the famous " Whizz Bangs " of the 5th Division, came into being. The troupe first started, under Brigade arrangements, in the small theatre of that town, and was then practically a Battalion show. Subsequently it was placed under the able leadership of Sergt. King of the 14th Warwicks.

In August Brig.-Gen. Maynard succeeded Brig-Gen. Wanless O'Gowan in command of the Brigade, and, a month later, Brig.-Gen. L. O. W. Jones became the Brigadier. In the winter, to the great regret of the other units of the Brigade, their old comrades the 2nd Bn. The Duke of Wellington's and the 2nd Bn. K.O.Y.L.I. were removed from the Division. The places of the two Yorkshire regiments were filled by the 14th and 15th Bns. Royal Warwickshire Regt., and at the same time the 14th Brigade was replaced by the 95th. The latter was, however, composed of three battalions of the 14th, and one other.

A good many changes took place in the Battalion. Lieut.-Colonel P. M. Robinson, C.M.G., was appointed to the command of a Brigade in September. He had commanded since November 1914, and the Battalion had been engaged under him at Hill 60 and at Pilkem, besides the difficult and costly trench work in Flanders. Major H. D. Buchanan-Dunlop, D.S.O., succeeded him, with Capt. Newton as Adjutant.

In August 2/Lieuts. A. D. Fleming and J. A. Fleming joined. Lieut. M'Clelland left, wounded, but rejoined in November. In September Major R. Lynch White left to take up a staff appointment ; Capt. E. J. Russell

LIEUT.-COLONEL H. D. BUCHANAN-DUNLOP, C.M.G., D.S.O.

(Present Commanding Officer.   Commanded in France for two years)

[*To face p.* 128

was wounded and evacuated. In October Capt. Parker left on being wounded. Capt. Whitty joined, but was transferred in a few weeks to the 8th Service Battalion of the Regiment; 2/Lieut. Scott also joined. In December Lieut. W. R. Cobb returned and 2/Lieuts. Clay, Cale and Bellman joined. 2/Lieuts. Carpenter and Burdett wer, detached for duty with the Brigade Machine Gun Company.

During this period, units of " Kitchener's Army " were sometimes attached for instruction in trench duty. Companies of our 7th Battalion, 7th Buffs, 12th Gloucesters, 11th Royal Welsh Fusiliers and 14th Royal Warwicks came to the Battalion at different times.

Towards the end of September, when the British attack near Loos and that of the French in Champagne were in progress, preparations were made for an advance of the 13th Brigade from Carnoy, in conjunction with the 18th Division from Fricourt. The British and German trenches were taped out near Bray and the assault on the latter was practised. The operation was only to take place should the advance of the British and French to the north and south make great progress, and the enemy in the Albert sector be weakened in consequence. It did not materialise.

As winter advanced, considerable trouble was experienced, as usual, in keeping the trenches safe and habitable. The wet destroyed much of each day's work. By December some of the communication trenches had become so bad that companies going into the trenches were obliged to move across the open, at considerable risk. Gum boots were issued as trench stores, and were a great blessing.

The accuracy and rapidity of fire of the Battalion

trench mortars earned special notice about this time. They could fire at the rate of about 12 rounds a minute.

Christmas Day was spent in the trenches, and both the Divisional and the Brigade Commanders visited the Battalion to convey their good wishes. A cordial telegram was received from the 3rd Bn. The Queen's Own Regiment.

On the 26th December, 2/Lieuts. Quinlan and Clay, with eighteen other ranks, visited the German trenches in the hope of capturing a prisoner. They did not succeed in this, but they thoroughly bombed a length of trench and got back without loss.

1916.

On the 6th January 1916 the Battalion came out of the trenches at Carnoy, on completion of its last tour of duty in this area, and marched via Sailly Laurette to Corbie, where it remained for a whole month. The weather was fine on the whole, and the companies were kept busy with intensive training. Games, too, were not forgotten. Football fixtures included a defeat in Association by the 355 Company A.S.C., a win in Rugby (6—0) by the Officers against those of the K.O.S.B., and a victory in Association by " C " Company, the winners of the Battalion League, over the rest.

On the 6th February the Battalion left Corbie, in fine weather, for Rainneville. At Querrieu, on this march, the 7th Service Battalion of the Regiment was passed and their drum and bugle band played the 1st Battalion through the village. The weather now broke, and the week spent at Rainneville justified the name of that place. It cleared a bit on the 13th, when the 13th Brigade marched to Ailly-sur-Somme.

The Battalion remained here another ten days, most of which were miserably cold and wet.

The great bugbear during the winter months in the Somme area was " trench feet," and it is interesting to note now, at the close of this tour on the Somme, that the Battalion had, it is believed, only one case. The immunity of the unit was due mainly to good organisation. Every night during these winter months, " rations " brought up dry socks for every man in the trenches, and took back with them the wet socks. These were washed and dried in the transport lines, ready for bringing up the next day. The Quarter-master employed two old soldiers, who fixed up a most excellent drying-room in Bray, and regularly, each day, all the Battalion's socks were dry and ready when the limbers were loaded up.

The whole of the 5th Division left the Somme area on the 24th February, the 13th Brigade marching via Flesselles to Doullens. The second day of this march was distinctly unpleasant. The road was frozen and every man in the Battalion had at least one fall. The C.O. sat down violently three times. Horses could hardly move, and riding was, of course, out of the question. It snowed hard, and there was a high, bitterly cold wind. The Brigade was delayed for a long time owing to the road being blocked for over a mile ; transport vehicles having got into difficulties on the slippery surface.

Arras. — After three days in comfortable billets at Doullens, the Brigade continued its march to Arras. The Battalion arrived at that town after dark on the 1st March, and the men were billeted in cloisters underneath the University.

The Battalion was destined to remain in the Arras area for nearly four months. The first tour of trench duty began on the 2nd March, when the Battalion relieved a battalion of the 83rd French Infantry Regiment north of Arras with its left on the Arras-Bailleul Road. The trenches were found to be good and comfortable, some of the dug-outs being very deep and lighted by electricity. But, judging from the virulence of the German snipers, the freedom with which they used their working parties and other indications, a general impression was conveyed to all that the enemy had been allowed recently to have matters very much his own way—a state of things which the 5th Division at once set to work to alter. On the whole, the area was found to be fairly quiet, though less so than the Carnoy sector.

Casualties in the Battalion were distinctly more numerous. This was no doubt partly due to the aggressive attitude adopted by the Division in the course of restricting the freedom of enemy action noticed on arrival ; an attitude which naturally led to retaliation. Later on, indeed, the French nicknamed the 5th " The Mad Division " on account of its habit of " asking for trouble," but, needless to say, this was taken as a compliment. Any attempt to avoid loss by refraining from injuring the enemy must, in trench warfare, tend to the latter becoming " top dog."

The tours of trench duty, which lasted about a week, were spent partly in the firing line and partly in close reserve. After the first tour of duty, the 13th Brigade took over the left sector of the Divisional Front and the Battalion was always afterwards in trenches on the extreme left, in advance of Roclincourt, next to the 51st Highland Division.

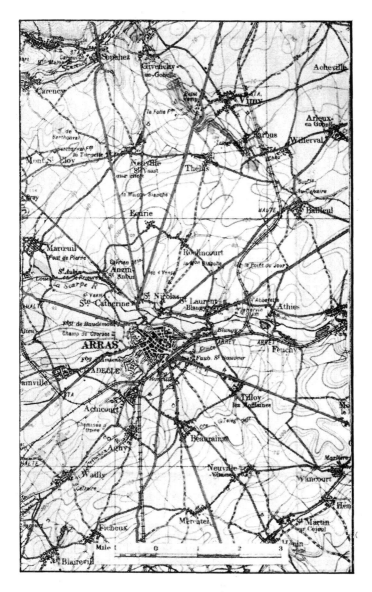

ARRAS

Some incidents of the actual fighting must be recorded. At 5 a.m. on the 9th April Capt. Gross (Commanding " D " Company), with Lieut. Dobie and C.S.M. Crossley, one of the heroes of Neuve Chapelle, was inspecting the work done during the previous night on the wire in front of one of his company's trenches. A thick mist appeared to ensure immunity from direct enemy action. Unfortunately the mist must have cleared somewhat without attracting the notice of the group of our men round the wire. The enemy suddenly opened a concentrated rifle fire from a concealed sap only about forty yards away. Both Officers, the Company Sergeant-Major and a Private fell at once—killed or mortally wounded—a heavy blow ! Sergt. Hammond and L/Cpl. Liddamore were afterwards awarded the D.C.M. for their courage in bringing in the wounded under intense fire.

On the 7th May, when the Battalion was in support, the enemy opened a particularly heavy bombardment which lasted for about three hours. As far as the Battalion was concerned the principal point of attack was a place called " Observation Redoubt," garrisoned by a platoon of " D " Company. It was calculated that nearly 700 shells fell on this one spot and, as can be well imagined, the Redoubt was knocked completely out of shape. Yet, so good were the deep dug-outs taken over from the French, that not a single man was hurt. The Battalion stood to in case the bombardment should prove to be the precursor of an attack, but nothing further happened.

An incident occurred on the 27th of May which, though of little importance in itself, is worthy of mention because it is an example of the grand spirit of the rank and file. During a specially heavy trench mortar

K

bombardment, L/Cpl. Harris was horribly mutilated by an aerial torpedo. Both his thighs were shattered, wounds of which he died a few days later. He managed to crawl to his platoon officer—not for sympathy, for delivering no last message, for nothing the officer could do to relieve his agony—but just to apologise for being wounded !

A curious and rather gratifying little episode occurred about this time. Another unit attempted a night bombing raid on the Hun trenches. Luck was against them and, through no fault of their own, the expedition was a failure. Next day the enemy shouted to the K.O.S.B., then occupying the trenches, " What about the West Kents now ? " The Bosche, who was usually better informed, evidently thought that it was the West Kents who had attempted this raid, and it is flattering to think that, knowing the reputation of the Regiment, they were exulting over our supposed failure.

When in rest the Battalion was billeted in one or other of the villages near Arras. Of course " rest " only meant cessation from fighting. A great deal of work had to be done, and large working parties were in constant requisition. Tunnelling under R.E. supervision formed no small part of the tasks in these days. Nominal rest did not imply certain immunity from enemy action. The " gas alert " was not infrequent, and once at least a whole company had to leave its billets and take refuge in dug-outs because of shell fire. During sick parade one day a shell entered the Doctor's Aid Post, but fortunately did not explode.

Each Brigade of the Division was relieved in turn and moved back to the neighbourhood of Agnez-lez-Duisans for training and rest.

In spite of work, time was found for games and amusements. A six-a-side platoon football competition took place in March and April, the winners being the Transport Team.

At Agnez-lez-Duisans, in June, there was a Divisional Horse Show. The Battalion, who took great pride in their transport, did very well. It was an easy first in the preliminary Brigade competition; in the Divisional Competition, open, of course, to mounted units as well as the three Brigades, it took the first for officers' chargers under 15·3, and third (first for infantry) for a pair of heavy draught horses. Cricket matches, tug-of-war, boxing, etc., helped to keep the men fit and provided a welcome change from war service.

Rats and mice were always present in force, and constant war was waged against them. " Peters," Colonel Dunlop's dog, was one of the ablest combatants on our side in this minor warfare. This dog had a wonderful capacity for getting lost and for reappearing when quite given up. He was twice recovered by officers of the Regiment serving on the Staff, many miles from the Battalion.

Another form of amusement was provided by the very excellent Divisional Pierrot Troupe called the " Whizz-Bangs," who gave first-class entertainments to all troops in the area. A cinema show was also much appreciated.

Shrapnel helmets, shortly to become universally known as " tin hats," came into fashion about March. They were not looked upon with much favour at first, but the men soon got accustomed to them and came to appreciate the extra security they provided.

It was about this time that a particularly brutal form of Hun frightfulness was discovered by the

Transport officer, who found a small hook-shaped piece of wire, sharpened at the ends, among the horse feed.

The losses suffered by the Battalion in operations in the Arras area from March to early July were :—

Capt. Gross, Lieut. Dobie, C.S.M. Crossley and 12 others killed ; 2/Lieut. Pracey and 56 others wounded— a total casualty list of 72.

There were some changes in officers. In March Capt. H. A. Waring, who had been Adjutant of the 3rd Bn. since the beginning of the War, arrived and assumed the duties of Second in Command and, at first, those of Adjutant as well. 2/Lieuts. Balch, G. P. S. Johnstone and Jarvis joined.

In April Capt. Gross and Lieut. Dobie were killed, Capt. Newton left to become a Brigade Major, and 2/Lieuts. Cornford, Fox, Martin and Pracey joined.

In May Lieut. Kerr, who had been wounded in October 1914, rejoined, and 2/Lieuts. Joel and Hyde came to the Battalion.

In June Capt. Ogle and Lieut. Bartlett joined. On the 15th June reinforcements of 92 were received. This draft included men of regiments other than The Queen's Own. Among these there were some 15 men of the East Surreys and, although most of these men had previously served with the 1st Bn. East Surrey Regiment in the 5th Division, sanction was refused for these men to be allowed to rejoin their old Battalion.

In order to keep them together they were formed into a special platooon (No. 8A) and attached to " B " Company. This platoon, which was composed of very fine men, most of whom had been wounded and re- turned, did excellent work during the Somme fighting.

This inclusion of men of other regiments in the draft for our Battalion was the first indication of the distressful system which was soon to become general, whereby men were sent to units with but slight regard to the regiment to which they belonged.

The reinforcements received on the 15th June brought the strength of the Battalion up to over 1100 of all ranks.

CHAPTER VIII

THE SOMME

THE great Somme offensive of 1916 opened on the 1st July. A plan entailing a subsidiary attack from about Wailly, five miles south of Arras, by the 5th Division had been formed. The Division was withdrawn from the trenches and concentrated some fifteen to twenty miles west of Arras. Here it was in G.H.Q. reserve, ready either to deliver the proposed attack or to operate, where circumstances might require, in the Somme area.

Each battalion of the 13th Brigade was put into the trenches at Wailly for forty-eight hours at a time, in order to get acquainted with that part of the front. When the Battalion took over its sector, Capt. Newton was found to be the Brigade Major of the Brigade occupying the trenches. He gave us a good account of the trenches, stating : " It is a quiet sector, there being only one old man in the trenches opposite and he has a white beard."

However, the Battalion had what might be called a lively time during its forty-eight hours, as on our side the artillery put down continuous smoke and gas demonstration barrages on to the German trenches, to which the enemy replied with every type of artillery fire. The old whit·-bearded gentleman, therefore, was not quite so somnolent as Capt. Newton had led us to suppose.

The Battalion handed over its trenches at Wailly on

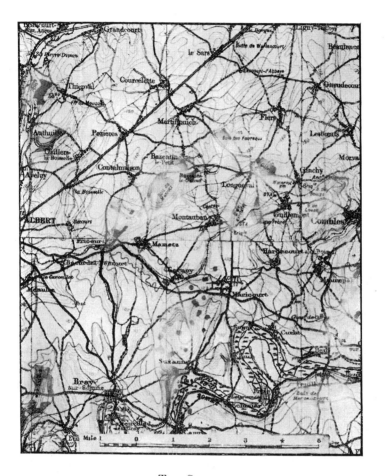

THE SOMME

[*To face p.* 138

the night of the 2nd of July.   Next day it was conveyed
in motor omnibuses to Houvrigneul, about eighteen
miles W. of Arras. It remained here for ten days, in
constant readiness to move at short notice, while the
situation was developing on the Somme. It was
whilst at Houvrigneul that a set of drums was received
by the Battalion, and Sergt. Donoghue got together a
Drum and Fife Band, which afterwards was much
appreciated in the Battalion.

Though in almost hourly expectation of orders to
advance, the 13th Brigade was kept employed in
experimental exercises, notably in schemes to test
co-operation between aeroplanes and infantry during
an attack. Thus, when urgent orders to move were
received on the 13th, one company of the Battalion
was engaged in such work seven miles away, while
another had been detached to construct new trenches
near Wailly. This was unfortunate, as it involved
much extra fatigue for the two companies. When the
Battalion was again concentrated at Outrebois, seven
miles west of Doullens, at 1.30 a.m. next morning, the
main body had marched sixteen miles, " C " Company
twenty-two, and " A " Company no less than thirty-one.
The southward move had been ordered because the
plan for an advance from Wailly had been definitely
abandoned, principally because it was found that the
contours of the ground there prevented our Artillery
from cutting the enemy's wire.

The 14th was a day of uncertainty and of contradictory orders and, for this reason, rather a trying
one. Suffice to say that the Battalion, having left
Outrebois at noon, did not arrive at Herrisart, on the
Amiens-Arras Road, until 1 a.m., though the direct
distance between the two places was no more than

16 miles. At noon on the 15th the march was continued to Franvillers, on the Amiens-Arras Road.
Though the distance was short it took $3\frac{1}{2}$ hours to
accomplish. Besides delays and uncertainties the day
was extremely hot, the road very dusty, and the men
had had two hard days, including much night marching.
For these combined reasons the march of the 15th
was a particularly exhausting one. The 16th was
spent in a welcome rest. At 9.30 a.m. on the 17th,
the 13th Brigade left Franvillers. The Battalion
reached Meaulte, a couple of miles south of Albert, at
1.30 p.m. The 7th Battalion of the Regiment had
just distinguished itself greatly at Trones Wood, and
now, having been relieved from the line, was bivouacked
near Meaulte.

The Division was now part of the XV Corps. Signs
that the Battalion was getting involved in the " Big
Push " were becoming very evident. Meaulte and the
vicinity simply swarmed with troops of all arms. The
18th was spent in Meaulte.

On the 19th the Battalion was ordered up to support.
Before entering the trenches, eleven officers and a proportion of N.C.O.'s and men were detached, in accordance with Army orders, and sent to remain with the
transport. Experience in the past had shown the
necessity for making sure of a nucleus of survivors,
should the unit suffer very heavy losses. Hereafter
this was always done before going into action, and those
left behind were called the " dumped personnel."

The Battalion marched soon after noon that day to
Mametz, crossing the old German front line, thus
seeing the country that most of the officers and men
had looked longingly towards in 1915. " A " and " B "
Companies dug themselves in between Bazentin and

Longueval in support to the K.O.S.B., while " C " and
" D " Companies occupied an old German trench
north of Montauban.　There was considerable artillery
activity during the day and night, but the Battalion
only suffered two casualties.

On the night of the 19th-20th, troops in the front
line attacked, with the result that the Germans were
slightly pressed back, and High Wood (Bois des
Foureaux) was partly occupied.　The Battalion moved
into the front line after dark on the 20th.　" A " and
" B " Companies occupied the track running from the
south corner of High Wood in a S.E. direction, " D "
Company was in support, and " C " in reserve.　The
Germans put a heavy barrage behind our front line
after dark, and one of our companies was badly caught
when moving up.　The 14th Royal Warwicks prolonged the front line to the right, towards Longueval.

The 21st was spent in the trenches.　During the
day and night, patrols were freely used in order to
fix, as far as possible, the exact situation of the enemy ;
for all knew that an attack was imminent.　Casualties
continued.　The Quartermaster, Capt. Rogers, who
had come out with the Battalion and served continuously, doing most splendid work, was wounded when
issuing rations to the carrying parties.　Colonel Dunlop,
recognising that the point to which rations and water
were ordered to be brought was a particularly dangerous
one, had tried to get it changed, but without success.
Numerous casualties occurred among the transport
and carrying parties.　The Battalion had lost about
ninety men since the 19th, the barrage through which
the companies had to pass on the night of the 20th
accounting for most of them.　Lieut. M'Clenaghan
was one of the wounded.

The situation on the evening of the 22nd July was as follows :—The enemy's main position was supposed to be along Switch Trench, but he was known to be occupying Wood Lane as an advanced position. An attack by several Divisions on Switch Trench was ordered for 1 a.m. on 23rd. As a preliminary operation The Queen's Own on the left and the 14th Royal Warwicks on the right were to seize Wood Lane at 10 p.m. The K.O.S.B. were to pass through our line later and, wheeling to their left, take part in the main attack on Switch Trench.

The two leading battalions were occupying a trench along the track running S.E. from the south point of High Wood, the left of The Queen's Own touching the Wood. The Battalion frontage was 400 yards. Wood Lane, the objective, was 400 yards in front. The ground sloped gently upwards for 350 yards and then fell for the remaining 50, so that the German trench was out of sight. Along the ridge 50 yards in front of Wood Lane ran a slightly sunken road. The enemy left this vacant by day, but occupied it with machine-guns at night. The situation on our left, in High Wood, was obscure. The Division on our left maintained at first that the whole of the Wood was in British hands, an assertion which Colonel Dunlop was convinced was a mistake. Later on, an assurance was received from this Division that the Wood would be secured before the Battalion gave its flank to it in the attack. There were rumours of a German strong point in the Wood, but where exactly situated was not known.

" A " and " B " Companies were ordered to lead the attack in two waves, the rear one carrying tools. " C " Company was to construct support positions and communications. " D " was to move up to our front trench and be ready to carry wire and stores up to the new line. A platoon of " C " under Lieut. Peachey was specially detailed to work up the flank of the Wood, to keep touch with troops of the Division on the left, and assist in the capture of the strong point, if this were found to be occupied by the enemy.

High Wood.—At 9.52 p.m. " A " and " B " Companies left their trenches, and, advancing without much loss, lay down close behind our barrage not far from the crest of the hill. At 10, when the barrage lifted, they rushed at the enemy, but both Wood Lane and the sunken road were strongly held by the Germans, who had suffered little from our artillery. A devastating machine-gun fire was poured into our men from the strong point in the Wood and from a position just behind the Wood. Nearly all the officers, including the commanders of " A," " B " and " C " Companies, were hit at once. The men made repeated efforts to get forward. " C " and " D " Companies were sent in to reinforce, and eventually some of the K.O.S.B. and the 15th Royal Warwicks (the reserve battalion) were drawn into the fight. A small party of " A " Company on the right succeeded in reaching the German trench, but, being assailed with bombs on their exposed right flank, they could not maintain themselves when their own supply of bombs became exhausted. On our left a platoon of " B " Company under Lieut. Scott eventually reached its objective and consolidated 40 yards of the enemy's trench, to which they clung for four hours. But as a whole our men, do what they might, could not get forward. The units on our left and on our right being equally unsuccessful, the attack was given up and the remnants ordered back to our original front line just as dawn was breaking.

Such, in short, is the history of this tragic failure. To elaborate it a little :—

It has been said previously that the enemy was not much damaged by our artillery fire. The latter, in fact, was almost ineffective, the batteries having only been notified of the coming attack at 8 p.m., when it was already getting dark. It was then too late to register properly on the enemy trenches, which were out of sight. Hence the artillery support, though heavy, was very inadequate, and this through no fault of the gunners, who were necessarily groping in the dark. The real obstacle to success was, however, the fire from the left flank. It was found afterwards that the strong point in the Wood most thoroughly swept no-man's-land with its machine-gun fire. The Division on our left failing to capture it, this strong point kept up an impenetrable curtain of bullets in front of the position throughout the attack. Our own platoon of " C " Company under Lieut. Peachey, which had been detailed to move up the edge of the Wood and, it was hoped, to protect the left flank of the attack, was practically exterminated, the officer being one of the first to fall. Thus the attack was delivered under quite different conditions from those that had been intended. The men tried most desperately to get forward. " Come on, boys—let's have another go ! " they would shout, and thus yet another heroic effort to achieve the impossible would be made.

The platoon of " B " Company which succeeded in reaching the enemy's trench and consolidated there, only numbered about 20. Later it was joined by

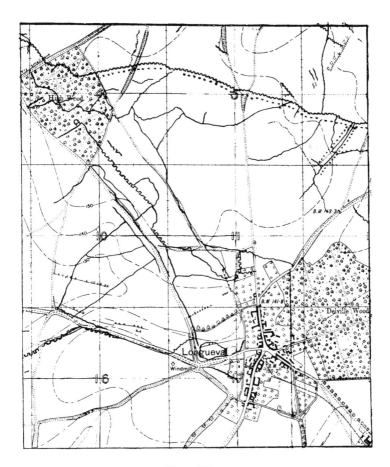

HIGH WOOD

To face p. 144

Lieut. Bartlett of " D " Company and the few men
that remained of his platoon. Though senior to
Lieut. Scott, Lieut Bartlett declined to take command
as he considered that the former officer must be more
in touch with the situation. He worked as a private,
putting up wire and using a rifle. He was, in all
probability, killed during the retirement, as he was never
seen again. A few men of the K.O.S.B. also got up
just before Lieut. Scott received orders to retire.

The great attack on the Switch Trench was also a
failure, partly, perhaps, because of the non-success of
the preliminary operation, but mainly because the
Division on the left could make no headway in High
Wood.

The officer casualties in the Battalion amounted
to 14. In " A " Company Lieut. Cobb, command-
ing, was wounded very early. His three subalterns
all fell, 2/Lieut. Lewinstein being killed, 2/Lieut.
F. A. Fleming and 2/Lieut. Cornford being reported
as " missing." Of " B " Company, Capt. Bennett,
commanding, was " wounded and missing," Lieut.
Letherdale " missing " and 2/Lieut. Fox killed. " C "
Company lost its commander, Capt. Ogle, Lieut.
Bullen and 2/Lieut. Peachey wounded, and 2/Lieut.
Cross " wounded and missing." In " D " Company
Lieut. Bartlett was " missing " and 2/Lieut. Gillett
was killed. Lieut Healey, the adjutant, who went
forward to ascertain the situation, was " wounded
and missing." It was ascertained afterwards that
Lieut. Healey was shot through the stomach when
quite close to the German trenches. His runner, at
Lieut. Healey's request, put him into a shell hole
under cover, and then returned for assistance. Unfortunately the runner was also hit on the way back,

and died next day in hospital. The runner, Pte. Noble, was only got in as day was breaking, so that it was by this time impossible to get assistance to Lieut. Healey—a gallant and able officer, who was a great loss to the Battalion.

Those reported as " wounded and missing " or simply as " missing " were undoubtedly all killed or mortally wounded, since not one of them was ever heard of again.

The losses in other ranks amounted to 407. Only some 250 survivors could be collected in the original front trench after the action.

It is always easy to find excuses for failure. Nevertheless it does seem to be the fact that the attack, as delivered, was quite impossible of success from the first. The factors that made it so may be here stated. Firstly, a night attack by a considerable force is proverbially risky. Such attacks have succeeded many times in this war, but that does not alter the fact that the element of chance plays an undue part in the proceedings. However carefully prepared the operation may be, a very small incident or a trivial obstacle may quite easily throw out all calculations. Secondly, the ineffective artillery support already referred to. Thirdly, the machine-gun fire from the left. This last factor would alone have prevented any chance of success. The stream of enfilading bullets made the ground actually impassable. Colonel Dunlop had recognised some part at least of the danger, and had received positive assurance that the safety of his left flank would be provided for by other troops. This, as has been seen, was not done.

A year or two later the Battalion formation for attack would no doubt have been different. By that

time it was well understood that a rifle or machine-gun
fire that can stop a platoon of good troops is equally
impenetrable by a company. Therefore the companies
would have been formed with more depth than they
were, so that only a portion of each, say one platoon,
would have been subjected to the withering machine-
gun fire. The remaining three platoons of each
company, more or less intact, would have been still
available for effort elsewhere. The principle that it is
useless to thicken a line already held up and that such
a course can only lead to heavier casualties, unheard
of before the war, was still imperfectly understood at
this time, when the whole success of an attack depended
on getting the attacking troops forward, before the
enemy's artillery barrage came down on our position.
So it is no disparagement to the Battalion that it did
not adopt a course in direct opposition to all previous
teaching.

General Stephens, the G.O. Commanding the 5th
Division, told Colonel Dunlop that success under
the actual circumstances was impossible. Addressing
the men, he said they had done right well, and that
it was no fault of theirs that the position was not
captured.

Numerous incidents of individual courage occurred,
very few of which can be recorded.

Lieut. Dando, the Scout officer, led his scouts past
the left of the enemy's trench, reconnoitred their
position, and brought back most valuable information.
A number of his party were killed.

Lieut. Cale, the Battalion Lewis Gun officer, assisted
by Sergt. Weston, the Lewis Gun sergeant, endeavoured
to carry out of action, under heavy fire, Lieut. Cross,
whose thigh was shattered.

During a bomb attack on Lieut. Scott's party, Pte. Butlin jumped over the bombs thrown by the enemy before they had time to explode and repulsed the Germans with his own bombs.

The work of the medical officer and of the stretcher-bearers is described by Colonel Dunlop as "almost superhuman." Captain Baines, R.A.M.C., attended to serious cases all that night and far into the next day in an advanced dressing station situated in the front-line trench. The trench was under constant artillery fire, and twice it was knocked in on top of him. Once when this occurred he had his fingers on a severed artery and, though partially buried, he maintained his hold. He was awarded the M.C.

Corporal Hatch of the stretcher-bearers, unable to get stretchers forward owing to machine-gun fire, went out alone into the bullet-spattered ground and placed the wounded under cover in shell holes, whence they might be brought in when the fire relaxed. He undoubtedly saved many lives. It was a marvel that he was not hit in the first five minutes, but he continued his wonderful work for hours. At last he was wounded. To the intense disappointment of every man in the Battalion, Corpl. Hatch did not receive the V.C. which, in the opinion of all, he had earned many times over that night. He was re-commended for it by his Commanding Officer, Brigade, Divisional, Corps and Army Commanders. He was awarded the D.C.M. and Médaille Militaire.

The Brigade was relieved in the front line on the night of 23rd-24th, and the woefully depleted Battalion was withdrawn to bivouac in rear. The work of reorganisation was at once taken in hand. The scenes of carnage, through which they had just passed, by no means weighed on the spirits of the survivors. Major Waring, the second in command, visiting the men in their bivouacs on the 24th, was much struck by their cheerfulness. He says it was "more like going round Christmas dinners, than a visit paid after the time they had been through." Resilience is certainly a quality strongly developed in the men of the home counties !

The Battalion remained in bivouac until the 29th July. Strong working and carrying parties had to be found every day and a few casualties occurred among these. One carrying party of an officer and one hundred men, working at night, were forced to wear gas helmets practically the whole time. Even so one or two were gassed. On the 27th the 15th Brigade captured Longueval and the Battalion stood by ready to support if necessary, but was not called on, except for strong digging and carrying parties.

Longueval.—On the 29th the Brigade returned to the line. The K.O.S.B. were in front in Delville Wood, with The Queen's Own in close support in trenches in and about Longueval. The immediate object was to consolidate the line from Delville Wood to High Wood. The companies left their bivouacs at five minutes' interval, the leading company starting at 10.30 p.m. Some confusion occurred when Longueval was reached owing to the inability of the guides supplied to find their way. This was not surprising, as the whole of the village and many sections of trench had been completely obliterated by shell fire. Consequently it took some time to establish communication between Battalion Head-

L

quarters and the companies. Longueval was under so heavy a shell fire that it was very difficult to get into touch with the K.O.S.B. in Delville Wood. This was ultimately accomplished by taking a route round the village. The Battalion then settled down to endure the shell fire, which lasted without intermission until they were relieved at 8 p.m. on the 30th. An officer describing the ordeal says : " Longueval was simply a mass of shell holes which changed shape as more shells fell. Our infantry sat tight through this hell on earth, under a perfect rain of 8-inch and 5·9-inch shells." The same officer records that several watches stopped in Longueval that day.

Delville Wood and Longueval will always remain in the memory of those who were there as a veritable nightmare.

When relieved the Battalion was found to have suffered sixty-four casualties, among whom was 2/Lieut. Jarvis, commanding " A " Company, who was killed. Heavy as this loss was in so small a battalion it was considerably less than had been feared, and the Battalion may be said to have come off lightly. Sergt. Bradman, who was acting Sergeant-Major of " A " Company, was also severely wounded, and it was only owing to the M.O. (Capt. Baines), and some volunteers from the Company that this N.C.O.'s life was saved. After the trench had been blown in on the top of Sergt. Bradman, the M.O. with some volunteers dug him out with their hands and, under a heavy shell fire, removed the mud from his wounds and carried him out of action.

On the 1st of August the 5th Division was with-drawn for a rest, and the Battalion marched *via* Meaulte, where it was met by the drums, to bivouac

CAPT. M. B. BAINES, M.C.
ROYAL ARMY MEDICAL CORPS
(Attached 1st Battalion R.W. Kent Regiment)

[*To face p.* 150

near Dernancourt. On the 4th it entrained at Merincourt and next day went into billets at Metigny. Here it remained for eighteen days.

Retrospect.—The Battalion had gone into the Battle of the Somme on the 19th of July with a total strength of over 1100. As comparatively few casualties had been suffered for nearly a year, the unit had not greatly changed in personnel during that time. The majority of both officers and men may be said to have been almost veterans, as far as length of fighting service went in those days. Eleven days later they came out of the line with their fighting strength reduced to 350. Seventeen officers and 575 other ranks had fallen, a large proportion of both being either killed or " missing " (synonymous terms then). The officers lost included the Adjutant, the Quartermaster, three company commanders and all four 2nds in command of companies. In those days of dreadful casualty lists such a loss was not exceptional. The feature that made it peculiarly sad for survivors was that their comrades had fallen, and the Battalion had been nearly destroyed without visible result. The only attack they had been called on to attempt had proved to be an impossible operation. It almost looked as if their Battalion had been thrown away !

Between the 31st of July and the 17th of August 16 officers and 325 other ranks joined the Battalion. The officers were Lieut. Nisbet, and 2/Lieuts. Harrison, Coltman, Press, Hallowes, Henfrey, Hill, Meakins, Jagger, Daubeny, Longstaffe, Molony, Brett, Jenkinson, Anslow and Young. Most of them were naturally inexperienced. It would take some time before they could adequately replace the fine officers who had fallen.

The men came from several different regiments, a few only being The Queen's Own. Most of them had received but little training and, though all good men, could by no means be considered as first-class soldiers for some time.

The Battalion was thus so changed in personnel that it might almost be supposed that the individuality of the unit would be changed too. This was not so. Nothing is more astonishing than the vitality of regimental individuality. Apropos of this, a senior officer remarks in his diary, " This is an old army battalion and it is extraordinary how things go on on the old lines, no matter who come and go." An elderly officer rejoining after eight years' absence, soon after the Battalion had suffered fearful losses, was amazed by the same discovery. There were not twenty individuals throughout the unit whom he knew. He expected to feel among strangers, he at once felt at home.

But, of course, the reconstructed Battalion was not, at first, of the same fighting value as it had been before its losses. The two and a half weeks at Metigny were utilised to the full in training the new men. Had they all come from battalions of the Regiment, the process would have been easier. It is presumed that the system of drafting men as reinforcements to units with little regard to regimental feeling was absolutely necessary. It was intensely unpopular, both with battalions in the field and training battalions at home. It added to the difficulties of the former, and tended to take the zest out of the work of officers and N.C.O.'s of the latter.

Leave up to forty-eight hours was granted in rotation. But, as it was confined to leave in

France, it was not of much use to the rank and
file.

Guillemont.—The 5th Division was brought back
into the line on the British right, near Guillemont.
The 13th Brigade was on the right of the Division
and in touch with the left of the French. The
Battalion, which had come up by rail to Dernancourt,
moved into front-line trenches during the night of
25th August. It was on low ground in a valley south
of Guillemont. A mile-long spur runs in a S.W.
direction from Leuze Wood ; Falfemont Farm stands
on the extremity of this spur and was occupied by
the Germans. The Battalion's trenches were some
600 to 800 yards to the S.W. of Falfemont. Headquarters and the reserve companies were on high
ground further to the west. The principal task of the
front battalions was to go forward at night and dig
a trench 400 yards nearer the enemy. It was required
as a " jumping off " place when the next attack should
take place. The work was pushed on during the
nights of 26th, 27th and 28th, and, after one false
start, a good, useful, well-placed trench was constructed. In the early morning of 28th, Lieut. Wright
of " D " Company, when reconnoitring, discovered
Germans occupying some old concrete gun pits 300 yards
from, and out of sight of, our front line. He tried to
dislodge them, but they were much too strong. When
captured a few days later, in the course of the big
attack, these pits were found to be held by about forty
Germans with several machine guns. Sergt. Sibbald,
the Battalion bombing sergeant, was killed on this
occasion. This N.C.O. had come out with the Battalion
and had served continuously without a day's sickness.

Full of energy and initiative and absolutely regardless of danger, he was a great loss. There was a lot of shelling during this tour of trench duty, and the weather was so bad that the men were never dry.

The Battalion was relieved on the night of the 29th August and withdrawn to Brigade reserve trenches. Casualties since the 25th numbered 65. Lieut. Nisbet and 2/Lieut. Young were wounded and 2/Lieut. Meakins was missing. The 13th Brigade left the front line on the 31st, but was brought up again on the 2nd of September with orders to attack Falfemont Farm and Wedge Wood next day.

Falfemont.—The Brigade attacked on the 3rd of September in conjunction with a big French attack on the right and other British troops on the left. The K.O.S.B., with Falfemont Farm, and the 14th Royal Warwicks with Wedge Wood as their respective objectives, were in front line. The Battalion was in support to the 14th Royal Warwicks.

The infantry attack began at 9 a.m. The K.O.S.B. reached the farm enclosure but failed, in spite of very gallant efforts, to take the farm itself. It was the old story of the murderous efficiency of the German machine guns. The 15th Royal Warwicks were sent in to assist the K.O.S.B., but also failed to reach the farm. All this was clearly visible from Battalion Headquarters.

From this point of vantage with the aid of a telescope could be seen a German machine gun, under the charge of an officer, which was brought out of a farm on a flank. This gun came into action from a position in a piece of trench near by, picking off every runner who tried to return with messages from the

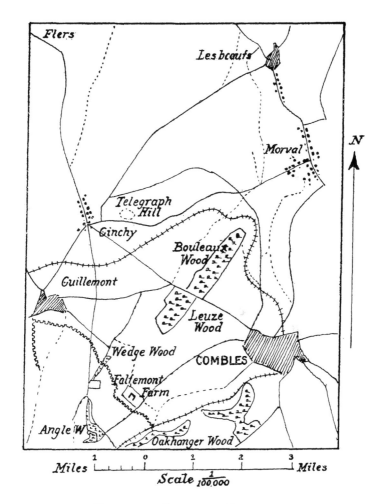

Flers

Les bœufs

N

Morval

Telegraph
Hill

Ginchy

Bouleaux
Wood

Guillemont

Leuze
Wood

Wedge Wood

COMBLES

Falfemont
Farm

Angle W

Oakhanger Wood

Miles   1   0   1   2   3   Miles

Scale $\frac{1}{100,000}$

FALFEMONT FARM AND GINCHY

To face p. 154

K.O.S.B. It was a very galling sight for, owing to
the distance that intervened, we could render no
assistance. Time after time a messenger would start
on his ill-fated journey, when—pop, pop, pop would
be heard, and down he would go.

From Battalion Headquarters, also, some German
reinforcements were observed endeavouring to get
down to the farm from Leuze Wood. Their endeavours
were, apparently, also spotted by a neighbouring
battery of French Heavy Artillery which gave them
a few moments' rapid fire, with the result that no
German reinforcements reached the farm, neither did
any return to the Wood.

In the meantime the 14th Royal Warwicks had,
after repeated and costly efforts, succeeded in capturing
a strong point held by machine guns in advance of
Wedge Wood, and had got a footing in the Wood itself.
The Battalion, which had suffered severely from shell
fire, moved up to reinforce the 14th Royal Warwicks.

That night the 13th Brigade, which had suffered
heavy losses, was relieved by the 15th Brigade, but
the Battalion remained in the trenches and was attached
to the 15th.

Another attack on Falfemont on the 4th was carried
out by the 15th Brigade, but being unsuccessful the
guns subjected the farm, for some hours, to a concentrated artillery fire. Though this failed to put all
the machine guns out of action, it materially lessened
their virulence. The infantry attack was then renewed
(in the afternoon of the 4th). The 1st Norfolks and
1st Cheshires advanced over the old ground, while the
1st Bedfords pressed in on their left.

It was a most exciting moment when the Norfolks
on the right facing the farm, were held up, and the

Cheshires and Bedfords, who prolonged the line to the left, swung round, taking the farm in flank and rear. This had the effect of cutting off the farm, and the Germans could then be seen running out with their hands up; any who tried to get away being caught in rear by our artillery barrage or by the fire of the Bedfords.

This attack, though very costly, succeeded, and Falfemont Farm was at last captured. The Queen's Own was at once brought forward in support of the Bedfords. Two companies advanced along the spur and dug in close to Leuze Wood, pushing patrols into the Wood itself. Luckily the ground was easy and a good, strong trench was constructed. These two companies were then the most advanced troops of the 15th Brigade. The advance made this day was the longest hitherto accomplished during the Battle of the Somme.

The Germans were fighting very well, but their idea of fighting to the last did not coincide with ours. Many who were encountered in shell holes fired at our men up till the end, and then, not relishing a bayonet encounter, put up their hands. This method of fighting was not approved of by the British soldier.

Citadel Camp.—The Battalion was withdrawn on the evening of the 5th, and marched to bivouacs between Fricourt and Bray. Considering that they had not been employed in the front of any of the attacks the losses were very heavy. The casualties were 10 officers and 191 other ranks out of a strength of 470 taken into action. The officers hit were : 2/Lieuts. Pracey, Martin and Hallowes, killed ; Capts. Paul and Bellman, Lieut. Press, 2/Lieuts. Hill, A. D. Fleming, Henfrey and Longstaffe, wounded. The four first-named wounded refused to leave until the action was over.

Lieut. Press was twice hit, but stayed on till the end.
The fighting strength of the Battalion was now reduced
to 270.

While in camp, on the 8th of September, the 13th
Brigade was inspected by the G.O.C. 5th Division.
He congratulated the Brigade on the recent operations,
explaining that the non-success of the first attack on
Falfemont was due to some failure of the artillery
support. He said that the attack by the 13th very
materially assisted the successful attack by the 15th
Brigade. The same day a wire was received from
General Sir T. Morland, commanding the XIV Corps,
in which he expressed admiration for the devoted
conduct of the 5th Division.

An officer gives a vivid glimpse of the extraordinary
sort of life led in modern war. He, himself, was shaving
at the entrance to his dug-out. " Behind, our own guns
were making a terrific noise, up and down the road
was a constant stream of motor ambulances, limbers
and other traffic and parties of men of all sorts ; just
over the road some men were kicking a football about ;
a hundred yards to my right a funeral was going on."

Leuze Wood.—On the 10th of September the 5th
Division provided a composite Brigade to relieve the
foremost troops of another Division. It was composed of the depleted battalions of the 13th Brigade
and isolated battalions from the other brigades of the
Division. The Battalion left the Citadel Camp at
9 a.m. and spent the day just west of Maricourt. At
6.45 p.m. it moved into front-line trenches in Leuze
Wood, with advanced posts along the edge.

The Battalion expected to attack next morning,
but orders to this effect were cancelled. A heavy

artillery fire was opened on the Wood in the afternoon and a German infantry attack was anticipated, but none came.

During the night the Battalion, except one company, was withdrawn to reserve trenches. This company was relieved the next night.

Casualties were again heavy, numbering 68. Capt. Bellman, 2/Lieut. Dando and 2/Lieut. Daubeny were wounded.

On the 12th Col. Dunlop, who had been suffering from dysentery for some time, was forced to go to hospital. The command of the Battalion devolved on Major Waring.

On the 13th the composite brigade was relieved and the Battalion, with a fighting strength reduced to about 200, went into billets at Mericourt, three miles S.W. of Albert. Next day Major R. Lynch White, D.S.O., rejoined from Staff Duty, and assumed command.

Since the beginning of September 2/Lieuts. Monypenny, Lewis-Barned, and 30 other ranks had joined the Battalion.

Waterlot and Ginchy.—The rest at Mericourt was not of long duration, for on the 18th the Brigade returned to the front line, and the Battalion occupied some very bad trenches with no dug-outs at Waterlot Farm. It remained until the evening of the 20th, losing a few men from shell fire, and then moved into trenches near Ginchy, where it was in reserve to the Division.

On the night of the 22nd it advanced into front line trenches facing Morval and began the construction of new assembly trenches in advance. 2/Lieut.

Monypenny was slightly wounded, but remained at
duty. Next day Battalion Headquarters was heavily
shelled and Major Lynch White slightly wounded.

The Battalion was relieved on the night of the
24th and bivouacked near Carnoy. Next day it
went into Divisional Reserve, south of Guillemont,
and supplied stretcher parties for Morval, which had
just been captured by the Guards, the 5th and the
6th Divisions. On the 26th it was again withdrawn
and went to the Citadel Camp.

Retrospect.—This ended the share of the Battalion
in the Battle of the Somme, as the 5th Division was
now withdrawn from the area. In less than two
and a half months it had lost in battle casualties,
31 officers and just over 900 other ranks. The fortune
of war ordained that the Battalion, numbering over
1100, which entered on these operations should be
terribly depleted in its first action and that its subsequent share in the glories of the 5th Division should
be rather a minor one. Yet if casualties be any test,
The Queen's Own had certainly borne its part. The
Division had captured Longueval, Delville Wood,
Falfemont Farm, Wedge Wood and Leuze Wood, and
assisted in the capture of Les Bœufs and Morval.
After the fall of the last-named place a message was
received from Sir Douglas Haig congratulating " the
Guards, the 6th Division and ' especially ' the 5th
Division."

Just before leaving the Somme area ten new officers
joined, namely 2/Lieuts. Sewell, Faunthorpe, Fender,
Smith, Fry, Gordon, Miles, Hill, Smellie and Radcliffe.

CHAPTER IX

O N leaving the Somme the 5th Division was transferred to the Festubert area. The Battalion went first to Les Planches, a suburb of Abbeville, where it arrived on the 29th of September. It then proceeded to the neighbourhood of Bethune, arriving at Essars, a mile N.E. of that town, on the 1st of October.

Festubert.—On the 3rd of October the Battalion moved into support trenches. The frontage allotted to the 13th Brigade was in the centre of the Division. It was 2700 yards long and ran in front of Festubert. Owing to the wet soil the defences mainly consisted of breastworks and, in some places, merely a chain of isolated posts. The support, or " village " line, contained eleven such posts with Festubert itself in the centre of them. On the 4th the Battalion took over the front line consisting partly of breastworks, partly of island posts. Three companies were in front with one in support. It was soon found that the area was a veritable " rest cure " after the Somme. During the six days the Battalion was in occupation of the line, not a man was hit. On some days hardly a shot was fired. On the evening of the 10th they withdrew to billets at Gorre, close to Bethune. Here they were visited by a troupe from Miss Lena Ashwell's concert party, which was greatly appreciated.

The next tour of trench duty was on the right, or Givenchy sector, of the Divisional Front. Moving up on the 17th, the Battalion remained in the front line until the 22nd. The enemy bombarded with trench mortars on the 20th, and five were wounded, 2/Lieut. Smellie and 2/Lieut. Faunthorpe among them, the former very slightly.

Next day two parties of four men each, under 2/Lieuts. Monypenny and Noakes, tried to capture a German sniper. They did not actually get one, but they did some damage. 2/Lieut. Monypenny's party crawled through the wire and got into the German trench. The sentry fled screaming with 2/Lieut. Monypenny after him. Unfortunately, however, although this officer fired all six chambers of his revolver at the flying German, he found he had forgotten to load his pistol and therefore scored a " wash out." A few Germans who were encountered were killed with bombs, and our two parties returned without a casualty.

The next few days were spent in the " village " line in support, the companies being employed in turn in working in the front line. On the 28th the Battalion returned to the Givenchy trenches and remained there until the 3rd of November without losing a man. They then returned to billets at Gorre.

A further period of trench duty from 9th to 15th cost four men wounded.

Lieut.-Col. Buchanan-Dunlop returned from sick leave on the 20th of November and resumed command. Major R. Lynch White becoming second in command and Major H. A. Waring adjutant.

On the 22nd, when in the Givenchy trenches, the enemy bombed the line with trench mortars, in

retaliation for an organised shoot on our part. Lieut.
Wall was wounded and two men killed—the first
fatal casualties since the Battalion came into the
area. On the 25th there was increased trench mortar
activity on both sides and the Battalion lost three
men killed and one wounded. Two more were
wounded in the same way next day.

An interesting incident occurred on the 8th
December. Two French soldiers, on leave from the
Somme, received permission to search for valuables
which they had buried near our present support line,
in the Autumn of 1914. The ground had changed
shape considerably in the interval from shell fire
and the many trenches dug in this neighbourhood.
They were about to give up this search when, to
their huge delight, but to the intense disappointment
of some of our men, they found a box. The feelings
of our men who were hoping to continue the search later
on, and who had been living, as it subsequently
proved, almost on the top of the box, can be imagined
when the finders informed them that the box contained
(according to them) money and jewellery to the value
of 15,000 francs. The spot had been in constant
occupation of troops for over two years—German,
French and British had occupied it and dug trenches
in turns, so they were very lucky to recover their
treasure.

Nothing worthy of note occurred during the remainder of 1916. The enemy's activity became more
and more marked and casualties were more numerous.
This was probably due to aggression on our part.
The 5th Division had to live up to its reputation as
the " mad division," and declined to purchase a
peaceful time at the expense of making life easy for

the enemy. Whereas the first tours of trench duty
had cost no casualties at all, quite a number of men
were hit in December. The total losses from 1st
October to the end of the year were eleven men killed,
and four officers (2/Lieuts. Smellie, Faunthorpe, Wall
and Noakes), and twenty-nine men wounded.

During the same months Lieut. Cobb and 2/Lieut.
Brett returned, and 2/Lieuts. Wall, Hyde, King and
Sampson joined. Lieut. and Quartermaster Thorne, an
old regular of the Regiment, also came. Five others,
including Captain Parker, joined, but were transferred
in a few days to our 6th Battalion.

When in rest at Gorre, many working parties were
required. But time was found for games, and
football, especially, was keenly enjoyed. The " Whiz
Bang " Pierrot Troupe helped to keep all ranks
amused, and bands, including the R.E. Band from
Chatham, did much to make life enjoyable.

On Christmas Day the Battalion was in billets at
Gorre, and so was not affected by a big organised
shoot arranged to prevent any chance of " fraternising."
The men had the best dinner possible under war
conditions and were visited as usual by the C.O. The
officers all dined together. Sergt.-Major Brown was
much delighted at receiving a postcard from the Prince
of Wales in reply to greetings sent to His Royal
Highness from the Sergeants' Mess.

1917.

The Battalion spent the first fortnight of 1917
at Beuvry in concentrated training. A brigade
training depot to instruct new drafts had been
organised. Much work was done and a great deal
of hard exercise in the way of games. Competitive

cross-country runs were arranged in teams of twenty men per company. A Battalion "Marathon" race was won by Drummer Grey. Two officers and several other ranks entered for a Brigade boxing competition. The "Whiz Bangs," bands and a cinema show kept things going in the evenings. As many as possible were allowed leave.

On returning to the line on the 14th of January the Battalion suffered a few casualties from trench mortars.

At 4.30 a.m. on the 8th of February, after half an hour's heavy bombardment, a small party of Germans succeeded in entering a sap occupied by men of "D" Company. Some confused hand-to-hand fighting ensued. We lost four men killed or died of wounds, six wounded and one missing. The German loss could not be accurately ascertained, but it was supposed to be about twenty, of whom five were certainly killed.

Raid of 10th February.—A very successful raid on the German trenches in the Givenchy sector was carried out by the Battalion in daylight on the 10th of February. It had been long prepared, orders authorising it being received as far back as the 13th of January. As in such cases success depends very greatly on preliminary preparations, these must be explained in detail. Colonel Dunlop decided that the raid should take place in daylight, and that there should be no preliminary artillery bombardment. On the very day the orders were received he explained his intentions to the company commanders, detailing "A" and "B" Company to carry out the enterprise. During the next tour in the trenches—from 14th to 20th January—the ground was very carefully ex-

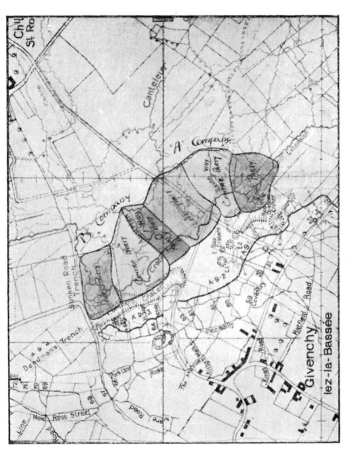

THE RAID, GIVENCHY

[To face p. 164

amined, and, as a result of the information then gained, it was decided that each company should attack in three parties. For it was found that there were just six places along the front where the mine craters, of which over fifty existed, could be crossed comparatively easily. Leaders for the parties were appointed and made responsible for finding their way. They observed by day and patrolled by night until all six knew exactly how to get across no-man's-land. Medium trench mortars bombarded the enemy front line every afternoon up to the day of the raid, a proportion of the bombs purposely being allowed to fall short in his wire in order to cut gaps. This also taught the enemy to expect a " strafe " every afternoon at the same time. On the day of the raid, instead of the usual " strafe," an artillery barrage was put down, and the raid carried out. Except for about two sentries all the enemy had taken cover in dug-outs in anticipation of the usual afternoon hate.

From the 20th to the 26th of January, while in reserve at Gorre and afterwards when in support, as far as circumstances would permit, the two companies were specially trained for the raid. Extra practice in bayonet fighting, bombing, cutting and crawling through wire and running over rough ground was given. Trenches to represent those to be raided were taped out, and the men well practised in rushing them, special attention being paid to the simultaneous rush of all the parties.

Extra artillery were brought up and batteries of 18-pounders and of 4.5-in. howitzers were duplicated. The new batteries fired alternately with the old, so that the enemy should not become aware of an increase in the number of guns.

M

The parties were specially equipped for the job. Over 100 body shields were issued. They probably saved many slight wounds. Lieut. Thorne, the Quartermaster, invented and had made carriers by which each man could take up six Mills Bombs. They were a great success. Each party had two specially prepared trench mortar bombs for use against dug-outs. Box respirators were replaced by the old gas helmets lest the enemy should get samples of our respirator. Each man carried a bandolier of ammunition. Flags to show the position of the parties in the enemy's trenches were provided. All identity marks were removed. Three extra medical officers and thirty-six extra stretcher-bearers were provided by the A.D.M.S. Dressing stations were selected.

The party leaders were : In " A " (Capt. Cobb's Company), 2/Lieut. Brett, 2/Lieut. Harris and Sergt. Donhou ; in " B " (Capt. Scott's Company), 2/Lieut. Jagger, 2/Lieut. Fry and Sergt. Lines.

Zero hour was fixed at 3 p.m. The morning was exceptionally still. The enemy sent over a few shells about noon, but otherwise remained absolutely quiet.

The Corps Counter-Battery Artillery — commonly known as the " Travelling Circus "—engaged the enemy artillery positions for half-an-hour before the raid was due to commence, in the hope of driving the German artillerymen into their dug-outs and cutting their telephone wires. It speaks well for the accuracy of this counter-battery work that no German artillery fire took place till twenty-seven minutes after the raid had commenced, and even then only from guns which were not opposite our front.

Quite suddenly, at 3 p.m., the stillness was changed to an inferno of noise as the British barrage opened and " A " and " B " Companies jumped out of their trenches. Everything went like clockwork. Not a single thing had been forgotten, and Col. Dunlop's careful preparation was amply rewarded. The Germans, completely surprised, made but a feeble resistance as their front trenches were overrun, the occupants being killed or captured. Our men were so eager that in some cases they got ahead of the time-table and ran into our own barrage—the only mistake made. The enemy's support trenches, the final objective, were entered earlier than had been anticipated. Some R.E. who had accompanied the raid blew in four mine shafts. The raiders withdrew after having been in the enemy's position for three-quarters of an hour, on a frontage of 800 yards and to a depth of 400 yards.

An officer and 26 others were captured. The lowest estimate of German killed, mostly in bombed dug-outs, was 150. This number is just half that claimed by the various parties. The German *communiqué* mentioning the raid stated that the " remnants " of the German Battalion were relieved the following night and withdrawn to La Bassée. This would seem to suggest that 300 is nearer the number of Hun casualties than 150.

Sergt. Lines' party went farthest and must have inflicted particularly heavy casualties. This N.C.O. was unfortunately killed. Pte. Thompson did great work with a Lewis gun, knocking out many Germans at a few yards' range.

The artillery barrage was excellent. Though many of our casualties were due to men running into the barrage, this was entirely due to the men's eagerness and was in no way the fault of the artillery. The counter battery work also seems to have been wonderfully effective, since it was twenty-seven minutes after the raid started before the enemy developed any sort of retaliation.

The Battalion's casualties were 4 sergeants—Lines, Avery, Toombs, and Wakeman—and 8 others killed, 54 wounded and 4 missing. Most of the wounds were slight. No officer was hit. Many of these casualties occurred in our trenches after the raid through artillery fire from the enemy who, for the rest of the day and following night, were very nervous.

The dash and keenness of the men were splendid. As always, their officers were full of admiration for them. It is indeed remarkable how, in every action, the men seem to have surpassed the expectation of their leaders, even of those who had seen them in action again and again.

This, the first daylight raid carried out by the Corps, earned many praises from Commanders. The Corps Commander was extremely complimentary, not only on the dash with which the raid was carried out, but on the infinite care devoted to all details of the plan. Major-Gen. Stephens, commanding the 5th Division, also expressed his admiration of the splendid manner in which the operation was conducted. He goes on to say : " The 1st Battalion Royal West Kent Regiment have a glorious record in this war, in which they have distinguished themselves from the very beginning. The dash and spirit with which they carried out this assault is worthy of their great reputation."

In *The Fifth Division in the Great War* it is recorded that " by far the most famous raid was a daylight one carried out by the West Kents at Givenchy on 10th February." The enterprise is then described in detail very much as above.

Next day, the 11th February, the Battalion was relieved and returned to Gorre. The Commander-in-Chief inspected them on the 13th. The Battalion was drawn up in line with their drums and transport. The latter was specially ordered on parade because the Battalion took great pride in it. After the inspection the companies marched past. The Commander-in-Chief was very complimentary.

Festubert.—The 5th Division remained in the area until the 15th March. The Battalion did the usual tours of duty in the trenches and rested at Gorre in between. Artillery and trench mortar activity gradually became more vigorous on both sides. On the 3rd of March an apparent intention on the part of the enemy to raid our trenches was nipped in the bud by our artillery, the guns getting to work extraordinarily quickly. Otherwise there was nothing of special interest to record.

Since the beginning of the year, Lieut. M'Clenaghan, Lieut. Nisbet and 2/Lieut. Press had rejoined. Capt. Wilberforce, an ex-regular officer of the regiment, and 2/Lieuts. Darlow, Cathcart, Lovelace, Gray and Winn joined. A draft of sixty-one other ranks was received.

Lieut. Nisbet was wounded for the second time a few days after he joined. Eleven other ranks were killed and thirty-one wounded since the beginning of 1917. These casualties do not include those sustained in the raid of 10th February.

Vimy Ridge.—The 5th Division was transferred to the Canadian Corps and, on the 16th of March, the 13th Brigade left Bethune and went into billets near Auchel, about 8 miles to the west.

For the remainder of March the battalions were

busily employed on special training grounds. The companies were reorganised according to a new system, each platoon being constituted as a complete unit with its proper proportion of riflemen, bombers, rifle grenadiers and Lewis gunners. A considerable amount of snow fell, but, as it did not lie, the training was not seriously interrupted.

Three officers, 2/Lieuts. Corke, Rogers and Lancaster, joined, as well as twenty-four other ranks.

On the 2nd of April the Brigade moved to Bois d'Olhain, 3 miles S.E. of Houdain, where the Battalion was under canvas. Attack by the whole Brigade over a taped course was practised during the next few days. Lieut. Nisbet rejoined.

The 13th Brigade was lent to the 2nd Canadian Division for an attack on Vimy Ridge, and on the morning of the 8th April the Battalion marched to Villers au Bois, where the men were supplied with bombs, rifle grenades, etc. At 9.30 p.m. the same day it moved by companies over difficult ground to Mont St Eloy and thence, by platoons at 100 yards interval, to assembly trenches at Neuville St Vaast, 3 miles S.W. of Vimy Village. The men were heavily laden and the going was very bad. The companies were in position at 3 a.m. on the 9th. Dumped personnel being subtracted, the battle strength was 20 officers and 655 other ranks.

The 2nd Canadian Division, to which the 13th Brigade was attached for this operation, was the centre one of three. The 1st Canadian Division was on its right, the 3rd on its left. In front of the 2nd Division were four objectives, the black line, the red line, the blue line, and the brown line (see Map). Two Canadian Brigades were detailed to capture the first two (the

A Road near Neuville St Vaast, 1917

[To face p. 170

black and red). The 6th Canadian Brigade on the right and the 13th Brigade on the left were then to pass through and attack the two farthest (the blue and the brown).

In the 13th Brigade, The Queen's Own on the right and the K.O.S.B.'s on the left were detailed as the assaulting battalions. The 15th Royal Warwicks were to be in support, and the 14th Royal Warwicks in reserve.

The task before the Battalion is shown on the map. " C " Company on the right and " D " on the left were to assault Thelus trench. When this was captured, " A " on the right and " B " on the left were to pass through and take Goulot Wood, establishing themselves on its western edge.

The Capture of Vimy Ridge.—Zero hour was fixed at 5.30 a.m. on the 9th of April and the Canadian attack then began. At 7.30 a.m. The Queen's Own left its assembly trenches in a snowstorm and, at 8.15, advanced in three waves in artillery formation. " C " and " D " Companies formed the two leading waves, " A " and " B " the third. The ground was fearfully cut up and very slippery, but the men kept well closed up and reached the Lille Road, punctually to time-table, at 9 a.m. When passing the German first-line trenches, the tanks, which were to have supported the attack, were found sticking in the mud and being shelled by the Germans.

At the Lille Road the Battalion deployed. The ground was reconnoitred and objectives pointed out. At 9.29 the first wave advanced to close under our artillery barrage. So intense was the barrage that watches could be compared and all the men notified as to when it would clear the objective with the greatest impunity.

Directly the barrage cleared Thelus trench, " C " and " D " Companies rushed it and captured a few Germans. Patrols from these two companies closely followed up the barrage and cleared all trenches up to Telegraph Weg. " B " Company then advanced past the North side of Count's Wood and entered Goulot Wood. It was found to be occupied by parties of Germans with, at least, one machine gun. They did not wait, however, but retired over the open ground to the N.E. Our Lewis gunners at once got on to them. " A " company coming up on the right of " B," the two companies pushed forward as soon as the barrage lifted and seized the final objective beyond the Eastern border of the Wood. Some casualties were suffered here from the German artillery. But it was found that all the ground to the front could be equally well commanded from the Western edge of the wood, where good dug-outs were discovered. So the men were kept back during daylight, and again pushed out to the brown line as soon as darkness fell. The line was then properly consolidated.

Nine guns were captured in the Wood, namely, four howitzers, four field and one 90-mm. gun. A few rounds were fired from them at close range as our men approached. The rifle-grenade section of one of the platoons at once came into action, while the rest of the platoon charged. The German gunners then bolted, but most of them were accounted for by our Lewis gunners.

The Wood was held by " A " and " B " companies with platoon posts along the brown line and company reserves in the Wood. Advanced posts were estab-

VIMY RIDGE

lished on the road, in front and in touch with those
of the Canadians on the right and the K.O.S.B. on
the left. The reserve companies (" C " and " D ")
were posted in Thelus trench, but at night " C " was
brought up in close support just behind the Wood.

The attack developed throughout with the utmost
precision. The shooting of the artillery and the
accuracy of their lifting barrage was splendid. Our
men behaved exactly as if carrying out a practice
attack.

The casualties of the Battalion were Lieut. Hyde,
killed ; 25 other ranks killed or missing ; 2/Lieut.
Lewis-Barned and 111 other ranks wounded. Some
of the latter died shortly afterwards. *The Fifth
Division in the Great War* shows 287 as the total
casualties suffered by the Brigade. Thus the Battalion
lost very nearly as many as the other three Battalions
combined.

Great difficulty was experienced in getting rations
up at night. Pack animals, including officers' chargers,
had to be used. The going was necessarily very bad
indeed, and improvised bridges had to be made over
old trenches. It took nine hours to reach Battalion
Headquarters and casualties occurred on the way.

The 10th of April was passed in the position gained.
The front companies were able to put the artillery
on to several good targets, as there was a lot of German
movement about Vimy. There was also a considerable
amount of sniping from that direction.

At 8.30 p.m. on the 10th the relief of the Battalion
by Canadians commenced. On its completion the
13th Brigade rejoined the 5th Division.

Many hearty congratulations on the operation were
received. That from the 2nd Canadian Division to

the O.C. 13th Brigade read : " Now that your Brigade has ceased to be attached to the Division, the G.O.C. wishes you to convey to all ranks under your command his admiration of their conduct during the time your Brigade has been under his orders.

" The Brigade had an exceedingly difficult task to perform, and they carried it through in the most dashing and workmanlike manner.

" The G.O.C. is proud to have had such a magnificent body of officers and men under his command.

" To you, personally, he wishes to convey his thanks for the masterly way in which you handled your Brigade.

" The G.O.C. regrets that he has not had an opportunity of personally thanking your Brigade, but he hopes that in the future he may again be associated with you and your gallant Brigade in victories as glorious as that of April 9th."

General Sir H. Horne, commanding the 1st Army, also congratulated Brig.-General Jones and the 13th Brigade, remarking that " The 5th Division is maintaining its high reputation of last year." In his message to the Canadian Corps, Sir H. Horne, after dwelling on the strength of the position, believed by the Germans to be impregnable, concludes : " The 9th of April 1917 will be an historic day in the annals of the British Empire."

Most cordial congratulations were received by the 13th from the other two Brigades of the Division —the 15th and the 95th.

The relief from Goulot Wood was not completed until 4 a.m. on the 11th of April. The Battalion then marched to Villers au Bois and the same evening to Gouy, a few miles to the North. On the 14th they

A VIEW OF VIMY

(Looking down on the town from the top of Vimy Ridge just after its capture)

[*To face p.* 174

returned to Villers au Bois, which is about seven miles
N.W. of Arras. Here they remained for a week,
furnishing large parties for railway repair work.

On the 22nd the 13th Brigade was moved up in
reserve to the other two Brigades of the Division,
who were to attack next day to the North of Vimy.
The following night after this attack the Battalion
relieved the Norfolks of the 15th Division in the front
line.

This attack, owing to the enemy's wire being uncut,
was a failure. The companies of the Norfolk Regiment
reached this wire and small parties actually cut their
way through, although the wire was of an average
depth of fifty yards. The Germans, who had begun
to put up their hands, when they saw that our attack
was being held up by the uncut wire, changed their
minds and their courage returned to them. They
brought up machine guns and inflicted heavy casualties
on our troops. The Norfolks, who had made valiant
efforts to get to grips with the enemy in his trenches,
could only, therefore, hold on to the position they
had reached by using shell holes as cover.

Owing to the heavy losses of the 15th Brigade, the
13th Brigade was ordered up to relieve the former
and the Battalion had the duty of relieving the
Norfolks. Thus it was possible for the Battalion
to repay in part its debt to the Norfolks, who had
relieved it on the 23rd July of the previous year,
after we had suffered such heavy losses in the attack
on Wood Lane trench, on the night of the 22nd-23rd.
On that occasion the Norfolks showed the greatest
consideration, taking over the trenches in daylight,
in order that our men might be got out before dark.

At La Coulotte, where the Norfolks had suffered

such heavy losses on the 23rd April, the Battalion relieved them that night, and it was gratifying afterwards
to learn that the Norfolks appreciated the manner in
which our companies did what they could to make the
relief as easy as possible.

There was heavy German shell fire, but the
Battalion avoided the shelled area and constructed
new trenches in positions unmarked by the enemy.
Next day, the 24th, was spent in these trenches in
comparative quiet, all ranks highly appreciating the
industry with which the Germans continued to shell
the old (vacated) trench area. They were relieved
after dark by a Canadian battalion and returned to
Villers au Bois. Casualties suffered were only one
killed and two wounded.

The Battalion remained at Villers au Bois until the
end of April. Heavy work, roadmaking and railway
repairing, was called for.

Captain Snelgrove, 2/Lieut. Homan and twenty-eight
other ranks joined.

The annual inter-company football competition was
begun while at Villers. " C " beat " B " and " D "
beat " A."

On the 2nd of May the Brigade moved to Roclincourt
between Vimy and Arras, and on the following night
the Battalion occupied trenches South of Farbus
Wood, South of Vimy, in reserve to the XIII Corps,
which was attacking N.W. of Oppy. Here they
remained until the 8th, furnishing carrying and
burying parties, etc.

Major Waring left on the 6th of May to take
command of a territorial battalion of the Lincoln-
shire Regiment, Captain Wilberforce taking over the
duties of Adjutant.

On the 8th the Germans bombarded with gas shells, Captain Bellman being gassed among others.

The same day the 95th Brigade was driven back from Fresney, three miles E. of Vimy, by a heavy German counter-attack, and the 13th Brigade was ordered into positions of readiness to attempt to take the ground lost. The attack was made at night. Two platoons were lent to strengthen another battalion. Otherwise the Battalion was not engaged. The attempt did not succeed.

The Battalion, having undergone a good deal of shell fire, was moved up into front lines near Arleux, a mile west of Fresnoy that night. Next day they lost four killed and twenty-five wounded from shell fire. Casualties continued during the next two days though the shelling was not so intense as at first.

A curious incident occurred here. In one of the trenches, which was just in rear of our front line, was found a British soldier who had evidently been killed by shell fire quite recently. Every stitch of clothing, including his boots, had been completely blown off by the effects of the shell, otherwise he was only slightly marked. It is believed that this occurrence was not unique.

On the night of the 12th the Battalion was withdrawn to reserve trenches near Farbus. Losses since the 6th amounted to 10 killed and 42 wounded.

On the 14th Lieut. M'Clenaghan rejoined.

The Battalion remained in reserve trenches near Farbus until 20th May. Every day large working parties were called for, and almost every day a casualty or two occurred among them. On the night of the 20th close support trenches were occupied, and a few more losses were sustained. On the 25th the

Battalion was withdrawn and moved by bus to Dieval, close to Bethune.

During a week spent at Dieval a great deal of musketry practice was got through.

2/Lieut. Mills rejoined on the 22nd, and Capt. Cobb on the 26th.

Lieut.-Col. Buchanan-Dunlop, D.S.O., had to go sick on the 26th of May. He did not return to the Battalion as, some time afterwards, he was appointed to the command of the 2nd Machine Gun Battalion. Wounded at Mons, he rejoined in November 1914, and succeeded to the command in September 1915. Under him The Queen's Own had been engaged in the heavy Somme fighting of 1916, the successful trench raid of February 1917, and the Vimy Ridge Victory, as well as in countless small affairs incidental to trench warfare. Lt.-Col. Lynch White, D.S.O., succeeded to the command.

The Battalion returned to Roclincourt on the 1st of June, remaining there until the 13th. Much work on railways and trenches was done, but time was found for games, and the final of the inter-company football was played off, " C " proving the winners. Baths were available ; officers and men were re-inoculated.

From the night of the 13th to that of the 16th the Battalion was in the front line near Arleux. It then went into Divisional reserve.

Major B. Johnstone joined on the 24th, and took over the duties of second in command.

On the 27th the Battalion came under the orders of the Brig.-General commanding the 15th Brigade, and moved up into Brigade reserve trenches. On the 28th the 15th Brigade carried out a successful attack and advanced the line. The Battalion was standing by to support if necessary, but was not called on. It

was withdrawn on the night of the 31st. While in
the line it rained incessantly and, as there was no sort
of cover, the men were never dry. But, as usual, the
more miserable became the conditions, the more cheerful became the men. The work done on assembly
and communication trenches was so good that it earned
the special thanks of the Brig.-General commanding
the 15th Brigade.

The 1st to the 5th of July was spent in camp at
training, musketry, bathing, etc. From 6th to 11th
the Battalion was again in the line in the Arleux sector.
Going up, " C " Company lost three men killed and
five wounded from a salvo of 4.2-in. shells which burst
in the middle of a platoon. The principal work consisted in consolidating, making new and improving
existing trenches, etc., but much patrolling was also
done. The enemy seemed to be so unenterprising at
this time that the opportunity was seized to train
new men in this rather nervous duty. A lot of valuable
salvage was recovered, some of it from no-man's-land.
Four more men were wounded.

From the 11th to the 17th of July the Battalion was
in support trenches. One man was killed. From the
17th to the 19th it rested, and on the evening of the
19th it returned to the Arleux sector, where it remained
until the 25th, losing four killed and two wounded.

After five days' rest the Arleux trenches were occupied again on the 31st.

On 25th August Lieut.-Col. Lynch White, D.S.O.,
quitted the Battalion to take command of a rest camp,
and Major B. Johnstone assumed command.

The history of the Battalion from now on until practically the end of the fighting has been contributed by
Lieut.-Col. B. Johnstone, D.S.O., who commanded it.

CHAPTER X

AUGUST-SEPTEMBER 1917.—The diaries for this period do not chronicle many things of particular interest, being mostly the record of routine moves into, and reliefs from, the trench system held by the Division. Weather is recorded as being mostly of an unpleasant type, rendering the upkeep of trenches, and improvement, matters of extreme difficulty, and necessitating large working parties. Delivery of rations and store materials was facilitated by the extension of the system of light railway, which had been worked on by the troops for some time. This light railway was of the greatest benefit in relieving the troops of carrying party fatigues. On an average night, preceding the railway extension, at least 100 men were required to perform two journeys over an average distance of 2 miles each way, in order to provision and water the Battalion and keep up the necessary supplies of S.A.A. and trench engineering material.

The enemy were not very enterprising during the tours of the Battalion in front line, this attitude being forced upon them by our constant patrolling, which had the effect of confining them to their own line. We had our first experience of gas dischargers during August, and from reports by prisoners who were taken shortly afterwards, the enemy were completely taken by surprise by our new methods.

Casualties for August were 1 man killed, 10 wounded.

LIEUT.-COLONEL B. JOHNSTONE, D.S.O.

September.—Early in September the Battalion received orders to move out of the line, with a view to a fairly prolonged rest and period of training, and the 4th of the month saw us *en route* for Berlencourt, where we arrived at noon on the next day. We found that we had the whole of the village at our own disposal and, all hands making themselves agreeable to the inhabitants, we were soon fixed up very comfortably. We were to enjoy the amenities of this pretty village in the valley of the Canche for a full three weeks. After the mud and work of the trenches, here was a very Vale of Avalon, untroubled by the sound of guns or the drone of planes, and the intense silence was almost uncanny at first. Games of every sort, together with concerts and visits to the small neighbouring towns, soon were the order of the day, and with a little training, tended to peaceful sleep at night, the latter a luxury to which most of the Battalion had been strangers for many months. But this was too good to last long, and rumours soon began to pervade the billets. Those who were in the know lay low and said nothing, and time passed peacefully on. On the 25th the long awaited orders arrived and the cat, on being let out of the bag, was found to be labelled " The Salient." The Battalion entrained for Wizernes, and thence proceeded to Vlamertynghe, in the Brandhoek area. We had scarcely got into camp and settled down when orders arrived. The Battalion was to come under the orders of the Vth Corps, and with the K.O.S.B. we marched up to Goldfish Château, where we remained for the next forty-eight hours, ready to move up if necessary to reinforce the Vth Corps, which was making an attack on the Wieltje Ridge. The attack was successful and the Battalion was not called on for actual fighting, but returned

N

to Brandhoek and thence proceeded to Godvaervelde
and Berthen, to be in readiness for its own fight.

It was providential that the Battalion had been
moved up to support the 59th Division, as on the night
of 27th-28th the camp at Brandhoek was bombed
by enemy planes, and the dumped personnel, who
had been left at this camp, suffered severely, 6 officers
and 24 other ranks being wounded, besides 5 of the
transport horses. The wounded officers were Capts.
Press, Bellman, M.C., and Nisbet, Lieut. Smith, and
2/Lieuts. Stephen and Nurse. Capt. Press and Lieut.
Smith remained at duty. Two of the wounded men
died. The Battalion itself was extremely lucky, as
both bombing and long-range h.v. gun fire continued
throughout the night, but no casualties were sustained.
The huts which would have been occupied by the rest
of the Battalion had they been in camp were badly
knocked about by the bombs, not one escaping more
or less serious damage. At Berthen we were again
bombed, and once more the transport suffered severely,
12 horses being knocked out. Bombing by night was
continuous and this, together with the unceasing roar
of the guns, rendered sleep almost impossible by night,
and the training and working parties demanded by
day occupied the waking hours, so that it was a very
weary Battalion which moved out on 1st October to
Bedford House to fit up for the actual fight.

During September Regt. Sergt.-Major Brown was
appointed to a commission in the Battalion. C.S.M.
Kill, C.S.M. Duffield, and Sergt. Ragfield received com-
missions in our 10th Battalion. 2/Lieuts. Cathcart and
Molony left to join the R.F.C., 2/Lieuts. Lovell, Oram,
Chauncy and Fayter joined. A draft of 248 brought the
strength of the Battalion, excluding officers, to 828.

CHAPTER XI

THE FIGHTING IN " THE SALIENT "

OCTOBER 1917.—Those of the Battalion (very few in number) who had had previous experience of the conditions in the Ypres Salient, had given us all some small idea of what the Battalion would have to face in the way of conditions of ground and artillery fire, but the oldest hands had to confess that the conditions in 1917 were beyond comparison, and considerably worse than those faced by the Battalion in its previous experience.

Firm ground simply did not exist within three to four miles of the front-line trenches. The whole area was reduced to a sea of more or less liquid mud, as a result of artillery fire and the weather conditions. Movement was calculated at a rate of one mile per hour, and even this rate was looked on as a maximum rate of progression (for it could not be termed marching).

On 2nd October six hours were taken over the relief of the trenches, which were to be the jumping-off point for the attack, and these trenches were only three miles from Bedford House, where the Battalion had halted to fit up with bombs, S.A.A., rations for three days, and the various other articles required for the attack and consolidation of a position.

Our trenches on the 3rd October ran from the Menin Road just S.W. of Veldhoek to a point 1000 yards north, the left of the Battalion resting on the back of the small stream called the Scherriabeke. In spite of the weather, and the shelling, the lines of trenches were traceable and were occupied without casualties, except for two men who fell into shell holes and were never seen again. Trench-board tracks were laid, but destroyed by enemy shell fire almost as soon as put into position.

On 3rd October the enemy twice attacked our front-line trenches, but were driven off on each occasion, although supported by very heavy artillery fire. Several wounded prisoners were left in our trenches and many dead were observed in front of our line. Very intense shelling was experienced throughout the day, the line of Battalion Headquarters and the Reserve Company (" D ") being particularly heavily shelled. During the day the Battalion suffered about 100 casualties, and the Regimental Aid Post was twice blown out and had to be moved. Good use was made of German pillboxes, which made excellent headquarters and regimental aid posts, the only draw-back being that their entrances faced the German lines and great care had to be taken in the use of lights at night.

During the night of the 3rd-4th the Battalion Head-quarters and the Reserve Company moved forward to battle positions, and all was reported in readiness for the attack, which was to be launched at 6 a.m. on 4th October.

During the night tapes were laid out on which the attacking companies were to form up. These tapes were laid by the Company Commanders, about one hundred yards west of their trench positions, so that the attacking waves could start off from a position parallel to their objectives. This arrangement proved the salvation of the Battalion, for at 5 a.m. the enemy put down a heavy barrage of shells of all calibres on the front-line trench and the area of Battalion Headquarters. But by 5 a.m. all the attacking waves had dug themselves in on their respective tape lines, and the barrage, passing over them, caused no casualties. The attack was launched to time and the Battalion took the objective assigned to it, being the right flank Battalion of the attack on Paschendaele. In spite of heavy casualties the Battalion maintained itself in position until relieved on the night of the 5th-6th October after the most sanguinary fighting. Seven counter-attacks were made by the enemy, three in great force, but in spite of an exposed right flank, which could not be adequately covered till the night of the 4th, and enfilade and, at times, reverse fire from enemy machine guns, the Battalion did not give up a yard of the ground it had taken. It was on this flank that L.-Cpl. Vaughan rendered an invaluable service by holding an isolated position on the flank with a Lewis-gun team, inflicting very heavy casualties on the enemy.

The greatest difficulty was experienced in communicating with Brigade Headquarters. About 300 to 400 yards in rear of our Battalion Headquarters was a large pillbox housing a few Brigade signallers. To this pillbox a very large number of messages were sent by lamp, each message being repeated three times. In spite of this, of about fifteen messages sent only one or two were received by Brigade Headquarters. Experience showed that the most rapid and reliable means of communication was by carrier pigeon, of which we were given a good supply and which did extraordinarily good work.

The losses were extremely heavy, amounting to 10 officers and 368 other ranks. Captain Cobb, M.C., 2/Lieut. Daniell, and 2/Lieut. Redding were killed; 2/Lieuts. Brett, Monypenny, Fleming, Joel, Faunthorpe, Gordon and Chauncy, wounded. Of the 368 other ranks hit, 69 were killed. The Battalion had gone into action on 3rd October mustering 18 officers and 651 other ranks. Special messages of congratulation were sent to the Battalion by the Brigade and Divisional Commanders, and a visit of congratulation was paid to the Battalion by the Corps Commander, who complimented the Battalion on the magnificent show put up by all ranks.

On relief the Battalion proceeded to Ridge Wood Camp and on the 10th moved back into Corps Reserve at Chippewa Camp, Reninghelst.

Here the Battalion was put up in a very comfortable hutted camp. It was sufficiently far from the line to escape hostile artillery fire, but in common with all camps suffered intermittently from the attention of enemy bombing planes. But as the rule of life was " early to bed and early to rise " and the planes only bombed lighted areas, the Battalion escaped casualties. During the daylight hours training was strenuous, for the Battalion received drafts of 4 officers and 354 other ranks to make up for the casualties sustained in the fighting of the 4th-5th-6th October. Much needed reorganisation was carried out, and preparation made for the further fighting which was known to be the programme of the Battalion.

On the 22nd October the Battalion set forth for the line again, and on the 24th was again actively engaged in taking over the line which it had won on the 4th October.

Conditions were again very bad, if possible worse than earlier in the month, the weather having been consistently bad in the interval, and the enemy shelling unceasing. However, in spite of all obstacles, the Battalion in line was relieved successfully by 1 a.m. on the 25th, at a cost to us of only six casualties, which number was only increased by seven during the twenty-four hours immediately preceding the attack.

26th October.—The attack was staged to begin on 26th October at 5.40 a.m. The Battalion side slipped to the north in order to allow the 7th Division to form up north and south of the Ypres-Menin Road. This operation left the minimum space available to the Battalion for the purpose of forming up. Careful dovetailing eliminated this difficulty and sufficient room was made. Unfortunately, in order to allow the artillery barrage to come down behind our own trenches, so as to obtain a barrage line to suit the peculiar conditions of the ground, and to give the 7th Division, on our right, a fair chance to go for their objective, the village of Gheluvelt, the attacking waves and all support waves had to quit their trenches and form up for the attack on a line nearly 300 yards in rear of the line gained on 4th October. This arrangement, however, proved to be a very costly one to the Battalion. When the attack was launched, the attacking waves had to fight for the trenches they had quitted half an hour previously. The enemy had proved a little more enterprising than usual and his dawn patrols, finding our trenches unoccupied, had promptly taken them over, and greeted the attacking lines with heavy machine-gun fire. A heavy artillery barrage had been put down by the enemy from 4.30

to 5.30 a.m. causing a certain number of casualties
which had weakened the attacking companies.

However, they pressed forward, and the two leading
companies took their objective. But the attack of the
7th Division was not successful. The ground over
which this Division's attack was carried out resembled
a lake rather than a swamp, and even slightly wounded
men were drowned when they fell on being hit. The
defences of Gheluvelt proved much stronger than had
been realised, and the losses sustained by the attacking
Brigades of the 7th Division were so heavy that the
attack lost its impetus, and after a short period of
fighting at close quarters against continually increasing
enemy reinforcements, was repulsed. This left the
attacking companies of the Battalion " in the air "
and open to an encircling counter-attack, which
developed in great force, and cut " B " and " D "
Companies off from effective support. Survivors who
have been interviewed since the Armistice, having
been wounded and taken prisoners on this occasion,
agree in saying that those who were able to use their
arms fought to the last.

The attack, so far as the 7th Division and the
Battalion were concerned, having failed, a defensive
line and flank were formed from the remnants of the
Battalion and any available men from the 7th Division,
and, after a period of intense anxiety, which was
lightened by the arrival of a company of K.O.S.B.,
and reinforcements of officers from the Battalion
" dump," the line was stabilised a little in advance of
that held by the Battalion and 7th Division north
of the Menin Road preparatory to the assault. The
Battalion was relieved at nightfall by the Norfolks
and proceeded to Ridge Wood Camp, having lost as

casualties twelve officers, Captain Press and 2/Lieut. Lovelace, killed; Lieut. Smith and 2/Lieuts. Harris, Dyson, Fayter, Quilley, Hill, Brown, Rogers and Oram, wounded; 2/Lieut. Fry missing; and 335 other ranks in eighteen hours' fighting.

After relief on 26th October the Battalion moved to three camps in succession, all of which were within ten miles of the line.

The officers joining during October were 2/Lieuts. Sansom, Quilley, Thorning, Streatfield, Churchill and Marke.

Indications pointed to more fighting still, and all the waking hours were devoted to reorganisation, re-fitting, and training, the reinforcement drafts received being somewhat lacking in experience of trench war-fare. Hard work, however, overcame this difficulty, and although the Battalion was warned to be ready to make a further attack, the weather became so foul that the idea of further attacking over the low ground near the Menin Road was abandoned, and the next trip to the line was a matter of simple relief of trenches. This was successfully carried out on the 7th November, the Battalion relieving the 1st Battalion East Surrey Regiment. Again on the way up to the trenches the Battalion suffered several casualties one enemy shell alone putting one officer and sixteen other ranks out of action. 2/Lieut. Streatfield was the officer hit. He died next day.

The trenches taken over were those which had been established by the Battalion on 26th October, for the ground had become steadily more water-logged, and impassable either to ourselves or the enemy.

In reality trenches did not exist, our line being formed of a disconnected series of shell holes, in the

side of which shelves had been made with great difficulty, with the aid of a few sandbags and whatever
other revetting material could be collected from
destroyed "Pillboxes." The Battalion remained in
this position until the 11th November, when relieved
by a company of 1/6th Cheshire Regiment. Casualties
during the tour in the trenches amounted to one officer
and twenty-six other ranks.

After relief the Battalion proceeded to camp near
Westoutre, where a number of men had to receive
medical attention, owing to the condition of their feet
and legs after the prolonged immersion in the line,
in spite of all possible precautions having been taken
to prevent trench feet.

On the 15th the Battalion proceeded by rail to Selles,
where it remained, training and resting until 26th
November, on which day it was sent by bus to
Neuville-au-Cornet.

Two days earlier, orders had been sent out recalling
all ranks from leave, detached duties and courses of
instruction. This portended a big move, but the
destination of the Battalion was kept a profound
secret, and November passed away without any further
information becoming available, in spite of a company
being detailed for loading duties at railhead. However, it was shrewdly imagined that the Battalion was
to leave the district of the Salient for good, and as will
be shown later, this assumption proved to be correct,
and no one soul regretted the prospect for a moment,
for all knew that whatever was in prospect could not,
by any possibility, approach the horrors and hardships
of the two months just completed.

Casualties for the month amounted to four men killed
and twenty-three wounded, besides 2/Lieut. Streatfield.

Officers joining were Lieut. Dodson and 2/Lieuts. Davis and Whitfield.

December.—Training was continued, and on 4th December the Battalion moved once again, on this occasion to Monchy-Cayeux, near St Pol, and what seemed more encouraging, actually on the railway line. Here training was continued, until the orders for entrainment were received on 10th December, and our destination was at last divulged, proving to be Italy. On 11th December the Battalion entrained in three portions, one company, " D," being detached from the Battalion to act as Divisional Loading Party.

The doings of the Battalion in Italy may fitly be left to another chapter.

CHAPTER XII

THE Battalion entrained for Italy at Anvin, near St Pol, and after considerable delay, owing to rations for the journey not being forthcoming—owing, as we discovered later on, to the fact that the supply train had been derailed by bombs from an enemy aeroplane—we found ourselves fairly started on our five days' journey. The railway journey through the Midi and South of France proved most enjoyable and a source of much pleasure to all ranks, and we realised that part of the country we had been fighting in truly deserved to be called " The pleasant land of France."

The daily uncertainty as to meals was an additional joy, indicating a complete break with the usual routine. For this additional amusement we were indebted to the French (and later, the Italian) railway authorities.

On commencing the journey, each officer commanding a train was solemnly presented with a sheaf of documents, amongst which was one entitled " Ordre de Marche du Train." On this document was set forth the principal stations through which the train would pass on the journey, the hours at which it would arrive at these places, and, lastly, the names of places at which *halte-repas* would take place, and the hour of arrival at and departure from such places. In theory, at a *halte-repas*, at least an hour's halt would be made by the train. Hot water was supposed to be in readiness, and facilities were provided for all to wash, and stretch their legs. In actual fact, only once on the journey did the train arrive at the appointed *halte* at the hour laid down. It happened on several occasions that a halt was made at the appointed hour (quite apart from the unauthorised and casual halts), but on such occasions there was no sign of any facilities for making a hot meal or washing, and, after a very short experience of the train vagaries, it was discovered that the only effectual way of overcoming the difficulty was to expend *largesse* of francs and rum to the driver and his assistant, and leave the " Ordre de Marche " to look after itself, taking the halt when it seemed most convenient for the troops, and as opportunity offered. By this means, and by eliminating " casual halts " for the good of the driver, by carrying the necessary material for such halts on the engine itself, good progress was made, and the train eventually ran fairly close to its schedule.

The route selected for the Battalion trains was by Macon, Marseilles, Les Arc and Nice, at which place we arrived just after dawn on 15th December. After a short halt, the train continued on its way and arrived at Ventimiglia at 9 a.m. Here we found that the policy of attending to our engine-drivers bore fruit, for we arrived three hours ahead of our schedule time, and in addition found that the station was congested by previous trains, so that we had four hours at our disposal before continuing the journey, including the difference between Italian and French time.

All ranks were allowed into the town, after breakfast had been served, and companies went for a march along the seashore for exercise, and returned loaded with fruit and flowers, partly purchased and partly the gift of the inhabitants and the British Colony.

The last forty-eight hours of the journey had been pure joy, and the Battalion was lucky, not only in being sent by this route instead of by the Mont Cenis Tunnel, but also because the most interesting part of the French Riviera had been traversed by daylight. For the last three days of the journey the Battalion had been greeted with great effusion by the inhabitants, and gifts were showered on the troops at every station where a halt was made. The remaining portion of the Battalion was not so fortunate, and did not have the opportunity of a trip into the town of Ventimiglia, perhaps owing to an insufficiency of *pour boire* to the engine-driver of their train.

The train moved off from Ventimiglia at 12.15 Italian time, and continued its way leisurely along the Italian Riviera until arriving at Savona at 10 p.m. At San Piere Barena, where a halt of an hour was made on the 16th of December, the local Syndic in his robes of office, supported by his Town Councillors and the local Red Cross Detachment, held a reception for all officers, and coffee and wine and fruit were distributed to the troops. We were lucky in having two Italian-speaking officers with the Headquarter train, and their speeches in acknowledgment of the Italian greetings were received with great applause.

At Savona the steam engines of our train were replaced by electric locomotives, and the train started the long climb into the mountains and across the Venetian plain. The warmth of the Riviera gave place to damp mist, and early on the morning of 17th December the Battalion arrived at Fontivilla, and detrained into two feet of snow.

The Battalion was in some ways more lucky than other battalions which arrived in Italy about the same time. The fact that there were Italian-speaking officers serving with the Battalion, enabled the preliminary difficulties regarding billeting and intercourse with the inhabitants to be surmounted fairly easily. The principal difficulty was in the billeting question. The Italian fashion of living together, several generations in the same house, with all the descendants of these generations, made the question of accommodation, even in houses of a very considerable size, most difficult. This was added to by the scarcity of farm buildings on the ground level, and in the end the troops were mostly put up in the upper stories of buildings, of which the lower story was given over to the family cattle. These upper barns were completely open on one side and access was to be gained only by the use of ladders. A little ingenuity, and the pressing into service of rick covers and all available wagon sheets, soon converted the most unpromising-looking straw store into a fairly comfortable billet, and the men declared, when they had got over the strangeness of having to retire to rest like fowls, that they were far more comfortable at night than they had been in France and Belgium.

Our first billets were around the palace of the Count of Bolzonella. The G.H.Q. of the Italian Aircraft was in possession of the palace itself, but the outlying buildings and farms were handed over to the Battalion. We had a visit here from Major-General W. G. B. Western, formerly O.C. 2nd Battalion in Ceylon, who then held the appointment of A.G. Italy.

From now on till the end of December, the Battalion was engaged in training, and various parties were sent off daily for reconnaissance of the mountain line above the river Brenta, which was held by the Italians.

These reconnaissances of mountain lines were of extreme interest to all ranks. The whole organisation was
completely different from anything we had seen before,
and the motor drive to Rubio a thing which no one
who did it will ever forget. Hair-pin corners were
negotiated at a speed of, say, 30 m.p.h., and the occupants of the vehicle had the certain knowledge that, if
anything were coming the other way, either they or
the others were fairly safe for a drop of 2000 to 3000
feet down the mountain-side. There were numerous
accidents of this kind to Italian lorries, the drivers
of which were very expert, but reckless.

The weather was very cold at night, but during the
day it was almost too hot for comfort.

On Christmas Day the time-honoured festivities
were held as usual, and on the 28th the Battalion
was inspected by the French General De Mestre, then
commanding the French Xth Army, to which the
5th Division was attached. The Inspection being
concluded, five officers and twenty-four other ranks,
who had been awarded decorations for the fighting
in October, were presented to the General, who congratulated them and presented them with the ribbons
of the decorations awarded.

The month had passed away quietly, and all ranks
appreciated the rest from heavy work. All spare
time was devoted to learning useful Italian phrases,
and the task was facilitated by the inhabitants, who
were only too pleased to help. This was the more
noteworthy as our reception on the Venetian Plain
had been none too friendly. The inhabitants had
been looking forward to a speedy conclusion of peace
as a result of the Caporetto disaster, and looked upon
the arrival of the French and British troops as likely

to prolong hostilities, of which they appeared to be heartily weary.

But this attitude soon changed towards the troops, whose discipline and tact in dealings with the people of the countryside, and their willingness to help in any way possible, had won all hearts.

Officers joining during December were Lieut. Doe, M.C., and 2/Lieuts. Quigley, Ouzman and Burden.

And so we came to the end of 1917, and looked forward to happy times and Peace to come in the New Year.

1918.

1918.—Naturally, on arriving in an absolutely new area, the facilities for training did not come up to those existing in France and Belgium, so a considerable amount of work was set in hand in order to remedy this state of affairs. An old training ground of the Italian Army was taken over and a rifle range constructed, and trenching, bombing and wiring was practised. Parties were sent up to the foot-hills north and south of the River Brenta, and from their billets undertook daily training in mountain climbing, the medical officers carefully compiling statistics as to the effect on the troops of carrying various kits and performing physical exercises such as trench digging, handling weights, with a view to avoiding casualties from heart strain when the troops relieved the Italians in the line on the Asiago Plateau, which was to be our destination. Continual reconnaissance was carried out in this direction, but the Battalion remained about Bolzonella until 22nd January, on which day a move was made to a new area. After two long and very tiring marches, the Battalion

o

arrived at St Andra, where a day's rest was given, and on the 25th of January took over from the 1st Battalion, 11th Regiment of the Italian Army.

The position taken over was that of reserve battalion to the regiment holding the line of the River Piave. We occupied the village of Arcade, which had only been damaged slightly by bombing and long range artillery fire. Billets were very comfortable, but the sanitary conditions of the area left very much to be desired, and all hands had to turn to and give the area a thorough clean up. Reconnaissance continued, and on the evening of 29th January the Battalion took over the river front trench line from the 15th Battalion Warwickshire Regiment. The line consisted of T heads cut into the bank and retaining wall of the River Piave. The river on the Battalion frontage was about 1200 yards wide, but the channel was occupied mostly by large and small islands of shingle, the actual water, then running, forming several channels between these islands. Only two of these channels were fordable, and as the enemy (Austrians) opposite our front were very inoffensive, our first preoccupation was to evolve some method of crossing the unfordable channels, so as to get at our opponents and stir them out of their lethargy. Various methods were tried, but the strength of the current was so great as to defeat us temporarily. Eventually a series of flying bridges solved the problem satisfactorily and patrolling became the ordinary nightly task. On account of the intense cold and the amount of wading which had to be done by the patrols, special arrangements had to be made to give hot meals and baths to all patrols on their return from the night's outings. The place where the men

used to go for their hot baths and food was one of the
few places which was regularly and fairly heavily
shelled. It was here that we first met a new type
of shell, which first burst in the air with a very local
shrapnel effect, and then continued on its course for
several hundred yards, finally bursting like an ordinary
percussion H.E. shell.

The enemy still remained quiet except for sporadic
shelling in reply to our artillery registration, and so
we were able to improve the trench system without
much interference. Work was somewhat different
from the tasks the Battalion had done in France and
Belgium. Here, on the banks of the Piave, there
was little or no earth, and once the surface soil had
been removed, one had to move nothing but pebbles,
all rounded by the water's effect, and the trenches
were riveted by boards on each face. In making
shelters, the wood shelter was made up complete, as
near as possible to the site to be occupied, and a hole
sufficiently large to receive the completed erection
was then dug in the shingle and the structure lowered
into the hole. Shingle was then piled all around and
above the wooden construction, and the shelter was
then complete. Such shelters would not have lasted
many days in France or Belgium, but here, by reason
of the lightness of the enemy artillery work, and the
fact that shelters were placed right against the river
embankment, so that shells had to fall almost per-
pendicularly to hit any of the shelters, only one of
those made and occupied by the Battalion was hit
during the whole period of our tenure of the river
line.

Artillery fire on both sides increased in activity,
but was principally directed on the back areas, and

the time of front-line duty was comparatively peaceful. We spent a lot of time on patrolling at night and in attempting to stir up the enemy, but without much success, as the various channels into which the river was divided, and the depth of the water in each varied immensely during every period of twenty-four hours, and patrol work eventually resolved itself into keeping the maps of "No Man's Land" up to date. The enemy refused to come out to meet us, and as we could not get across to their side of the river, we just sat and watched each other till the end of the month.

Officers joining during January were 2/Lieuts. Stenning, Steele, Stephenson and Mattison. Sixteen other ranks came. Casualties for the month, one man wounded.

February.—During February the enemy began to be more aggressive, but not in the way of infantry action. They confined themselves to action from the air, and apparently had imported an aeroplane circus from some other front. Night after night was disturbed by the drone of the double engines of their bombing planes, and the shrill whistle of the " anti-aircraft alarms." The troops had to leave their billets and take to the trenches in the fields, until, at last, one was glad when the period of so-called " rest " had come to an end, and one was able to seek the repose of the front-line trenches.

About the middle of the month, preparations were made for a large scale raid on the enemy across the river, and the carrying and reconnaissance in connection with this operation involved an extra amount of labour. Artillery activity increased, and several heavy enemy shoots were directed against our front

and support lines. A few casualties were caused by
these shoots, but on the whole life continued to be
fairly peaceful, at any rate in comparison with what
it had been in France and Belgium. The enemy
aircraft increased in daring, and on several occasions
an armoured plane flew all along the river quite close
to our bank, so close, in fact, that it was possible to
see our bullets from machine guns and rifles ricochet
from the fusilage of the machine.

Padova, the G.H.Q. of the British troops in Italy,
was bombed continuously by night, and extra work
was thrown on the troops in support and reserve, in
mounting anti-aircraft machine guns. Practically all
available Vickers and Lewis guns were disposed in
successive lines along the line of flight of the enemy
planes, and these guns opened fire whenever an enemy
plane came in sight against the stars. Had it not been
for this continual disturbance by night, and the incessant call for working parties by day, life would have
been fairly pleasant, but as things went, we all found
that life in the Sunny South was decidedly strenuous.

Casualties for February were Lieut. Collins and
one man wounded.

2/Lieut. Garbutt and forty-three other ranks joined.

March.—Routine trench life continued, together
with work in preparation for the projected operations,
for the first fortnight of the month. On the 16th the
Battalion was suddenly relieved by the 2nd Battalion,
270th Italian Regiment. Three days' heavy marching
followed, and on the 18th the Battalion arrived at
Fassalta, in the Padova area, and immediately set
to work training in anticipation of the projected move
to the Asiago Plateau.

On the 26th we found ourselves on the move again, to Villafranca. Here we had a couple of days' rest. On the 30th a Brigade competition was held, and points were awarded for marching, transport turnout, tug-of-war and relay race. The Battalion gained the " Silver Bugle " for turning out most winning teams, and also the transport and marching competitions.

The 31st, being Easter Sunday, was given over to Church Parades and rest. This was to be our last day on Italian soil, for movement orders had been received for the 5th Division to be prepared to move to France at two hours' notice, and the actual move orders arrived on the afternoon of this day.

Drafts totalling fifty-six other ranks were received during March.

CHAPTER XIII

APRIL.—April the 1st dawned, and many were the japes at the expense of the 13th Infantry Brigade, for whose benefit, the Superior Authorities, wittingly or not, had reserved the day for the purpose of entrainment back to France. The 5th Division, badly battered in the fighting of October and November in the Ypres Salient, had been sent off at short notice to Italy to assist in stemming the Austrian advance and to stiffen the resistance of that portion of the Italian Army which had escaped being involved in the Caporetto disaster. And now the Division was called back from its comparative repose in the Venetian Plain, to assist in beating back the waves of German soldiery which had overwhelmed the Fifth Army and was daily making more ground in the direction of Amiens, with a view to cutting the French and British Armies apart, and seizing the Channel ports. Rumours of the enemy advance had reached us, but no details, so the gravity of the situation was not yet appreciated, except by those in high places. So, on the whole, the journey back to France was looked upon as a more or less pleasant interlude, in spite of lingering regrets that the pleasant days in Italy had come to a close.

All ranks had the consciousness of work well done, for, although the Battalion had not had the luck to take part in any large scale operations, it had borne its share of the labours of the British Army in Italy, and had gained golden opinions from all with whom it had come into contact, both officially and unofficially, and the Corporate Body knew in its inmost heart that it was ready and able to undertake, and to carry to a successful conclusion, any task which could be entrusted to it.

The five days' train journey soon came to an end, and the Battalion detrained at Frevent. On the return journey to France, the Battalion again had the good fortune to travel by the southern route along the Riviera, and by a fortunate combination of circumstances, passed in the daylight hours all the places of interest which had been passed through by day on the journey into Italy.

The Battalion concentrated at Barly, in the Frevent area, on the 7th April, and the next three days were days of strenuous activity. The Battalion found large working parties at rail-head, and at the same time had practically to refit with all those necessaries of warfare which had not been brought back from Italy; the material having been left for the use of the Divisions which had not been recalled to France.

The 10th saw the Battalion on the march again, and on the 11th we entrained for Thiennes.

Early on the morning of 12th April the Battalion detrained and marched into cover of the Bois D'Amont, the southern portion of the Forest of Nieppe, which covered the approaches to Hazebrouck. Before detraining at Doullens on 6th April we had seen part of the effect of the German drive, the fields along the railway line being filled with the camps of refugees from the lately overrun territory, and here at Thiennes, and in the immediate neighbourhood, the roads were blocked by every description of vehicle, containing the

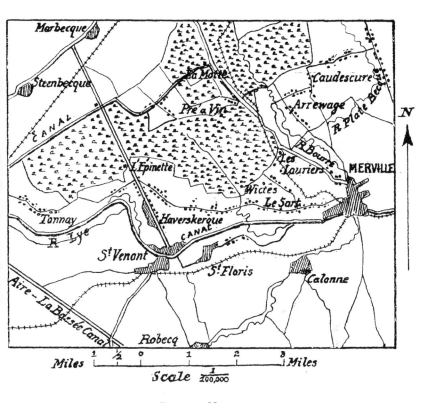

Marbecque

Steenbecque

CANAL

La Motte

Pré a Vin

Caudescure

Arrewage

R. Plate Becq

L'Epinette

Les Lauriers

Wictes

Le Sart

MERVILLE

R. Bourre

N

Tannay

R. Lye

Haverskerque

CANAL

St Venant

St Floris

Calonne

Aire - La Bassée Canal

Robecq

Miles ⌐ 1 ½ 0 1 2 3 Miles

Scale $\frac{1}{200,000}$

BOIS DE NIEPPE

[To face p. 204

household goods of the wretched peasants who had abandoned everything but their most cherished and most portable belongings, in the effort to escape from the on-rushing German hordes.

The situation was grave. The Divisional Commander, coming to the conference of Brigade and Battalion commanders, did not mince words. He told all those present that there was nothing to be done but to hold on to the eastern edge of the Forest of Nieppe, and that the Division would have to do everything for itself. There was no formed body of troops available to assist the Division, and that on the Division the safety of Hazebrouck and the communications with the Channel ports depended.

On the principle that the best defence is to attack, the Divisional orders were then issued for an advance on Merville, which town had been occupied by the enemy, in spite of the resistance put up by the 51st (Highland) Division, which had been transferred north after suffering appalling losses in the fighting retreat of the Fifth Army. The 13th Brigade was ordered to attack, the Battalion being in reserve. The attacking battalions of the Brigade were soon heavily involved with enemy machine-gun detachments and, suffering heavy losses, succeeded in making good a line about 200 yards east of the edge of the Forest. Here they dug in, and the Battalion moved up into close support and dug in, this being the third line of trenches dug by the Battalion in eight hours.

On the 14th the Battalion, which had moved up into close support of the 14th Warwicks on the night of the 13th, and had dug yet another line of trenches, took over the post line from that battalion. In the abortive attack on Merville, which had been broken off by orders from Division, the 14th Warwicks had suffered heavy casualties, and had not been able to do much beyond digging rifle pits. The Battalion was set to work improving these pits, and a beginning was made of a wired line. The crops were high, and continual patrols were out by day and night. The enemy were in possession of several farmhouses, from which our position could be overlooked. With the aid of our howitzers, and by firing Very Flares into the thatched roofs of the buildings, these houses were destroyed, and life was more peaceful for twenty-four hours. But on 16th April the enemy began to get his artillery into position, and the usual bombardments began to take their daily part in our lives. But here, in the Forest of Nieppe, the enemy, instead of confining his shelling to the use of high explosives, made use almost entirely of gas. All descriptions of gas were used by him daily. Blue cross, green cross, yellow cross (the so-called " mustard gas ") were used by day and by night, and the troops were compelled almost to live in their gas masks. Aeroplane activity increased day by day, and at times almost reached the intensity that had recently been experienced in Italy.

Continual digging was carried out, and although internal reliefs were carried out within the Division, there was little or no rest, and relief meant only an opportunity for the troops to have a hot bath and a much-needed change of under-garments.

By the end of the month a really good front-line system of trenches had been made and thoroughly wired, in spite of all difficulties, and it became apparent that wherever the enemy might attempt to break through, he would not be successful on the front held by the 5th Division.

During the last fortnight of April the Battalion had suffered a considerable number of casualties, but, luckily, the majority of these were of a slight nature, being mostly the effects of mustard gas, which had not been sufficiently neutralised in various areas of the Forest, where working parties were engaged.

Casualties for April were three killed, 2/Lieut. Thorning and nine others wounded.

May.—During May the Battalion side-slipped to the north for a few tours in trenches at the extreme north of the sector held by the 5th Division. The change was a welcome one, as this portion of the line was open country and the continual gassing by the enemy was not so much felt here. Work in the line was of a heavy and exhausting nature, as continual little advancements of the general trench line took place, and each of these involved fresh dispositions and further digging and carrying parties. The rest periods were filled with work on the supporting lines in rear of the front-line system, and the Battalion was congratulated on several occasions by the Higher Authorities for the work done. Casualties were not heavy during the month, but nevertheless the Battalion suffered losses every time it went into the first-line system, and this steady drain began to have effect on the numbers available for fighting or work. The position had been absolutely stabilised, and, in spite of tentative offers to attack on the part of the enemy, which were easily disposed of, the Battalion had got back to a regular routine manner of life.

The next thing to be done was to make things as unpleasant as possible for the enemy, and to this end activity in patrolling was redoubled, and the dispositions of their troops accurately ascertained, and also their general routine. These points being disposed, active preparations for an attack were set in hand.

Officers joining during May were Capt. Kay, 2/Lieut. Blott, 2/Lieut. Clarke, Lieut. Smyth, 2/Lieuts. Hines, Tuck, Arlett, Shepherd and Purchase. The six last-named came from our 7th Battalion. 2/Lieut. Clarke died a few days after joining. A draft of thirty other ranks was received.

Casualties for the month were five killed ; 2/Lieuts. Ouzman and Harding, and Lieut. Harrison, and about thirty others wounded.

June.—The attack to take place, naturally, was the object for careful practice. The normal trench routine reliefs were not interfered with, but a practice trench system was laid out, and on every occasion when the Battalion was relieved from front-line duty, the troops to be engaged were trained over this practice system. Even more care than usual was taken over this work, for the Battalion and other troops of the 5th Division were to have the distinction and honour of making the first set-piece attack on the enemy, which had been made since their successful onrush in March. This attack was, for some reason unknown to us, postponed on two different occasions. Once the Battalion had actually been issued with bombs, extra ammunition, etc., and was about to move off to its assembly positions.

The attack, however, took place on the morning of the 28th June, and was a brilliant success. The orders were that no one should leave the trenches until a period of two minutes had elapsed from the time of the com-

mencement of the barrage. Such was the keenness of
the Battalion, that our assembly trenches were empty
and the men dashing forward within half a minute of
the barrage coming down. No praise could be high
enough for the excellence of the barrage supplied by
both artillery and the machine guns. Hundreds of
Germans were seen who had been killed by machine-
gun bullets, presumably when they tried to leave the
protection of their trenches and run away. Unfortunately, however, the keenness of our men resulted
in our sustaining a good many more casualties than
would otherwise have taken place.

The objective assigned to the Battalion was captured
without a check, and many prisoners were taken.
But what was more satisfactory to all taking part
in the affray, was the fact that the Battalion found
that the troops opposed to it were stout fellows and
stayed to fight awhile. One platoon alone of the
Battalion accounted for 36 of the enemy in one farm-
house, and this with the bayonet only ; other platoons
did a fair share of the work to be done and, after about
five minutes' real fighting at close quarters, the balance
of the enemy broke and fled, only to be shot down
by our Lewis guns. All objectives assigned to the
Battalion had been captured before the allotted time.
The casualties to the Battalion were 120 of all ranks.
Officer losses were Captain Scott, Lieut. Monypenny
and Lieut. Smyth killed ; Lieut. Blott, Lieut. Arlett,
2/Lieut. Cox and 2/Lieut. Garbutt wounded. Of
the 120, 22 were killed, and 16 missing. Of this 16,
14 were afterwards found to be wounded, and were
recovered by our stretcher-bearers. The total loss
to the enemy on the Battalion frontage was 180 killed
by actual count, and 30 prisoners ; the other battalions

engaged inflicting similar losses. The position taken was rapidly put into a state of defence, in anticipation of the naturally expected counter-attacks, which were duly developed by the enemy as soon as darkness fell. Our attack had been launched at 6 a.m., and all objectives had been taken by an hour afterwards, and, as the special parties carrying materials and tools for entrenching the captured position had fulfilled their mission within twenty minutes of the capture of the final objectives, and had stopped to assist in digging trenches and getting out wire, the counter-attacks were easily beaten off, and the enemy was forced to acquiesce in his infantry defeat and confine his further action to artillery and machine-gun demonstrations. The whole affair had been a triumphant success, marred only by the number of casualties sustained. The Battalion remained in the positions it had captured till late on the night of 30th June, when it was relieved and returned to well-earned rest in Brigade reserve.

Colonel Johnstone's narrative is here interrupted to insert an amplification of the battle of the Plate Becque by Major Kay.

Major Kay's Narrative.—" The Battalion moved up from Steenbecque and occupied assembly trenches on the night of 27th-28th June. Disposition of companies in assembly trenches is shown in attached sketch. The Battalion was in position by 12 a.m. Patrols and listening posts were sent out and with-drawn at dawn. No enemy patrols were encountered. All our wire on the Battalion front was cut by 1.30 a.m. Zero hour was received at 1.30 a.m., and companies informed. Watches were synchronised at the same time. Activity shown by enemy artillery

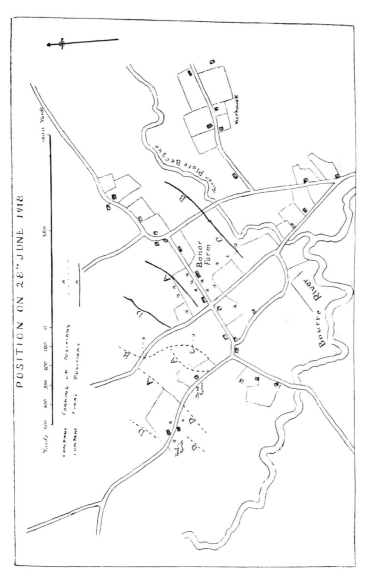

POSITION ON 28TH JUNE 1918

Yards 500 400 300 200 100 0 500 1000 Yards

COMPANY FORMING UP POSITIONS
COMPANY FINAL POSITIONS

Bonar Farm

River Plate Becque

Verhouck

Bourre River

PLATE BECQUE AND BONAR FARM

[*To face p.* 210

and machine guns during the night was rather below
normal.

" At 6 a.m. our barrage came down, and all companies
left their assembly trenches and closed up under it.
Two companies ('C' and 'B') formed the first wave.
Each company advanced with two platoons in the
front line and one in close support. One company
('A') formed the second wave and followed closely
behind the first wave. One company ('D') was in
reserve and advanced in sections in file.

" The right company ('C,' under Lieut. Monypenny, M.C.) advanced and went straight through
the enemy front line to his support line. Little resistance was met except at one point, where the
enemy's machine guns were posted. Sharp hand-to-
hand fighting took place about here, a number of
the enemy being bayoneted. The company pushed
rapidly on and took its final objective, driving
what was left of the enemy towards the Plate Becque.
A heavy Lewis gun and rifle fire was opened on
them and many were killed whilst attempting to
cross the stream. Patrols were pushed forward to
the line of the Plate Becque. Sergt. Hirschfield,
accompanied by a sapper, went forward and blew
up the bridges. One of these was made of stone
and these two men were driven back by heavy
machine-gun fire. It was not until the third
attempt that the bridge was finally destroyed. The
whole of the work involved in the demolition of
these three bridges was carried out under heavy
machine-gun fire.

" Touch was maintained with the 15th Royal
Warwickshire Regiment, on the right, throughout the
advance. Lieut. P. J. Blott was severely wounded

before reaching the German front line, his platoon
sergeant taking command of the platoon during the
remainder of the day. The company suffered about
40 per cent. casualties in reaching its final objective,
Lieut. Arlett was wounded during the advance but
remained in command of his platoon, organising the
defence till late in the afternoon.

" The left company (' B,' Captain J. J. Scott, M.C.)
advanced and captured the enemy's front line. A
considerable number of casualties occurred soon after
the advance commenced. This was partly from our
own barrage, owing to the eagerness of all ranks to
engage with the enemy, and partly from enemy
machine guns. In spite of this, however, the advance
was continued without a check. Those of the enemy
who had not been killed retired rapidly towards the
Plate Becque. As soon as the final objective was
reached, a heavy fire was opened with Lewis guns and
rifles on the retreating enemy, a large number of
whom were killed. Patrols were sent forward and
repeated attempts were made by several men of the
company to destroy the bridge by hand. But this
they could not do, owing chiefly to the strength of
the bridge and to the heavy machine-gun barrage.
On account of the somewhat severe losses incurred
during the early part of the advance, there was at
one time a considerable gap between the two leading companies. The close support platoon, led by
2/Lieut. Burden, immediately pushed forward and
filled the gap. Touch was maintained with the
K.O.S.B. on the left throughout the advance. The
company had fifty-nine casualties during the advance,
including the company commander and next senior
officer (Lieut. E. P. Smyth), both being killed.

"The second wave ('A' Company, Lieut. Lewis-Barned, M.C.) followed closely in rear of the first wave. A dozen or more Germans, many of them wearing what appeared to be a red cross armlet, were encountered in the orchard. As these men were throwing bombs into the rear of the first wave which had swept over them, the whole of the party were bayonetted at once. The German support lines was then occupied. Parties of moppers-up went on to Bonar Farm and other houses and at these places a few of the enemy were killed or captured. The Company had about twenty-five casualties during the advance, including 2/Lieut. Cox, who was wounded. The O.C. Company, appreciating the fact that the left company's front line was weakly held, immediately sent forward three sections to assist in consolidating and holding the line.

"The Reserve Company ('D,' Captain Dodson) proceeded to occupy the German front line, which they reached at 6.15 a.m., carrying forward with them picks, shovels, and S.A.A. drawn from the battalion dump the previous night. Carrying parties under 2/Lieut. Garbutt and 2/Lieut. Whitfield went forward to the final objective, pressing through the enemy barrage with great determination, and reached the forward companies within three minutes of the objective being gained. 2/Lieut. Whitfield rendered great assistance to 'B' Company, who were short of officers, in organising the consolidation. The parties then returned to 'D' Company in reserve."

General.—" 1. Owing to the complete surprise of the attack and the eagerness displayed by all ranks to get to close quarters with the enemy, strong resistance was only met here and there. In those places

P

where the enemy remained, no half measures were adopted.

" 2. Direction was well maintained. In cases where leaders became casualties, subordinate leaders at once took their places and were well acquainted with the task they had to perform.

" 3. Visual communication was found to be impracticable and telephone lines to companies were constantly cut. Lance-Sergt. Davis and three signallers worked on the line throughout the day—at times under very heavy shell fire—and towards evening telephone communication to all companies was established. In the case of the support company, the O.C. Company was actually talking by telephone to the Adjutant, from his newly-occupied position, within three minutes of his arrival there, and, owing to the extraordinary fine work of the Battalion signallers, was in communication practically ceaselessly throughout the day.

"4. The stretcher-bearers worked unceasingly through the day, regardless of casualties and of the almost continuous heavy shelling.

" 5. ' B ' Company during the advance had three Lewis guns destroyed by shell fire. The O.C. 2nd K.O.S.B. generously lent two of his guns to O.C. ' B ' Company which were a great help in making the situation secure.

" 6. Six machine guns, one heavy trench mortar, ammunition, with maps, documents, etc., and over thirty prisoners were captured. Owing to the extensive use of observation aeroplanes by the enemy, the Brigadier (General Jones), had all the serviceable captured German machine guns brought up and concentrated near the front line ; their job being to fire solely and only at enemy aircraft."

Colonel Johnstone's narrative is now resumed :

July.—During July nothing happened of interest. The line captured on June 28th was worked on continuously, and a very large amount of work was done by the Battalion on the support, reserve, divisional and corps lines of entrenchments. For the rest, ordinary trench reliefs were carried out, with more or less interference from the enemy. His interference took the form of heavy shelling with gas shells, together with intensive bombing from aeroplanes. On one occasion a trench relief, which was normally complete in about two hours, commenced at 8.30 p.m., but was not completed till 4.30 a.m. the following morning.

The periods of duty out of trenches were short, and on several occasions the Battalion was aroused in the middle of the night and marched towards the front line, to be at hand to take a share in repulsing enemy attacks.

Long range artillery fire was developed by the enemy against the camps which had been established in the Forest. These camps, and the light railway which had been constructed through the forest by Canadian railwaymen, were objects of particular attention by the enemy guns and planes, and the Battalion when at rest had to evacuate its camp on three occasions, and spend the night in the refuge trenches. And by the fate which pursued the Battalion during this month, whether in line, support, or reserve, the occasions on which the enemy was most pressing in his attentions, were the occasions on which the weather was on its worst behaviour.

Slowly but surely the month drew to a close, and the night of the 31st found the Battalion relieved by the

1st Battalion Cheshire Regiment and *en route* for Arcade Camp, in the Forest of Nieppe.

Officers joining (or rejoining) during July were Capt. Edwards, Lieut. Fulcher, 2/Lieuts. King, Tice-hurst, Stern, Glass and Nott. Drafts amounting to 111 other ranks were received.

Casualties for the month were four killed, and Capt. Edwards and eleven men wounded.

August.—The Battalion had seen the last of the Forest of Nieppe, after its last relief on 31st July. The 5th Division was relieved, and was concentrated in the area west of Hazebrouck again, and refitting was the order of the day, coupled with the inevitable training, forced on us by the continual arrival of rein-forcement drafts. But the training carried out during the first fortnight was of a more interesting description than that which had hitherto been the rule when out of the line. Here, instead of creeping barrages and trench to trench attacks, the Battalion trained entirely for manœuvres. This was interesting to all ranks, coming as it did on top of the news of the enemy reverses at the hands of the French and our own troops, and all ranks were eager to try their hands at what was, to the vast majority, a quite new species of warfare. The weather remained good, and the whole Battalion spent day after day marching across country and fighting imaginary battles. On the 13th the Battalion entrained for the Frevent—St Pol area, and on the morning of the 14th went into billets at Sibiville. Here training was continued until the 19th, on which day the Battalion enbussed for Marieux, and thence marched to Couin in the Authie Valley. The troops rested whilst the officers reconnoitred the roads and tracks leading to the east. This looked like business, and proved to be so, for on return from reconnaissance, the officers found that orders for the move had arrived, and at 10.30 p.m. the last men of the Battalion had left the cover of Couin Wood, and were on the march towards Gommecourt Wood. The Battalion was in position by 2.35 a.m. on 21st August, having taken over the position vacated by a Battalion of New Zealand Infantry, which had side-slipped to the south.

CHAPTER XIV

A UGUST 21ST.—The night of the 21st-22nd August was spent in expectation. The 13th Brigade was in reserve to the 5th Division, and the role of the Brigade was to support and carry through the attack to be made by the 15th and 95th Brigades, which in their turn were to carry on the initial attack launched by the 37th Division.

These two brigades of the 5th Division attained their objectives, having passed through the line gained by the 37th Division. Progress to the south had not been so rapid, so the two brigades had to fall back somewhat to conform to the general line.

On the 22nd the fighting continued, and was particularly severe on the 5th Division frontage. The weather was not propitious, heavy fog covering the whole country till about mid-day. The attacking brigades suffered heavy casualties but continued to advance. On the evening of the 22nd, the 13th Brigade was ordered to be ready to advance to the support of the leading brigades, and early on the morning of the 23rd, the Battalion set forth to carry on the attack of the 95th Brigade, which had had a very hard fight. The Battalion moved off in the direction of Grevillers and Achiet le Petit. In the late afternoon, at 4.50, orders were received that the Battalion was to attack and seize the village of Irles. Hitherto the Battalion had been advancing due east, and the

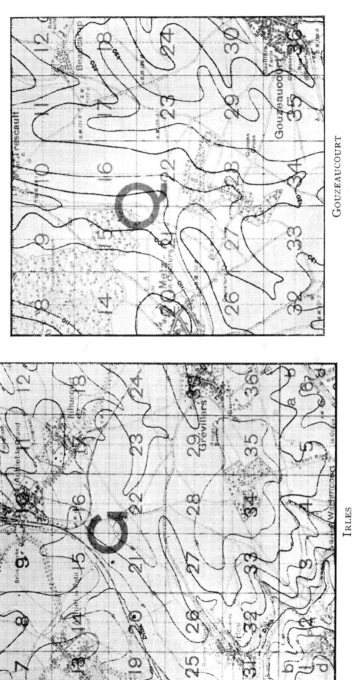

IRLES

GOUZEAUCOURT

THE ADVANCE, 1918

[To face p. 218

new orders involved a complete right-angled wheel to the south.

The other battalions of the Brigade continued straight east and south-east, but in spite of the complicated nature of the manœuvre, all went well, and the Battalion deployed from artillery formation for attack just west of the railway line between Miraumont and Achiet le Grand.   The railway had been cleared by the 95th Division in spite of their heavy losses. The tanks detailed to the Brigade had been knocked out at close range while attempting to surmount the railway cutting.

The Battalion attacked in the last remaining hours of daylight, and on entering Irles found the village had been evacuated by the enemy, and was in the possession of a couple of patrols of the 12th Glosters.   The C.O. of this unit had been badly wounded, and arrived at Battalion Headquarters in the railway cutting, and laid formal claim to the capture of the village. The three attacking companies of the Battalion, finding that their allotted task had already been performed, pushed on and succeeded in gaining a position on the high ground a thousand yards beyond the village, and established a line of posts there.

The high ground to the south dominating Miraumont was also occupied, and the right flank of the Battalion was refused, in order to keep actual touch with the New Zealand Division, which had had severe fighting around Beauregard Dovecot. Casualties in the Battalion were not heavy, when balanced against the value of the positions won, which absolutely dominated the enemy positions to the east and south, and afforded an excellent *point d'appui* for the continuance of the advance.   Actual casualties were

Lieut. Steele, killed ; Capt. Winn, Lieuts. Collins, Quigley, Glass and Cotterell, wounded ; and 100 other ranks, of whom seventeen were killed. About half the casualties were sustained during the actual attack, and the balance whilst the position gained was being entrenched.

Casualties were all from machine-gun fire, which swept the crest of the ridge and the reverse flank alike, from about 2000 yards range. This machine-gun fire continued intermittently during the night, as the objective of the troops on the left of the Battalion (Loupart Wood) was not taken until the following day, owing to the distance to be covered and the strenuous resistance put up by the enemy during the evening attack. During the night contact patrols were sent out and collected a few prisoners, but the total captures could not be ascertained until the morning of the 24th. At dawn on the 24th the Battalion was ordered to prepare the position for defence in order to give the right flank attack an opportunity to come up into the general line. This work was set in hand, and whilst it was being carried out a large number of the enemy were seen assembling behind their lines to the east.

This movement was dealt with by long-range fire from machine and Lewis guns, and the enemy soon disappeared. During the afternoon the Division on our right advanced on Miraumont. As the advance developed the enemy were seen to come out from their underground shelters in the village, and form up in column of route, the column being preceded and closed by men carrying white flags. Strong patrols were thereupon sent forward from the Battalion, and these patrols brought in 13 prisoners from various dug-outs,

THE RAILWAY CUTTING NEAR ACHIET LE GRAND

A view of the Railway Line taken immediately after its capture by the British in August 1918

[To face p. 220

and also some machine guns and trench mortars. One patrol brought in four prisoners who had remained with a battery of 4.2-in. guns which the enemy had not been able to remove. The total captures by the Battalion were one 5.9 gun, the four 4.2 guns mentioned above, eight infantry trench mortars, and fourteen machine guns. All this booty was brought back to the railway cutting, which presented an extraordinary sight, as all the material captured by the 95th Brigade was also piled there. Here we came across the first specimens we had seen of the enemy special anti-tank rifle, an unwieldy weapon firing a huge bullet. Except that the weapon was built as a rifle the cartridge resembled a small pom-pom shell, one cartridge weighing a quarter of a pound.

The Battalion remained in position during the night of 24th-25th August. During the day two more casualties occurred among the officers of the Battalion, Lieuts. Milford and Thorning being wounded. Loupart Wood on the Battalion left flank, and about 2000 yards away, had not been thoroughly cleared (or had been re-occupied by enemy machine-gun patrols), and these guns fired at odd intervals during the day.

The New Zealand Division passed through the Battalion during the morning to carry on the advance, and the Battalion transport being moved up, supplies were issued, ammunition made up, and the Battalion made ready to follow up the attack. Orders were received early on the 25th, and the Battalion moved off to the north-east. The Brigade dug itself in near Grevillers, and after a very wet night moved off in the morning of the 26th, and occupied a position of readiness just west of Favreuil. During the move to this position two men were killed and thirteen wounded, by trip wire " booby traps " concealed by the Huns in the long grass. The area was searched, and found to be liberally sown with traps of various descriptions, but only a few were ready for action, the speed of the advance having prevented the enemy from completing them. Late in the evening the K.O.S.B. and the 14th Warwicks attacked and captured Beugnatre, and, on the 27th, in pursuance of the leap-frogging principle of advance which had been adopted as the standard, the Battalion moved up to take the place of the battalions which had attacked. The night passed fairly quietly, but in the early morning of the 28th the enemy put down a heavy barrage, and continued to shell spasmodically during the day, but only caused three casualties to the Battalion, the shooting being very wild.

During these latter days the 5th Division had pushed on, as a rule, more rapidly than the troops on its flanks, but on the 29th information was received that the New Zealand Division had passed through Bapaume, and the Battalion received orders to push forward strong patrols, and to back these up as opportunity offered. The first patrol on the left flank lost three men almost immediately by machine-gun fire, and the Stokes mortars attached to the Battalion were pushed forward to deal with these guns, which they put out of action. The patrol movements developed into an action covered by our artillery, a simultaneous forward movement being made by the Division on our left, and eventually the Battalion made good the high ground about Beugny, overlooking the railway from Bapaume eastwards.

Two officers (Lieut. Darlow, killed ; 2/Lieut. King, wounded) and forty other ranks became casualties, mostly from machine-gun fire, and the Battalion took twenty prisoners and killed about 100 of the enemy. The high ground gained was of importance, being needed as a jumping-off place for the attack which was to take place on the morrow. During the night of the 29th, patrols kept touch with the enemy, and the Battalion was relieved by the 95th Brigade attacking battalion, the 1st Devons, and moved into reserve to the Division, remaining in reserve during the remainder of the month. During these days reinforcements joined the Battalion and all things were made ready for further action.

Captain Kerr, Lieut. Gordon, Lieut. Lewin, 2/Lieut. Bernard and seventy-seven other ranks joined during August.

September.—The Division moved into army reserve for a period, and remained in the area just north of Bapaume until the 13th of September. During this period various drafts of reinforcements joined the Battalion and all spare time was devoted to training, and making preparation for further movement forward. The Battalion eventually moved on the afternoon of September 13th, passing through Bapaume, and subsequently took over an area from the 2nd Auckland Battalion, New Zealand Division, about Metz en Couture, immediately south of Havrincourt Wood. Active movement forward by the Corps had not taken place for some days, in order that the advances of the enormous number of troops engaged should be brought up to a comparatively level frontage. Small actions to obtain possession of local points of vantage had been carried out, but no attacks of a serious nature. The Battalion spent

two short tours in the line, that had been gained up
to date, and for the rest devoted its attention to further
training, and the improvement of the bivouac area
assigned to it.

After a period of rest the Division again took up
position in the line, the 13th Brigade being in reserve.
On the 25th the Brigade relieved the Brigade in the
line, and the Battalion took over the right sector
from the 1st Battalion, East Surrey Regiment. All
preparations had been made for the continuance
of the forward movement, and after twenty-four hours
of increased activity an attack was launched by the
whole Corps. The objective of the Battalion was
African Trench. This was the most forward trench
which had been constructed by our troops after the
surprise attack towards Cambrai in the previous
year. It had been very strongly fortified by the
enemy, and had been a cause of many casualties to
our troops, who had made several individual battalion
attempts to take it. The advance had to be made
over a crest, which was swept by machine-gun fire
by the enemy, and exposed to machine-gun fire from
the high ground above the village of Gouzeaucourt,
about 1800 yards eastwards.

The 13th Brigade attacked, with the 95th Brigade
on its left holding the flank. Troops also attacked
on the right of the Battalion, but very little progress
was made. The frontage assigned to the Battalion
was just over 1000 yards, and with the strength
reduced by its previous casualties and the number
of machine guns employed by the enemy, the task
was too great for it, and indeed also for the other
troops engaged, to carry out successfully. Added
to these difficulties the enemy had heavily bombarded

our support line on the early morning of the 27th, and unfortunately knocked out most of our heavy trench mortars, under cover of a hurricane barrage from which our troops were to attack. Thus the Brigade was deprived of any covering fire, except a light barrage from our field batteries, which was not sufficient to make the enemy take refuge in his dug-outs. He had had ample warning of the operations in progress, for the Divisions to the north had attacked at 5.20 a.m., whereas the 5th Division attack did not commence till 7.52 a.m., in accordance with the plan of the higher command.

As soon as our men topped the crest they were met by a withering machine-gun fire, alike from the front and the flanks, where the enemy were holding strong points, constructed from abandoned tanks. The tanks taking part in our attack were ditched and burnt out, and in spite of local reinforcements the Battalion was unable to take its objective. By 11 a.m. the few survivors of the Battalion's attacking companies had dug themselves in in a line of posts, about 200 yards east of the jumping-off line. The troops on the right had got into African Trench, but the Germans were in too great strength and bombed them out again.

Enemy artillery fire continued to be heavy against the front and support line until darkness fell. During the night patrols crawled forward and ascertained that the enemy was still holding his position in strength. An attack at 2.15 a.m. on the 28th evidently shook his resolution, for patrols, hearing movement in the enemy trench, went forward to reconnoitre, and found that the enemy was moving eastwards. Eventually the enemy's trench was occupied about daylight, five belated Huns being taken prisoners. Further patrols were immediately sent to follow up the Huns, who were still keeping machine-guns in position to cover the movement of their rear-guard. These patrols were ordered not to advance further east than absolutely necessary to discover the enemy's movements, for the 95th Brigade was assigned the duty of continuing our eastward advance.

When this Brigade had passed through our line a thorough search of the field was made, and several wounded were brought in, including two of the Northumberland Fusiliers, the Battalion which had attacked on our right; also five wounded Germans were gathered, who reported that their comrades had retired hastily at 2.30 a.m. This statement was borne out by the condition of their trench. Equipment of every description was littered about everywhere, and ten machine guns in working order, with numerous others which had been rendered unserviceable, were found in the trench, together with numberless rifles, and 300,000 rounds of S.A.A. in boxes, besides that in the machine-gun positions and dug-outs ready for immediate use. The Battalion casualties in the action were heavy, especially taking into consideration the then low effective strength. Lieuts. Hemmerde and Lewin and 2/Lieut. Stevens were killed; 2/Lieuts. Burden, Nott, Luscombe, Thorning, Smith and Bernard, wounded, and of other ranks 59 were killed., 3 died of wounds, 118 were wounded while 10 wounded slightly remained at duty. In addition, 37 were missing at the roll call, and of these 35 were found later, having been collected and taken to hospital wounded, without passing through the Regimental Aid Post.

Whilst the other Brigades of the Division were performing their allotted task of following up the retreating enemy, until relieved by other troops, the 13th Brigade remained on the captured ground, and on the 30th the Battalion withdrew into Brigade Reserve and reorganised.

Drafts numbering sixty-eight were received during September.

Brig.-General L. O. W. Jones, who had commanded the Brigade since the autumn of 1915, and who was much beloved and trusted, died of pneumonia in September. He was succeeded by Brig.-General Beckwith.

General Jones had originally come to France as Captain and Adjutant of the 2nd Bn. The Essex Regiment. After commanding that Battalion for a short while, he was promoted Brigadier-General and took over command of the 13th Infantry Brigade in September 1915, being probably the youngest officer of that rank at the time.

In spite of an utter disregard for danger, General Jones was never wounded during his four years' continuous service in France. He was a fine soldier who knew no fear and it was a tragedy that his promising career should be brought to a close, not by wounds, but by disease.

One wishes that, anyway, he might have been spared until the war was finished, and cannot help thinking that he himself would have preferred to have been killed in action.

October.—For the first eight days of October, the Battalion rested in reserve, training, reorganising and absorbing the reinforcements of officers and men who had joined during the fight and subsequently. The 12th Gloucester Regiment had been broken up on the reorganisation of the Brigades of the Division into three battalions in place of four, and the Battalion received 165 other ranks from this source. This reorganisation had become necessary on account of the shortage of reinforcements now available for the British Armies in France. The new men soon settled down, and very rapidly became enthusiastic members of the Battalion.

Early morning of the 9th of October found the Battalion on the move eastwards again, to take its share in the pursuit of the still retiring enemy, who was fighting a sustained rear-guard action in order to ensure the safety of his artillery, and give himself time to fortify his next position, selected for a defensive action. The march forward continued for four days and, on the night of 13th October, the Battalion took its place as reserve battalion to the 13th Brigade, on a line east of Viesly, overlooking the valley of the River Selle, and the railway line from Le Cateau to Solesmes, which ran along the rising ground just east of the valley. Here the Battalion remained till the night of the 16th, when a move to the front line was made in relief of the 2nd K.O.S.B. and the 16th Royal Warwickshire Regiment. The Battalion remained in this line until the night of the 19th, when it was relieved by the battalions it had relieved on the 13th. During the period in the line active patrolling took place by day and night, and very useful information was obtained, which proved most helpful to the relieving ¡attalions which had come into the line to make an a¡tack on the morning of the 20th. On relief, the Battalion proceeded to

Bethencourt and thence to Caudry, the first more or less undestroyed town that the Battalion had rested in since leaving Doullens in April, nearly seven months previously. Here the Battalion remained until the end of the month.

During October, Captain Anstruther, D.S.O., M.C., and 2/Lieuts. Beckett, Burgess, Carnold, Barrett, Druce, Johnson, Vincent, Evans, Philpott, Wilkinson, and Mulcock joined. 2/Lieut. Stephenson was wounded.

The 5th Division had been more or less continuously engaged in battle since its return from Italy. Many casualties had been sustained and the Battalion had had, if anything, more than its fair share of these. The Division remained at rest whilst other troops continued the pursuit. But the rest was a rest only in name, for wherever the enemy suspected that troops were billeted, he made the night one continual alarm by means of his bombing planes, though gradually this nuisance was abated by the exploits of our night-flying pilots and the vigilance of the anti-aircraft guns, both of the artillery and infantry. The days were spent in training, and a reasonable amount of recreation, for although all ranks knew that the enemy had been badly hit during the past three months, it was expected that he would still be able to reorganise his shattered forces and put up more than one stout fight before he was eventually driven back within his own frontiers. With a view to the impending operations, all ranks, therefore, set themselves to train cheerfully and make themselves absolutely ready for the tasks which lay before them.

Q

CHAPTER XV

L IEUT.-COL. JOHNSTONE, D.S.O., proceeded on leave about the middle of October, and so the great advantage of a participator's personal narrative is no longer available, but fortunately there is little more to record as the fighting was practically over. Major Kay, D.S.O., succeeded to the Command.

Across the Sambre.—The Battalion was on the move again in the early days of November and, advancing through Mormal Forest, crossed the Sambre in the front line on the 8th. The Germans when they retired had mined every cross-roads in the Forest, and all of them blew up very successfully, with one exception. When we passed this intact one, we found there a very worried Quartermaster of the Norfolks, who was billeted in a house situated exactly at the cross-roads, and who was wondering at what moment his cross-roads were going up too. It was very difficult to resist the temptation to tip-toe off his particular piece of mud and pavé.

Very early next day the Battalion was pressing forward all ready for battle. " B " and " C " Companies were leading, with patrols well out to the front, and advancing in line with the troops on the right and left. These companies arrived on the position, which had been held by the Germans the day before, just about dawn. They were told by the inhabitants of La Payé that the Germans had said that the British would arrive at about 8 a.m. the next morning, and would want some hot coffee. One of the first persons seen in the village was a little girl, who was wearing a regimental cap badge of The Queen's Own. She said that she had been given it two days before by one of a party of prisoners who had been marched through the village. (This man must have belonged to the 7th Battalion of the Regiment, which was not far away on our flank.) At 9 a.m., when the leading companies had arrived at Ferrière la Petite, three miles south of Maubeuge, orders to halt were received, and an outpost line was taken up.

Lieut. M'Clenaghan was killed on the 9th, by a shell, when he was riding back towards the Sambre from Pontigny, where he had been reconnoitring for an advanced Brigade Headquarters. He was the last casualty the Battalion suffered and, except for Major Brown, M.C., must have had more war service with the Battalion than any other officer present at the time.

The Armistice was concluded two days later, on 11th November. The last German we saw before the Armistice was a flying man in a multi-coloured monoplane, who, flying very low indeed, visited each company in turn, and also the transport, peppering them severely with a machine gun. The total bag was a very slight wound in the foot of one of the cooks.

The action of the 9th, therefore, proved to be the last warlike operation of the 1st Battalion, The Queen's Own Royal West Kent Regiment. Thus the Battalion concluded its share in the Great War fifteen miles from the position on the Mons Canal, where it had fought its first great battle four and a quarter years earlier.

But little remains to be told. The Battalion remained in billets between Mormal Forest and Le Quesnoy for more than a month, during which time not a complaint was received from the inhabitants as to the conduct of the men or damage to property. It then moved to Noville les Bois, in the neighbourhood of Namur, arriving on the 22nd December. Not a single man fell out in the ten days' march, though the weather was trying and the roads very bad. The attitude of the Belgian people was at first slightly suspicious; they appeared to distrust the " licentious soldiery "; but this feeling was soon changed into cordiality when they experienced the conduct of the British soldier.

Months were passed in training, education and games, but demobilisation began almost at once, and the Battalion slowly dwindled. A large block of officers, including Lieut.-Col. Kay, D.S.O., was transferred to the 6th Battalion of the Regiment at Cologne. So it was a very small battalion that disembarked at Dover, under the command of Major R. Brown, M.C., on the 23rd April 1919.

Major Brown originally came to France in December 1914, and took over the duties of Regimental Sergeant-Major when R.S.M. Doe was given his commission. From that date till the Armistice he served continuously with the Battalion, his work as R.S.M. always earning the highest praise of all who came into contact with him. His initiative during the early days and the subsequent heavy fighting, contributed no small quota to the success of the Battalion's operations. The establishment of the very essential advanced " rear " Headquarters were always his first care, thus perfecting the liaison between Battalion Headquarters and the transport lines.

Major R. Brown, M.C.

R.S.M. Brown was commissioned as Second Lieutenant in September 1917. His services as an officer were mentioned by all successive commanding officers as being of the greatest value to the Battalion. He was awarded the M.C. and subsequently a bar to that decoration, for great gallantry and devotion to duty during various operations.

Thus it is doubtful whether a better custodian of the Battalion for its journey back to " Blighty " could have been found.

POSTSCRIPT

A prominent politician, writing about a certain battalion some decades ago, was bold enough to state that it was " undoubtedly the finest battalion in the world." We are not sure of the exact words, but that was the meaning of his remarks.

A French General is said to have remarked about Sir John French's army, some months after the fighting began, that " no better army was conceivable." Again we can only give the sense of the remark.

" Comparisons are odious." They are more than usually odious when they deal with army units, about which all good soldiers are superlatively sensitive. Therefore we will not affront all other regiments by saying that the descendant of the glorious old " Dirty Half Hundred " was, throughout the War, the " finest battalion in the world." We would much prefer to paraphrase the French General and to say that " no better battalion was conceivable."

These remarks are appended because it is felt that the foregoing pages do not sufficiently speak for themselves. Had the task of arranging the Record fallen into more able hands, no doubt would have been left in the mind of a reader that the 1st Battalion, The Queen's Own Royal West Kent Regiment, was a super-excellent one.

If so, why ?

If this question were put to a patriotic man of Kent, of course he would maintain that the county from which the Regiment gets its recruits explains everything. It would certainly be difficult to imagine a *bad* regiment recruited from Kent. But, for all that, one cannot believe that this alone accounts for it. There would not seem to be, indeed, much to chose between one district of the British Isles and another as regards fighting value. North, East, South and West England, the Lowlands, the Highlands, Wales, North and South Ireland have all supplied units of outstanding fighting merit.

Then there is another thing : Sir Arthur Conan Doyle calls the " West Kents " a " shire regiment, raised from the very soil of England." Now, with all due respect to that eminent author and historian, that statement is, unless the soil of London be considered as part of " the very soil of England," quite misleading. The regimental recruiting area extends well into Greater London, and at least two out of every three men recruited in normal times, though genuine men of Kent, are indistinguishable from Londoners. They are none the worse fighting men for that !

To look for other than territorial reasons—the Regiment has the advantage of very great traditions. Sedulously instructed in them when he joins, constantly reminded of them throughout his service by all sorts of means (not least among which must be counted the excellent Regimental Magazine), The

Queen's Own " other rank " is very strongly imbued
with " Regimental Pride." That in itself goes a long
way to make him an ugly fighter. A humble regiment,
if there be such a thing, can be of very little use except
for show purposes !

And now for the reasons that far outweigh all others.

In the first instance, the Battalion was exceedingly
fortunate in its successive commanding officers. Every
one of them belonged to the Regiment and was imbued
with its own particular spirit ; thoroughly understanding the men and how to get the most out of them.
When it is considered how very greatly the efficiency
of a unit depends on its commanding officer, it must
be acknowledged that the Battalion owes much of its
continued fighting renown to the officers who succeeded
to the Command.

Secondly, the officers, warrant officers and N.C.O.'s,
who " set the pace," contributed no small share to
the high standard of the Battalion. One dare not
mention any who are still alive, but one can say of those
who had the great glory of giving their lives for their
King, their Country, and their *Regiment*—of Major
Buckle, of Major Pack-Beresford, of Major Hastings,
of C.S.M.'s Crossley, Penny, Ransome, of Sergts. File,
Verrall, Fitzgerald, Barden, Fisher, Powell, and many
others too numerous to mention here, that they were
all magnificent men and soldiers in the very best sense
of both words. *They* made the Battalion what it was.
To their unremitting conscientious and unostentatious
toil of years ; to their force of character, judgment
and tact, the fighting efficiency that the Battalion
proved itself to possess is to be attributed.

Thirdly, all ranks worked together in a splendid way
for the good of the Regiment. If an officer became a

casualty the N.C.O. carried on, and if the N.C.O. became a casualty the private carried on.

But, it may be said, this only refers to the first few months of the war, because after Neuve Chapelle but comparatively few of the original men were left in any rank. True ; but the impetus had been given. The Battalion had already made a great name. Things had been said by the Great Ones that must have filled all ranks with a great pride. The new-comers, officers and men alike, had a standard set that they *dare* not lower.

For the first year or more—indeed until the system of indiscriminate reinforcements was invented—the Battalion was extremely well served by its feeding unit. The drafts received were most excellent. This may be considered as an additional reason why the early standard was maintained, and the 1st Battalion owes a heavy debt of gratitude to the O.C. 3rd Bn. and his staff for the good officers and the splendidly trained men who came from Fort Darland, Chatham.

Still another cause that contributed to the maintenance of the high standard set by the officers and men of the Old Army was the attractive force of a good name. Sufficient of the doings of the Battalion got to be known in England to make the Regiment a marked one. Thus *Punch* chose a Queen's Own private to illustrate one of his cartoons. A good type of officer and a good type of man was in this way induced to choose as his regiment one so famous as " The Queen's Own."

The history of the 1st Battalion during the Great War, especially the part it took in the operations about October 1914, could never be complete without special mention of the late Major M. P. Buckle, D.S.O.

Major Buckle was temporarily in command of the

Battalion from about 13th October to the date of his death.

Apart from the training the Battalion had received in Peace time and the experience gained by it during the first two or three months of war, there was one other factor which helped it to play the magnificent part that it did in the operations of this period. This was recognised by the N.C.O.'s and men who survived.

During Peace time the sterling qualities of Major Buckle had helped to gain such a great influence over everyone that, whilst he was in Command, the men naturally looked to him for guidance and encouragement ; needless to say, it was not denied them. All will agree that he was everywhere, regardless of danger to himself, always encouraging, helping and setting by his own magnificent conduct, such a great example that the Battalion, though worn out and weary, was ready to attempt the impossible. It is certain that the great personal influence of this officer, over the whole Battalion, was one of the greatest factors which helped to bring it through the critical days at the end of October 1914.

This was recognised and appreciated by the men, and it was with the greatest regret that the news of his untimely death, whilst attempting to rally the men of another corps, was received by the survivors.

No man gave up his life more willingly in the carrying out of his duty—holding the line intact—than Major Buckle. Everyone felt his death deeply, and it was recognised that the Regiment had lost a great leader and a great soldier.

Finally, it should be recorded as one of the most satisfactory outcomes of the war, that the Battalion established a close friendship with the 2nd K.O.S.B.

The two Battalions served side by side from Mons
till the Armistice, and a strong feeling of mutual
respect and confidence was established. When the 1st
Battalion, The Queen's Own, shall again be called
to the battlefield, and have the responsibility of handing
on the glory of the Regiment unsullied to futurity, no
better fortune can be wished for it than that it may
again be brigaded with the 2nd Battalion, The King's
Own Scottish Borderers.

" Quo fas et gloria ducunt."

APPENDIX

APPENDIX

THE names contained herein are of those who were brought to notice for special acts of gallantry and good work.

The list was compiled and kept up to date at Battalion Headquarters during the War, and is therefore as complete as possible, though undoubetdly there are many others whose actions were equally good but, owing to being unwitnessed, were never reported.

Some received rewards. Unfortunately all could not, sometimes owing to death, but also because the number of rewards issued was necessarily limited.

Those in this list who received no reward may be consoled by the fact that their actions were none the less appreciated by their comrades.

PART I

August 1914 *to March* 1916

MONS—NEUVE CHAPELLE—HILL 60

Lieut. HENRY BASIL HAYDON WHITE ⎫
2/Lieut. JAMES REGINALD RUSSELL ⎭ 1st R.W. Kent Regt.

At Neuve Chapelle in October 1914 these two junior officers brought the Battalion out of action after ten days' continuous fighting in the trenches, when all other officers had become casualties.

No. 5259. C.S.M. F. CROSSLEY ⎫ were specially noted for
No. 6694. Sergt. M. STROUD ⎪ their excellent work during
No. 6031. —— PALMER ⎪ the fighting at Neuve
No. 7316. Pte. E. ALLISON ⎬ Chapelle in Oct. 1914,
No. 9401. Sergt. W. MARSLIN ⎪ when all the officers in
No. 7934. Pte. G. WARD ⎪ the Battalion, except two
No. 9879. Sergt. J. GILBERT ⎪ junior subalterns, became
No. 8129. C.Q.M.S. S. J. CRONK ⎭ casualties.

No. 6694.   Sergt. M. STROUD.

Left the trenches on 27th October 1914 with two privates, when volunteers were called for to reconnoitre the enemy trenches.   In spite of the enemy's heavy fire, he carried out this duty satisfactorily, although the two privates, having both been hit, had to return after going a short distance.

No. 8345.   C.S.M. A. REYNOLDS.

As Sergt.-Major of " D " Company, did exceptionally good work, especially when his company was commanded by a very junior officer.

No. 7261.   L.-Cpl. D. WRIGHT.

On 25th October 1914, at Neuve Chapelle, volunteered to reconnoitre a trench which had been dug close to our firing line by the enemy.   He brought back information that the trench was unoccupied, and then took forward a covering party while the trench was being filled in.   This N.C.O. had been conspicuous on many occasions for gallant conduct and useful work.

No. 7982.   L.-Cpl. G. JOHNSON.

At Neuve Chapelle, on the 27th October 1914, went forward from the firing line to an abandoned field gun about 200 yards from the enemy's position, in broad daylight.   He removed the sights from the gun ; returned with them ; handed them to the officer in command of the gun ; and, returning on a second occasion, removed the breech-block of the gun.

No. 6025.   Pte. FRANK FLOYD.

In the trenches, between the 23rd and 26th October 1914, when exposed to a very heavy bombardment at Neuve Chapelle, continually carried messages under heavy fire.

No. 8192.   Pte. J. TURNBULL.

Between the 13th and 19th November 1914, when in the trenches near Ypres, repeatedly left the trenches and recon- noitred the enemy position at night under heavy fire.   He accounted for six German snipers, and brought back their rifles or part of their equipment as proof of their death. He also brought back valuable information regarding the position of the enemy trenches. He was eventually wounded while performing this duty.

Lieut. and Q.M. HARRY GEORGE ROGERS.

Brought up rations and hot tea to the trenches under shell and rifle fire between the 13th and 19th November 1914, and was highly efficient in the discharge of his duties during the campaign.

No. 888.   Pte. WILLIAM CRAMP.

When in trenches on 8th March 1915, climbed over the parapet within 25 yards of the German line by night and reconnoitred a crater which separated the two lines and which was connected by a communication trench with the enemy's trenches.

No. 7847.   Actg. Sergt. E. DENNINGTON.

On 26th March 1915 went to a portion of the fire trench which had been destroyed by shell fire, and, assisted by a private soldier, dug out a lance-corporal who had been buried under the fallen parapet, within 30 yards of the enemy. He worked for over an hour, lying on his stomach until the lance-corporal had been rescued.

No. 7292.   Sergt. ERNEST BRADMAN.

At Ypres, in March 1915, when the trench occupied by his platoon was being heavily bombarded by enemy artillery and minenwerfer, Sergt. Bradman showed great courage and coolness, walking up and down the trench and steadying his men. The trench was knocked in at many places, and these portions were under hostile machine-gun fire.

No. 240.   L.-Sergt. JAMES YOUNG.

Picked up a burning hand grenade, which had been thrown into his trench by the enemy and had fallen among a group of men, and threw it back at the enemy. The grenade exploded as it left his hand. This occurred on Hill 60 on the 17th April 1915.

No. 9046. Sergt. WILLIAM FISHER.

On 17th April 1915, on Hill 60, was noted for great gallantry.

No. 168. Pte. JOHN HISSEY.

At Hill 60, on 17th April 1915, took command of a small party (no N.C.O. being available), and took up an important position, not previously occupied, by which the flank of the line was protected.

No. 8226. Sergt. JOHN RABBIT.

Displayed great gallantry on Hill 60 on 17th April 1915.

No. 9917. Sergt. GEORGE BOTTING.

During the attack on Hill 60, on the 17th April 1915, displayed great gallantry.

No. 8927. Sergt. GEORGE WESTON.

As Machine Gun Sergeant on Hill 60, on 17th April 1915, went out in front of our trenches and attacked a German. He himself was armed with only a bayonet.

No. 5793. Pte. THOMAS CORK.

When performing the duties of a stretcher-bearer near Hill 60 on 7th May 1915, went to the assistance of a wounded comrade in broad daylight, who was lying in an exposed position under close infantry fire. He took him food and water, crawled with him on his back some 300 yards to a sheltered position, where he left him until he had brought up a stretcher. The position of the wounded man was known by the Medical Officer, who had decided it was impossible to reach him by daylight. Pte. Cork performed this act without orders and entirely on his own initiative.

No. 8759. Sergt. ALBERT FRANCIS ROBINSON.

When acting as Signalling Sergeant during an attack carried out by the Battalion at night over unknown ground in May

1915, was the only person in the Battalion who had previously been over the ground in daylight, when laying telephone lines. He volunteered to go forward and get in touch with the companies which had lost direction in the darkness. He twice went forward under heavy shell and rifle fire, got in touch with companies and brought valuable information as to the situation back to Battalion Headquarters.

No. 8136.   Pte. M. SKEAN.

At St Eloi in July 1915, during a bombardment of our trenches by enemy minenwerfer, Pte. Skean was buried. After being dug out he volunteered to accompany the Battalion sniping officer into a ruin just behind a gap in our front line : while there an enemy bomb fell on the ruin, again burying him and wounding him. He was dug out by the sniping officer, who was himself wounded whilst doing this. Pte. Skean, though wounded and badly shaken by having been twice buried, remained with the officer, binding up his wound and helping to get him to our trenches.

PART II

March to June 1916

ARRAS

No. 6348.   Sergt. A. HAMMOND.
No. 1036.   L.-Cpl. F. LIDDAMORE.

At Arras in the early morning of 9th April 1916, when it was misty, Capt. Gross and Lieut. Dobie, with C.S.M. Crossley, went out to inspect the wire in front of the fire trench.   While they were doing so, the enemy suddenly opened fire.   Lieut. Dobie fell dead into a crater, the others got back except Capt. Gross, who was left out wounded.   C.S.M. Crossley, Sergt. Hammond and L.-Cpl. Liddamore crept out under fire and succeeded in dragging Capt. Gross back to the trench.   He, however, died a few minutes later.   In doing this C.S.M. Crossley was killed and L.-Cpl. Liddamore got a bullet through his clothing.   Sergt. Hammond was untouched.

No. 8740.   Pte. THOMAS WHITE.

As a Battalion runner for nearly two years never failed to deliver his messages.

No. 8702.   Pte. C. BARR.

Was conspicuous for his devotion to duty at all times.

No. 7640.   L.-Cpl. WILLIAM SMITH.

During a very long period in the trenches it was noticeable that L.-Cpl. Smith always volunteered for any particularly dangerous duties.

No. 7882.   Cpl. SIDNEY JAMES ASH.

Was noted for continuous good work in the trenches, both on patrol duty and sniping.   He inflicted many casualties on the enemy by his skill and daring when sniping.

No. 8839.   Sergt. FREDERICK WILLIAM MANN.

Was conspicuous for good work in charge of patrols, always setting a fine example of coolness under fire.

No. 5618.   Pte. WILLIAM SCARBOROUGH.

As a company runner never failed to deliver his messages, having frequently had to pass through heavy barrages to do so.

PART III

July to September 1916

THE SOMME FIGHTING

No. 7725. Cpl. GEORGE HATCH.

The Battalion, when advancing to the assault of the German trenches in the vicinity of High Wood on the night of 22nd-23rd July 1916, came under very heavy machine-gun and shell fire, and a large number of men were wounded. As the intensity of the fire did not diminish, it was impossible for the stretcher-bearers to go out and collect wounded. However, Cpl. Hatch, who was in charge of the stretcher-bearers, went out by himself, walked about in the open and carried wounded to cover in shell holes. This was done some 200 yards in front of our own lines and within very close range of the enemy machine guns. He afterwards carried back many of these men to our own lines. He continued his work with the utmost coolness and disregard for personal safety for about seven hours and until well after daylight, when eventually he was himself wounded. He was under very heavy fire the whole time. He was seen to carry back at least fifty cases, and there is no doubt that he saved the lives of a large number of men.

No. 5029. Pte. WILLIAM BUTLIN.

Near High Wood on the night of 22nd-23rd July 1916 was one of a platoon that got into the enemy trench while the Germans were holding the same trench on both flanks. The enemy on the left started to attack by bombing down the trench. Pte. Butlin sprang over some enemy bombs which were about to explode at the bottom of the trench and threw one of his own at the enemy. His action undoubtedly saved the flank of the platoon. Throughout the engagement he displayed the greatest gallantry and coolness.

1916] APPENDIX

No. 7524.   Sergt. WILLIAM SIBBALD.

On the night of 22nd-23rd July 1916, when the Battalion assaulted the enemy trenches near High Wood, was one of a bombing party which was sent in search of an isolated enemy trench to the flank.   Although wounded early in the engagement, he refused to go to the dressing station, and throughout the night displayed the greatest coolness and contempt for danger.   During the night of 21st July he did valuable reconnaissance work, and with a bomb killed two German snipers whom he found concealed in a shell hole.

Sergt. Sibbald was killed in a later action on the Somme.

Temp. Lieut. JOHN JAMES SCOTT.

When the Battalion attacked the German trenches near High Wood on the night of the 22nd-23rd July it was met by a very heavy machine-gun and shell fire, and Lieut. Scott's platoon was the only portion of the assaulting party that was able to remain in the enemy trench.   Lieut. Scott at once set to work to consolidate the position, holding off the enemy in front of him and on both flanks.   He held this isolated position with his platoon for four hours.   He showed great gallantry in the attack, and great coolness and ability when in occupation of the enemy trench.

2/Lieut. GEOFFREY WRIGHT DANDO.

Near High Wood on the night of 22nd-23rd July 1916 led a party of bombers past the enemy trench, which the Battalion was assaulting, and searched for a small isolated trench on the flank.   Failing to find the existence of this supposed trench, he returned to Battalion H.Q. to report.   He then twice returned to the firing line (the enemy trench) in order to report on the situation.   Previous to the assault 2/Lieut. Dando had carried out a reconnaissance in daylight, bringing back useful information.   On two occasions the N.C.O. accompanying him was wounded.

2/Lieut. REGINALD HARRY CALE.

On the night of 22nd-23rd July 1916, when the Battalion assaulted the German trenches near High Wood, 2/Lieut.

Cale, who was Battalion Lewis Gun Officer, followed the
assaulting party with his sergeant. Having lost his way in
the dark, he commenced to return to our trenches when he
found a badly wounded officer. Owing to very heavy rifle
and machine-gun fire at a range of about 100 yards, the party
had to crawl, and he carried the wounded officer on his back
for a short distance. The wounded officer, however, who had
a broken thigh, could not bear the pain, and 2/Lieut. Cale
then took him on his shoulders and walked upright with him.
After going a short distance further the wounded officer had
to be placed on the ground, and the party left him in search of
a stretcher. This all took place under heavy fire.

Temp. Capt. MARK BLAKISTON BAINES (R.A.M.C.).

At Longueval on 29th and 30th July 1916, owing to the
very heavy and unceasing German bombardment, movement
was practically impossible, and no regular Battalion dressing
station could be established. Capt. Baines moved about in
the trench, which was little else than a series of shell holes,
dressing the wounded with complete disregard for his personal
safety. Several of the wounded were buried and Capt. Baines
assisted in getting them out, notably in the case of an N.C.O.
who was very severely wounded and had some three feet of
earth thrown over him. Capt. Baines removed the earth
with his hands, got the N.C.O. out, and was able to dress the
wounds.

Previously, when near High Wood on 22nd-23rd July,
Capt. Baines worked for thirty-six hours attending to seriously
wounded men in an old trench just behind our firing line,
which was under continuous shell fire. On two occasions the
trench was blown in and earth was thrown over him, his
instruments, and the man he was dressing, but Capt. Baines
continued to work with the utmost coolness and disregard for
danger.

His great devotion to duty was also conspicuous at Hill 60,
in the operations north of Ypres in April 1915, and at the
second attack on Hill 60 in May 1915.

No. 8535.   Sergt. WILLIAM TRAILL.

On the night of 20th-21st July 1916, when the Battalion was proceeding to take over front-line trenches in the vicinity of High Wood, it had to pass through a heavy hostile barrage. This N.C.O. showed the greatest coolness and gallantry in keeping the platoon (of which he was in command) together, and it was due to his efforts that the platoon passed through the barrage with very few casualties.   Later, when the company was digging in, Sergt. Traill walked up and down under shell fire and displayed the greatest cheerfulness and coolness.

Again, on the night of 22nd-23rd July, when the Battalion assaulted the German trenches near High Wood, this N.C.O. established himself with a few men some fifteen yards from the enemy trench.   He collected men from various companies and made them dig in there.   He killed several Germans who tried to capture our wounded, and the latter he brought back with him when he returned to our trenches.   He held this advanced position for some hours, during which he kept in constant touch with the rear.   He showed great presence of mind in helping in wounded, and behaved with great gallantry throughout the action.

No. 4949.   Pte. CHASE AVIS.

When the Battalion assaulted the German trenches near High Wood on the night of 22nd-23rd July 1916, accompanied one of the assaulting parties as a runner and shortly afterwards returned to Battalion H.Q. with a message.   As soon as he had delivered his message he immediately volunteered to return to the firing line and, as a fact, made two more journeys. He had to work across open ground under heavy shell fire, and throughout the night he showed great coolness and gallantry.

No. 6433.   L.-Cpl. CORNELIUS BUTLER.

When the Battalion took over the front-line trenches near High Wood on the night of 20th-21st July 1916 this N.C.O. laid the telephone wire from the front-line trench to Battalion H.Q. under heavy shell fire, and twice had to go the full length of the line to relay wire and mend breaks caused by shell fire.

Again on the night of 22nd-23rd July he was in charge of a signal station in the front line when the Battalion assaulted the German trenches. Early in the night his lamp was broken and his line cut, but he remained in the open under heavy shell and machine-gun fire mending the breakages. He eventually got in touch with Battalion H.Q. by means of an electric torch. On both occasions he acted with the utmost coolness.

No. 8505.   L.-Sergt. BENJAMIN DAVIS.

On the night of 20th-21st July 1916, when the Battalion took over front-line trenches near High Wood, laid the telephone wire from the front-line trenches to Battalion H.Q. under heavy shell fire, and when the wire was broken by shells, went out and laid another wire. He acted throughout with great coolness.

No. 4826.   Pte. WILLIAM ROBINSON.

When the Battalion assaulted the German trenches on the night of 22nd-23rd July 1916, near High Wood, this soldier formed one of a party of bombers that went on the left flank of the attack and searched for an isolated enemy trench. The party having lost touch with the company on the right, he volunteered and went out alone to regain touch. Later in the night he became separated from his own party and joined with a party of the 4th Battn. Gordon Highlanders in a bombing attack on High Wood. Throughout he displayed great cheerfulness and disregard for danger.

No. 6042.   Cpl. NICHOLAS LOFT.

The company to which this N.C.O. belonged suffered heavy casualties on the night of 22nd-23rd July 1916, near High Wood, during the assault on the German trenches. By 3 a.m. on the 23rd inst. all the officers and senior N.C.O.'s were out of action. Cpl. Loft then took command of the company and continued to command it till it was relieved that evening. The company was in the front-line trenches during this time and under continuous fire. Cpl. Loft showed great coolness and considerable initiative and ability under trying circumstances.

No. 7501.   Pte. BERNARD MIRES.

When the Battalion assaulted the German trenches near High Wood on the night of 22nd-23rd July 1916 the enemy trench had been reached and Pte. Mires volunteered to go back to a signal station to report that our artillery fire was dropping short. To do this he had to pass over ground that was swept by a very heavy machine-gun fire—and he recrossed this ground after he had delivered his message. Throughout the engagement he showed exceptional coolness.

No. 7456.   Sergt. GEORGE FRANKLIN.

During the assault on the night of 22nd-23rd July 1916 was the only N.C.O. of a platoon that got into the German trench and remained there four hours, although the Germans were in the same trench on both flanks. He rendered the greatest assistance to the officer in command of the platoon in consolidating the trench under heavy shell fire, and did much work himself. He also made a barricade at the left end of the trench during an enemy bombing attack on that flank. His great coolness and steadiness throughout the action did much to give his men confidence.

No. 5593.   Pte. SAMUEL FIGG.

The platoon to which this soldier belonged lost touch with the O.C. company on the night of 22nd-23rd July 1916 near High Wood, and Pte. Figg went up to the enemy trench, that was being assaulted, under heavy machine-gun fire in search of him. He returned to our front-line trench to report and he was then sent to a platoon which had entered the enemy trench and was in need of reinforcements. This was a particularly dangerous task as he had to cross about 600 yards under very heavy machine-gun fire. Pte. Figg performed his duty cheerfully and well.

No. 10206.   Pte. HENRY TRAINER.

On the night of 22nd-23rd July 1916, near High Wood, when the Battalion assaulted the German trenches, was employed as a " runner " to one of the leading companies and repeatedly crossed and recrossed ground that was swept by a very heavy rifle and machine-gun fire. He showed great coolness and complete disregard for danger.

No. 4007.   L.-Cpl. WILLIAM RUTH.

In the absence of the platoon sergeant on the night of 22nd-28rd July 1916, near High Wood, during the Battalion's assault on the German trenches, performed his duties and rendered the greatest assistance to the officer commanding the platoon (who was with another party) by keeping him constantly informed as to the situation, and by leading a charge on a trench that was believed to be held by the enemy. Later he volunteered to take a patrol to get in touch with a platoon that was in the enemy trench and isolated. All this took place under very heavy fire. L.-Cpl. Ruth was cheerful during the action, and did much to keep up the spirits of the men.

No. 10236.   Pte. VICTOR WARBY.

Near High Wood on 21st July 1916 was with a sergeant on patrol duty in front of our lines. Two German snipers were located in a shell hole, Pte. Warby crawled round to the far side of the shell hole to ensure that the snipers should not escape, and then the sergeant threw a bomb and killed them. Throughout the operations at this time Pte. Warby displayed great coolness and gallantry under fire.

No. 38.   Sergt. GEORGE SIMMONDS.

At Longueval on 30th July 1916, when our trenches were subjected to a very heavy and continuous bombardment by the enemy's heavy artillery, and the company runners had become casualties, voluntarily performed their duties and, on at least four occasions, left the trench under very heavy shell fire in order to keep touch with the adjoining companies and Battalion H.Q. These journeys entailed very great personal risk, as he had to cross open ground in view of enemy snipers and under a heavy bombardment.

No. 10604.   L.-Cpl. ALFRED ROBSON.

On the night of 22nd-23rd July 1916, near High Wood, was one of a platoon that got into the German trenches and remained there four hours, although the Germans were in the same trench on both flanks.   He volunteered to take out the covering party in front of the trench.   This he did with great coolness and courage in spite of the heavy bombardment and machine-gun fire.

No. 6143.   Pte. JOHN LEARY.

Was one of a platoon that got into the German trenches during our assault on the night of 22nd-23rd July, and remained there four hours although the Germans were in the same trench on both flanks.   When all the N.C.O.'s, with one exception, had become casualties, he took command of the men in the right of the trench.   After he had consolidated the right flank he went out in front of the trench to find the covering party facing very heavy machine-gun fire, and he afterwards visited them on several other occasions.   His conduct throughout the action displayed great coolness and courage.

No. 9525.   Sergt. FREDERICK WILLIAM BODY.

Previous to the Battalion's assault on the German trenches near High Wood, went out in command of a reconnoitring patrol to gain information as to the enemy trenches.   He crept up through standing corn to within a few yards of the Germans. Having seen all they required the patrol shot at a German officer and then returned safely to our own lines.   The information that Sergt. Body brought back was most valuable and complete, and afterwards proved to be very accurate.

No. 8020.   C.S.M. JOHN STANLEY GLAZEBROOK.

When the Battalion took over the front-line trenches near High Wood on the night of 20th-21st July 1916, the relief had to take place under a very heavy German barrage.   C.S.M. Glazebrook displayed great coolness and resource in getting the company through the barrage, and by his conduct he undoubtedly saved many casualties.   This warrant officer, who for some months performed the duties of Regtl. Sergt.-

Major, showed considerable ability, capacity for hard work, and coolness under fire.

No. 6265.   Cpl. CHARLES THURLING.

On the night of 22nd-23rd July 1916, near High Wood, during an attack on the German trenches, was one of a bombing party sent to deal with a " strong point " on the east of the Wood.   When within about twenty yards of the "strong point" the officer in command of the party was wounded in the leg and unable to move.   Cpl. Thurling crawled round in search of the officer and, on finding him, dragged him back to a place where the wound could be dressed.   He displayed great bravery in doing this, as he was under direct fire from machine guns, and also heavy shell fire.   As soon as he had got the officer back he went forward and took charge of the bombing party.

Temp. Capt. CHARLES TUDOR BENNETT.

Was in command of one of the leading companies in the Battalion's assault on the German trenches near High Wood on the night of 22nd-23rd July 1916.   During the advance he was wounded in the stomach, and when men came to his assistance he ordered them to leave him and go on with the attack.

Capt. Bennett commanded a company for many months previous to this action, and always evinced great ability, capacity to command, and coolness in emergency.

No. 5310.   Cpl. ERNEST HOYLE.

On 11th September 1916, when the Battalion was in occupation of the front-line trenches in Leuze Wood, and the situation was involved and uncertain, volunteered to go out in daylight and reconnoitre.   He remained out for two hours, crawling about in the open, within view of the enemy and under constant fire.   The information he brought back relating to the position of the enemy was most useful.   A few days previous, on 4th September, when after the attack on Falfemont Farm and Wedge Wood the company was digging an advanced trench near Leuze Wood, Cpl. Hoyle set a fine example to his men under heavy shell fire.

No. 10619.   Pte. HERBERT THOMPSON.

During attacks on Wedge Wood and Falfemont Farm on 8rd and 4th September 1916, the Battalion was in the front system of trenches, with many dead and wounded men lying in front of them.   Pte. Thompson, under heavy machine-gun, rifle, and shell fire, went out to assist the wounded that could not be moved.   He dressed them, dug cover for them, and took out food and water.   His conduct was admirable, and he proved himself most useful in every way :   his skill in " first aid " undoubtedly enabled a man, whose leg was blown off, to be taken to the dressing station alive.

No. 10335.   Pte. JOHN CALLAGHAN.

On the afternoon of 29th August 1916, when the Battalion was in occupation of the front-line trenches south-west of Guillemont, the trenches of Pte. Callaghan's company were being heavily shelled, and the company was also suffering considerable casualties from our own shell fire.   Pte. Callaghan volunteered to carry back a message to Battalion H.Q., although at the time any movement was most dangerous. He carried back the message in very quick time across the open, and afterwards rejoined his company, although buried by a shell on the way.   This man distinguished himself by his coolness and courage on many other occasions.   During 28th and 29th August he brought many messages from an advanced trench to Company H.Q. under heavy fire.   On the morning of 29th August he volunteered to bring in wounded, and brought them in, although under fire at close range.   When the N.C.O.'s of his platoon became casualties he discharged the duties of an N.C.O. and set a splendid example to the other men.   This man was susbequently wounded.

No. 8759.   Sergt. ALBERT FRANCIS ROBINSON.

On 23rd September 1916, when the Battalion was in the line before Morval, the trench in which Battalion H.Q. was situated was subjected to heavy artillery fire, and practically destroyed.   The acting Regtl. Sergt.-Major was badly wounded and buried.   Sergt. Robinson rushed to him and dug him out,

at the risk of his own life.   He then, with another man, got a
stretcher and carried the Sergt.-Major up a sunken road to the
dressing station.   This road was at the time under a heavy
barrage.   This N.C.O. had already been awarded the D.C.M.
for gallantry.

No. 7564.   Acting-Cpl. WILLIAM FEAST.

Feast was conspicuous for good work and devotion to duty
throughout the period that the Battalion was engaged in the
operations on the Somme, and especially near High Wood
on 22nd-23rd July, at Longueval on 29th-30th July, at Falfemont Farm on 3rd-4th September, at Leuze Wood on
10th-11th September, and before Morval on 22nd-24th
September.   During these operations Cpl. Feast was in charge
of the Battalion " runners."   He took constant messages under
trying, and often very dangerous conditions.   He never
hesitated to go anywhere and displayed the greatest cheerfulness
on all occasions.   The example he set and the manner in which
he superintended the work of other runners facilitated to a
great degree the important and difficult work of getting messages
through in action.

PART IV

October 1916 *to March* 1917

No. 7435. Pte. H. HERBERT.

Near Festubert, on the afternoon of 20th December 1916, the enemy opened a systematic and very heavy trench mortar bombardment of our trenches. The O.C. company wished to get into communication with the artillery, but the telephone wire was cut. Pte. Herbert at once volunteered to carry the message to the next telephone. To do this he had to pass along a trench that was being bombarded. He successfully delivered his messages, although knocked over on more than one occasion and wounded. When Pte. Herbert volunteered to undertake this dangerous mission he knew that he was due to go to England in a few days' time on a month's special leave.

Temp. 2/Lieut. DONALD ALEXANDER BRETT.

The Battalion raided the German trenches at Givenchy-lez-La Bassée on 10th February 1917, when 2/Lieut. Brett was in command of one of the raiding parties. He led his party out of our trenches and took them to within about forty yards of the enemy front line. Finding that he was getting too close to our barrage, he halted his men and made them take cover. He himself calmly sat down in front of them and, with his watch in his hand, timed the lifting of the barrage. The moment it lifted he at once led his men forward again and gained all his objectives, bombing many dug-outs as he went. There is no doubt that his gallant and cool behaviour had a magnificent effect on the men during the assault, and his coolness in handling the party both during the assault and the withdrawal saved casualties.

No. 10176.   L.-Cpl. WILLIAM BLACKMAN.

On 10th February 1917, when the Battalion raided the German trenches at Givenchy-lez-La Bassée, was in command of a section of the raiding party.   He led his men with great skill and dash, setting a splendid example, bombing several dug-outs, killing many of the enemy, and taking seven prisoners single-handed.   He also entered dug-outs by himself to ensure that no live Germans were left there.

No. 7782.   Sergt. HORACE JEFFERY.

When the Battalion raided the German trenches at Givenchy-lez-La Bassée on 10th February 1917 was in command of the second wave of one of the raiding parties.   He led his party over the top, and was the first to reach the enemy trench. With the utmost coolness he stood on the parados of the enemy trench and directed his men as they worked along and cleared the German trenches.   He was twice wounded, but he remained on the top of the trench giving orders to his men.   He continued to do this until ordered to withdraw.   Throughout he set a magnificent example of cool initiative, and his personal gallantry had a great effect on the men.

No. 18105.   Pte. WALTER COLE.

In the raid of the Battalion on the German trenches at Givenchy-lez-La Bassée on 10th February 1917, with one other man attacked a party of six Germans who were in a strong position and were not prepared to surrender.   They successfully bombed the party, killing or capturing them all. This party of Germans threatened to stop communication between two of the raiding parties.

No. 7691.   Pte. WILLIAM THOMAS CAVE.

During the raid on the enemy trenches at Givenchy-lez-La Bassée on 10th February 1917, accompanied by one other man, found a party of six Germans who were in a strong position and not prepared to surrender.   He at once dashed forward with bombs and killed or captured them all.   This party of Germans threatened to stop communication between two of the raiding parties. His prompt action and personal gallantry prevented what might have caused a " hitch " in the attack. When the withdrawal was ordered he assisted a wounded man back to our lines.

No. 23332.   Pte. ALBERT PANNELL.

When the Battalion raided the enemy trenches at Givenchy-lez-La Bassée, on the 10th February 1917, dashed forward at the head of his party and cleared the way for the mining party, R.E., that was with them. He captured two of the enemy and bombed others that were barring the way. He undoubtedly greatly assisted our miners in getting to the enemy mine shafts quickly.

No. 7030.   Cpl. WILLIAM DAVID NICHOLSON.

During the raid on the enemy trenches at Givenchy-lez-La Bassée, on the 10th February 1917, was in command of a party of ten men whose duty it was to make a " stop " on the right of the raiding party. He bombed his way along the trench and made his " stop " at exactly the right place. He held on to this point until the whole raiding party had withdrawn. Throughout he set a fine example.

No. 7585.   L.-Cpl. ALBERT DIMMICK.

On 10th February 1917, when the Battalion raided the enemy trenches at Givenchy-lez-La Bassée, was in charge of a Lewis-gun team which accompanied the second wave of one of the raiding parties. After leaving our trenches he took up a position on the far lip of a crater, and shot a number of Germans that were advancing from the enemy support line to the front line. His presence of mind and initiative greatly helped the raiding party.

No. 4800.   Pte. NORMAN BASHFORD.

When the Battalion raided the German trenches at Givenchy-lez-La Bassée, on the 10th February 1917, was the first man of his party to enter the enemy trench. He quickly went along the enemy trench and killed two Germans. He then

s

came to some dug-outs which he bombed, killing several of the enemy and capturing two. He searched for, and procured from a dug-out, samples of rations and gas-helmets (special orders had been issued that these were to be procured if possible).

No. 4007.   Cpl. WILLIAM RUTH.

When the Battalion raided the enemy trenches at Givenchy-lez-La Bassée, on the 10th February 1917, was in command of the second wave of one of the raiding parties. He led his men over the top, bombed several dug-outs, and engaged a party of the enemy that was resisting : in this he personally accounted for several Germans. Throughout he showed a complete grasp of the situation and behaved in a gallant and cool manner. He was the last of his party to leave the enemy trenches, and, when he did so, he assisted a wounded N.C.O. back.

No. 23321.   Sergt. FREDERICK DONHOU.

During the raid on the German trenches at Givenchy-lez-La Bassée, on the 10th February 1917, was in command of the right raiding party which had the additional duties of guarding the right flank and covering a party of miners that were to attack the enemy mine shafts. He carried out his duties with the utmost dash and coolness, and handled his men with great judgment. During the raid an enemy bomb store exploded within a few feet of him, but, although temporarily dazed and slightly wounded, he carried on with his work and was the last to withdraw : he personally accounted for several Germans, including an officer. Previous to the raid it was his duty to reconnoitre the route over the craters he was to take, this he did with complete success.

Temp. Capt. WILLIAM RALPH COBB.

Throughout the raid on the enemy trenches at Givenchy-lez-La Bassée, on 10th February 1917, was in command of one of the raiding companies. Previous to the raid he trained his company with great thoroughness, going into the smallest

details and showing great ability and resource. He brought
his men to a pitch of the greatest keenness. When the raid
took place he handled his company with great judgment.
Owing to his careful timing of the start of the raiding parties
and his orders given for the withdrawal, his company suffered
few casualties. This officer was largely responsible for the
success of the raid.

On the 8th inst. when the Germans raided our trenches,
Capt. Cobb's company was in support, he immediately went
to the front line on his own initiative to ascertain the situation,
and then took command of the front line while the O.C. the
front line company went to Battalion H.Q. to report. This
officer had previously done much good work. He was wounded
at the second battle of Ypres in April 1915, and again at High
Wood in July 1916.

No. 4948.   Cpl. GEORGE ACKLAND.

During the raid on the enemy trenches at Givenchy-lez-
La Bassée, on 10th February 1917, was with a company holding
our front line when he rendered great assistance in getting in
wounded. The next morning it was reported that a dead
man was lying out in the craters. In broad daylight he went
out with a party of four men to bring the body in. This he
successfully did, although the Germans were watching him
from the other side of the craters. He then went out again
and, covered by a Lewis gun, fired at the Germans who had
been watching ; they quickly disappeared.

2/Lieut. BASIL CHARLES BARWELL JAGGER.

On 10th February 1917, during the Battalion's raid on
the enemy trenches at Givenchy-lez-La Bassée, was in command of the left raiding party and led his men with great
coolness, initiative and dash. In his particular area of the
enemy trenches there were several dug-outs. These he system-
atically cleared. Then he discovered there were three dug-
outs beyond his objective, and he actually went forward into
our barrage and dealt with them, killing some Germans and
bringing back others as prisoners. He took great pains in

the training of his men, and during the raid handled his men in a most cool and capable manner. During ordinary trench warfare he had proved himself a zealous officer, ready at all times to go anywhere and do anything.

No. 10619. Pte. HERBERT THOMPSON.

In the raid on the enemy trenches at Givenchy-lez-La Bassée, on the 10th February 1917, was in charge of a Lewis-gun team, whose duty it was to cover the advance of the left party. He was over the parapet the moment the order was given, and took his gun and party right up to our barrage. Here, with the utmost coolness, he fired his gun at all targets that presented themselves. The moment the barrage lifted he dashed forward and kept right up to the barrage, actually going into our barrage before it lifted from the enemy second line. Here he, with his Lewis gun, cleared two dug-outs. Throughout the raid he was always in evidence, showing an absolute disregard for danger, and taking his Lewis gun to the attack of any of the enemy he could see. He was a most prominent figure throughout, and set a magnificent example of complete fearlessness. On his return he found an officer of the Bde. M.G. Company, who had had a gun team put out of action ; he immediately volunteered to take the place of this team, although he was alone with his gun. Remained at this post by himself for quarter of an hour under heavy shell fire till relieved by a new M.G. team.

Pte. Thompson was also noted for good and gallant work on the Somme.

No. 8609. Sergt. WILLIAM EDWARD SWINYARD.

When the Battalion raided the enemy trenches at Givenchy-lez-La Bassée, on the 10th February 1917, accompanied one of the raiding parties and throughout led his men with great dash and gallantry, showing much ability and resource. He captured three Germans and destroyed a mine shaft and a dug-out. The splendid way his party worked was very largely due to his fine example, and the energy and enthusiasm he displayed when training the men for the raid.

No. 5520.   Sergt. CHARLIE SMITH.

On 10th February 1917, when the Battalion raided the enemy trenches at Givenchy-lez-La Bassée, was with the left raiding party. He led his men with the utmost dash and did much to encourage them by his own example. This party went rather too far and ran into our barrage. Sergt. Smith did much to assist his officer in reorganising the party and preventing casualties. He had on previous occasions done good work. He was wounded at High Wood in July 1916.

No. 15687.   Pte. SAMUEL FREDERICK CARLTON.

During the raid on the enemy trenches at Givenchy-lez-La Bassée, on 10th February 1917, was one of the first men to reach the enemy trench, and throughout behaved with the greatest gallantry and with complete disregard for his own personal safety. He did great work in clearing enemy dug-outs, and himself took several prisoners. There is no doubt that his fearless conduct inspired those who were near him. He had on other occasions shown himself to be a reliable man in an emergency.

No. 7709.   Cpl. WILLIAM BUDGEON.

On the 10th February 1917, when the Battalion raided the German trenches at Givenchy-lez-La Bassée, and the N.C.O. in command and the next senior N.C.O. of one of the raiding parties became casualties, Cpl. Budgeon at once took command of the party, reorganising his men when they got too close to our barrage, and then leading them even beyond the enemy support line. Several dug-outs were bombed, and there is no doubt that the party under command of this N.C.O. inflicted very heavy casualties on the enemy. Throughout he displayed fine courage and initiative and led his men with great dash. The party exactly carried out the task allotted to it, in spite of the loss of the senior N.C.O.'s. It penetrated further into the enemy lines than any other party in the raid, and inflicted more casualties on the enemy. The credit was due to Cpl. Budgeon, who also displayed great keenness when training for the raid.

No. 4648.   Pte. JOHN LAWRANCE.

During the raid on the German trenches at Givenchy-lez-La Bassée, on the 10th February 1917, was runner to the O.C. one of the raiding companies. When telephonic communication was broken, he took a message to Battalion H.Q. through the enemy barrage, which was then at its heaviest. Throughout the raid he behaved with great coolness and courage, always readily volunteering to carry any messages that were sent. He had several messages to take, and he never failed in the quick delivery of them.

No. 24326.   Pte. GEORGE DENNY.

On 10th February 1917 the Battalion raided the German trenches at Givenchy-lez-La Bassée. This soldier showed great dash and determination throughout the raid. He was always one of the leading men of his party, and personally killed several Germans with the bayonet, and bombed dug-outs. He set a great example of courage. He later assisted in bringing in the wounded.

No. 21085.   Pte. HARRY LORD.

On 10th February 1917, when the Battalion raided the German trenches at Givenchy-lez-La Bassée, showed great dash and determination throughout the raid. He was always one of the leading men of his party, and personally killed several Germans and bombed dug-outs. He set a great example of courage. He later assisted in bringing in the wounded.

No. 10613.   Pte. PHILLIP JOHN COOK.

During the raid on the 10th February 1917, at Givenchy-lez-La Bassée, was in charge of a Lewis gun. He behaved with great courage and coolness, and the quick and accurate manner in which he handled his gun caused many casualties among the Germans who were observed behind their front line. Later he rendered great assistance in getting in wounded.

No. 9264.   Sergt. ERNEST NOEL ROOTS.

Was conspicuous for devotion to duty and great zeal extending over a long period as Battalion Transport Sergeant.   This
N.C.O. came to France with the Battalion at the commencement of hostilities in August 1914.   A good horse-master, a
strict disciplinarian, and an untiring worker, he always took
the greatest pride in his work and produced most excellent
results.

2/Lieut. (Acting-Captain) JOHN FRANCIS BELLMAN.

Was noted for devotion to duty and good work extending over
a considerable period.   He joined the Battalion in December
1915.   He took command of a company at the end of July 1916
(after High Wood, 22nd-23rd July), and commanded it during
the remaining fighting on the Somme.   He was twice wounded,
but on each occasion remained at duty.   Capt. Bellman
always showed considerable zeal and ability, coupled with a
cheerful manner and great coolness in emergency.

No. 7811.   C.Q.M.S. THOMAS TAYLOR.

Was conspicuous for devotion to duty and good work extending over a long period.   He came to France with the Battalion
at the commencement of hostilities.   When the Battalion first
went to the Somme he was a platoon sergeant, but later acted
as C.S.M. and, as such, did extremely good work.   In October
1916 he was promoted C.Q.M.S., and always discharged his
duties in a zealous and able manner.

No. 9036.   Sergt. GEORGE LINES.

On 10th February 1917, when the Battalion raided the
enemy trenches at Givenchy-lez-La Bassée, being in command of one of the raiding parties, showed great enthusiasm
during the previous training and great determination in leading
the attack until he was wounded.   He instilled a splendid
spirit into his men, and his party did especially well during the
raid.   Sergt. Lines was two and a half years in France and
he always proved himself most reliable, resourceful and
courageous.   He died of wounds received on 10th February.

No. 9265.   Sergt. JAMES TOOMBS.

When the Battalion raided the German trenches at Givenchy-lez-La Bassée, on the 10th February 1917, was with one of the raiding parties and showed great courage and initiative.   He was killed by a shell after his return to our trenches.

Previously (during his two years in France) he had done very good work in the trenches, especially in patrol work.

PART V

April 1917

VIMY RIDGE

No. 4746. Sergt. GEORGE BRYDEN.

On 9th April 1917, when the Battalion took part in the attack on the Vimy Ridge, set a great example of coolness, gallantry and initiative throughout. He showed great energy in the after consolidation, and was always moving about encouraging his men and watching for any movement on the part of the enemy. He had previously done good work on the Somme.

No. 8691. Pte. ALFRED ELLIS.

When the Battalion took part in the attack on Vimy Ridge on 9th April 1917, showed great resource and vigour. He was employed as a sniper, and by constantly moving about by himself and on his own initiative, he was able to keep excellent observation on the movements of the enemy's infantry and artillery. The information he gained proved most useful.

2/Lieut. PHILLIPS BURNEY STERNDALE GYBBON-MONYPENNY.

On 9th April 1917, when the Battalion took part in the attack on the Vimy Ridge, showed great gallantry and resource. He had to form with his platoon an advanced post some 350 yards in front of the outpost line : this he successfully did, although under machine-gun fire. He set a fine example to his men.

This officer had previously done good work in trench warfare, leading patrols in a most fearless way and always showing keenness and energy.

No. 7585. L.-Cpl. ALBERT DIMMICK.

During the attack on Vimy Ridge, on the 9th April 1917, was in command of a Lewis-gun team. He handled his gun with great gallantry and coolness, and greatly harassed the enemy by his fire. He had previously been brought to the notice of the Divisional Commander for good work during the raid at Givenchy-lez-La Bassée.

No. 1215. Acting-Sergt. WILLIAM JOYCE.

On 9th April 1917, in the attack on Vimy Ridge, commanded his platoon with very great skill and initiative. By his judgment he saved many casualties when his platoon was under machine-gun fire, and set a fine example.

He did very good work during the fighting on the Somme.

No. 6253. Pte. ARTHUR NORMAN.

When the Battalion took part in the attack on Vimy Ridge, on 9th April 1917, did most valuable work as a company runner. He carried his messages under fire quickly and without hesitation, and was the means of important messages getting back to our artillery without delay.

No. 23025. Pte. JOSEPH OSBORNE.

During the attack on Vimy Ridge, on 9th April 1917, did valuable work as a platoon runner, keeping the platoon in constant touch with Company Headquarters. He showed great gallantry and coolness, and set a fine example to the other men.

No. 7095. L.-Cpl. JOHN BOTT.

On 9th April 1917, during the attack on Vimy Ridge, behaved with great courage and coolness, when in charge of a Lewis-gun team ; he was constantly ensuring that his gun was in good working order and looking out for any enemy movement of which he could take advantage. He had always proved himself a most reliable man under fire.

No. 5754.   C.S.M. WILLIAM HAIZELDEN.

Proved himself of the greatest assistance to his Company Commander in the attack on Vimy Ridge on the 9th April 1917.   When there was some danger of the company losing direction and the situation was difficult, he showed great resource and ability in reorganising the company.

He had been over two years in France, and had done much valuable work, particularly during the fighting on the Somme.

No. 5161.   Pte. JOHN FRYER.

On 9th April 1917, at Vimy Ridge, volunteered to perform the duties of platoon runner when two previous platoon runners had become casualties.   He showed great courage in carrying messages across the open under fire from machine guns and snipers.   Eventually he was wounded through both legs, but even then he reached his destination and delivered his message, although hardly able to walk.   He did good work during the fighting on the Somme.

No. 23253.   Pte. GEORGE GOULD.

Was in charge of a Lewis-gun team during the attack on Vimy Ridge on the 9th April 1917.   He handled his gun in a most daring and able manner, pushing his gun forward as opportunity offered, with utter disregard of danger.   At night he went forward to a very advanced post, and remained there, covering the party that was consolidating.

He did good work on 10th February 1917 when the Battalion raided at Givenchy-lez-La Bassée.

No. 5095.   Pte. ALFRED AUGUSTUS BARTRAM.

As company runner during the attack on Vimy Ridge on the 9th April 1917, carried many messages over the open, under heavy fire from shells, machine guns and snipers.   He delivered all his messages and constantly volunteered to carry them whenever required.   He did good work during the fighting on the Somme.

No. 14504.   Pte. JOSEPH PEACHEY.

On 9th April 1917, at Vimy Ridge, was No. 1 of a Lewis-gun team. He handled his gun with great ability and courage, and, by taking up a position on an exposed flank, inflicted many casualties on the retiring enemy.

He had previously done much good work.

No. 5003.   Pte. THOMAS FRANK JARRETT.

Was employed as a company runner at Vimy Ridge on the 9th April 1917, and carried many messages across the open under heavy fire from shells, machine guns and snipers. He worked unceasingly and almost without a rest.

He had previously done good work during the fighting on the Somme.

No. 59.   Pte. HOWARD VICTOR EVERETT.

At Vimy Ridge, on the 9th April 1917, was employed as a company runner and carried many messages under heavy fire from shells, machine guns and snipers. Throughout he displayed great courage and considerable resource.

He had previously done good work, notably when the Battalion raided the enemy trenches at Givenchy-lez-La Bassée.

No. 8075.   Cpl. FREDERICK MUNRO.

On 9th April 1917, during the attack on Vimy Ridge, led the men of his platoon with the greatest dash and determination, cheering them on and reorganising them whenever opportunity arose. Throughout the engagement he did most valuable work.

No. 23850.   L.-Cpl. FRED MOSELEY.

Early in the attack on Vimy Ridge, on 9th April 1917, was hit in the leg, but, with great pluck, went forward with the attack and remained at duty for over three hours. He only gave up when a second wound in the foot made it impossible for him to continue. His example had a most inspiring effect on the men of his platoon.

No. 6266.   Pte. Francis Chambers.
No. 4109.   Pte. Frederick Maskell.

During the attack on Vimy Ridge, on the 9th April 1917, were employed as company runners. They worked with untiring energy and almost without rest, carrying their messages often under heavy fire.

They had both been in France since the commencement of the war, and had done much good work.

No. 9995.   Acting-Sergt. Frederick Jupp.

Whilst in charge of a bombing section of a platoon, during the attack on Vimy Ridge on the 9th April 1917, behaved throughout with great coolness, and set a fine example of courage to those under him.   He showed considerable initiative, sending out constant patrols to ascertain the situation.

He had twice been wounded in the campaign, and had been in France since August 1914.

No. 5071.   Sergt. Peter Mackenzie.

Was platoon sergeant during the attack on Vimy Ridge on the 9th April 1917.   Although wounded early in the engagement, he remained at duty and set a fine example of courage. On reaching the enemy trench he showed much resource in organising his platoon.   He twice volunteered for patrol work when volunteers were called for.

He had been at the front over two years, and had been twice wounded.

No. 9071.   Acting-Cpl. Edmund Tumber.

On 9th April 1917, during the attack on Vimy Ridge, was in charge of bombers who had to take an advanced trench. He led his men with great coolness and courage, holding the trench until reinforced.

He previously did good work when in charge of Battalion bombers.

No. 4060. Cpl. WILLIAM RUSSELL.

At Vimy Ridge, on the 9th April 1917, showed considerable coolness and ability when in command of a section. When his platoon sergeant was wounded, he took his place and carried out his work in an excellent manner.

No. 4948. Cpl. GEORGE ACKLAND.

During the attack on Vimy Ridge, on the 9th April 1917, was in charge of the company Lewis guns, and showed great capability in the handling of the guns. He behaved with great courage, and set a fine example.

He had been in France for two and a half years, and had been previously noted by the Division for his good work.

No. 10350. Cpl. THOMAS FORAN.

Did excellent work during the assault on the enemy trenches at Vimy Ridge on 9th April 1917, behaving with great courage and resource. Later he showed great coolness when in charge of an advanced post that was being shelled.

He had previously done good work, especially during the fighting on the Somme.

No. 9190. Cpl. WILLIAM UINGS.
No. 10114. L.-Cpl. THOMAS HAYNES.
No. 23272. L.-Cpl. WILLIAM WISE.

On 9th April 1917, when the Battalion took part in the attack on Vimy Ridge, these N.C.O.'s acted with great coolness and courage. When those senior to them became casualties, or were not within reach, they showed considerable initiative and readiness to act on their own responsibilities.

They had all previously done good work in this campaign.

No. 428. Cpl. HARRY WICKHAM.

During the attack on Vimy Ridge did excellent work, showing much ability and courage in advancing on an isolated trench, and later when in command of his platoon.

He had previously done good work, especially during the fighting on the Somme.

No. 2102.   L.-Cpl. ROBERT BRAZIER.

L.-Cpl. Brazier performed valuable work throughout the attack on Vimy Ridge, especially in the advance on isolated trenches beyond Counts Wood and the cross-roads at Goulot Wood. He was sent back to report, and gave valuable information. Subsequently he showed ability and resource when in command of a platoon that was occupying scattered posts.

No. 3031.   Pte. CHARLES TIDD.

In the attack on Vimy Ridge, on 9th April 1917, was employed as a company runner. He did excellent work and showed great courage, carrying messages across open country under fire. On one occasion he was slightly wounded and knocked down by a shell, but carried straight on.

No. 5001.   Pte. PERCY HAMMOND.

On 9th April 1917, during the attack on Vimy Ridge, was employed as a company runner. He did excellent work and showed great courage, carrying messages across open country under fire.

He had previously done good work in the campaign.

No. 6292.   Pte. EDWARD ELEY.

Was employed as a company runner in the attack on Vimy Ridge, and showed great courage in carrying messages across open country under fire. He was twice hit, but never hesitated to go on.

He had previously done good work in the campaign.

Captain WILLIAM WILBERFORCE.

In the attack on Vimy Ridge, on the 9th April 1917, led his company with great judgment. He showed great resource and skill in the handling of his men. He gained all his objectives, and by attacking from a flank some enemy guns, which were still in action, materially assisted the advance of the troops on either side.

2/Lieut. (Acting-Capt.) JOHN FRANCIS BELLMAN.

On the 9th April 1917, at Vimy Ridge, led his company with great coolness and judgment. He gained all his objectives and showed great resource and initiative in the handling of his company. This officer had done much good work, both in trench warfare and in the battle of the Somme in 1916, when commanding a company. He had been twice wounded, but remained at duty on both occasions.

No. 10396.   Pte. JAMES MILES.

On the night of 9th-10th April 1917 was runner and guide to a ration party proceeding to the front line. This party came under shell fire, and he showed great courage in maintaining touch between the front and rear of the party and in assisting to readjust the loads of pack animals which had been wounded.

He had on many occasions done good work in this Battalion since the commencement of the campaign.

No. 9780.   Cpl. CHARLES JOHN CUTTER.

On the night of 9th-10th April 1917 was, with the Transport Officer, taking a convoy of pack animals with rations to the front line. The party came under shell fire, and four horses were hit, one of them being unable to move. Cpl. Cutter went to this horse through a barrage, removed the rations from it and carried them (a total amount of 60 men's rations) to safety. He then returned to the animal, shot it, and brought back all the saddlery. He behaved with the greatest coolness. He had been out since the commencement of the war, and had done much good work.

No. 8971.   Sergt. ARTHUR SMITH.

On 9th April 1917 was acting C.S.M., for the attack on Vimy Ridge, of an assaulting company. During the advance he displayed great gallantry and coolness, and did much to keep the company together. When the objectives were captured he was of the greatest assistance to his Company Commander in reorganising the company. He came to France at the commencement of the campaign, and had been wounded three times.

No. 7355.   Sergt. GEORGE WILLIAM TWEEDDALE.

During the attack on Vimy Ridge did extremely good work, showing much courage when employed as a stretcher-bearer, and when collecting wounded under fire.

For some time he had been N.C.O. in charge of stretcher-bearers in the line. He had been with the Battalion since the commencement of the war and had rendered most valuable services in many engagements.

No. 6325.   Pte. THOMAS GARRETT.

Was employed as a stretcher-bearer in the attack on Vimy Ridge, and did most excellent work carrying wounded under fire. He was leader of a squad which carried a stretcher over exposed ground where he knew a previous party had been heavily fired on. He had been with the Battalion since September 1914, and had done much good work in numerous engagements.

No. 7482.   Pte. SAMUEL AUSTEN.

On 9th April 1917, at Vimy Ridge, was employed as a stretcher-bearer, and did most excellent work carrying wounded under fire. He showed great courage throughout. He had been with the Battalion since October 1914, and had done much good work in numerous engagements.

No. 7767.   Pte. HERBERT JOHN REEVES.

At Vimy Ridge was employed as dressing orderly to the Medical Officer and, as such, did most excellent work, showing an utter disregard for danger. He had been with the Battalion since the commencement of the war, had been through many engagements, and had always behaved in a most cool and courageous manner.

T

No. 8759.   Sergt. ALBERT FRANCIS ROBINSON.

Behaved with the greatest gallantry and coolness on 9th April 1917 at Vimy Ridge, in establishing and maintaining communication. Throughout he displayed a complete disregard for danger. This N.C.O. had already been awarded the D.C.M. for gallantry in May 1915, and was again recommended for his admirable conduct during the fighting on the Somme.

No. 7564.   Cpl. WILLIAM FEAST.

Was in charge of the Battalion runners in the attack on Vimy Ridge. He showed great coolness under fire and disregard for danger, and organised the runners in an excellent manner. He was at all times willing to do any work that was required, and throughout rendered valuable services. He had already been granted the Military Medal for previous good work.

No. 8092.   L.-Cpl. JAMES JOSEPH HARRIS.

During the attack on Vimy Ridge rendered great assistance, both in establishing and maintaining telephonic communication to the companies. He repaired telephone lines on two occasions under heavy shell fire.

He had been out in France since 25th August 1914, had never been away from the Regiment, and had always done fine work.

No. 8759.   Sergt. ALBERT FRANCIS ROBINSON.

When in action near La Chaudiere, on 24th April 1917, the Battalion held the front line as an outpost line, without any regular system of trenches. Anyone going from Battalion H.Q. to the front line had to cross ground that was under complete observation by the enemy and was being constantly shelled, sniped, and swept by machine-gun fire. During the day Sergt. Robinson on three occasions voluntarily crossed this area to lay or repair telephone wires, thus enabling the front companies to keep communication with Battalion H.Q. This N.C.O. was awarded the D.C.M. for gallantry early n the war. He was particularly noticed for his courage and devotion to duty on the Somme, and again on 9th April 1917, when the Battalion took part in the capture of Vimy Ridge.

No. 5003.   Pte. THOMAS FRANK JARRETT.

Showed conspicuous gallantry on 24th April 1917, when the Battalion was in action holding the front line near La Chaudiere. The Battalion was holding the front line as an outpost line without any regular system of trenches. Anyone going from Battalion H.Q. to the front line had to cross ground that was under complete observation by the enemy, and was being constantly shelled, sniped, and swept by machine-gun fire. Pte. Jarrett was employed as a runner to one of the companies holding the front line. On several occasions by day and night he brought messages from his company to Battalion. H.Q. In the evening the enemy suddenly opened a heavy barrage on the front-line trenches, when he brought back a most clear and accurate account of the situation. He showed complete disregard for danger, and rendered most valuable services under difficult conditions in keeping his company in touch with Battalion H.Q. He had already been specially noted for his good work on 9th April 1917, when the Battalion took part in the capture of Vimy Ridge.

Lieut. and Q.M. ROBERT THORNE.

Was Q.M. to the Battalion from December 1916 and had, at all times, displayed exceptional zeal and ability, and had regularly brought up rations to the Battalion under fire. His work was particularly noticeable at Vimy on 9th April and at Fresnoy in May, when the weather conditions and heavy shelling made his task a very difficult and dangerous one.

2/Lieut. PHILLIPS BURNEY STERNDALE GYBBON-MONYPENNY.

Was conspicuous for devotion to duty and great zeal over a long period. He had led several successful patrols, and had distinguished himself on several occasions when the Battalion was in action by the bold and skilful handling of his platoon.

2/Lieut. JOHN DUDLEY WARD.

As a platoon commander for a long period, always showed great zeal and devotion to duty. He set an excellent example to all ranks by the skilful and courageous handling of his platoon at all times and by his cheerful manner under shell fire.

No. 4911. Sergt. HARRY MARSH.

Was specially noted for courage and devotion to duty over a long period (three years). Through his *sang-froid* and contempt for danger, he, as a platoon sergeant and acting C.S.M., had never failed to inspire the men under him with complete confidence, and to set them an excellent example.

No. 5003. Pte. THOMAS FRANK JARRETT.

Performed continuous good work, showing great devotion to duty and courage. As company runner throughout the Battle of the Somme and the Battle of Vimy Ridge and the ensuing combats near La Coulotte and Fresnoy, he did most valuable work.

No. 10337. Cpl. C. HARRIS.
No. 6266. Pte. FRANCIS CHAMBERS.

Were both conspicuous for continuous good work and devotion to duty.

PART VI

THE BATTLE OF THE MENIN ROAD
AND ITALY

2/Lieut. HARRY ALBERT GRAY.

As leader of the assaulting wave on the left of the Battalion, showed great courage and resource in maintaining direction. Later when his company commander became a casualty he reorganised the company, which had lost more than 60 per cent. of its strength. Then with the greatest coolness and energy he beat off several minor attacks. He remained in a shallow trench with his men, regardless of personal danger, during a particularly heavy bombardment and reorganised them after it.

The good work done by this company was mainly due to his example.

Temp. Capt. OLIVIER ARNAUD JAMES MURISET (R.A.M.C.).

During the attack N. of the Ypres-Menin Road worked continuously, under extremely heavy shelling, from the 3rd October until after relief on the 5th-6th and refused to leave until he had disposed of every man and had ascertained, as far as possible, that all wounded were in.

His aid post was under constant shell fire.

2/Lieut. CAMPBELL SEYMOUR MILFORD.

Led his company with conspicuous success and did valuable work throughout. When the front line was counter-attacked, he led his company to reinforce through a heavy barrage and succeeded in reorganising his portion of the front line, which was on a threatened flank.

Lieut. JAMES LAWRENCE CATHCART SUTHERLAND.

Preceding the attack N. of the Ypres-Menin Road, was sent on three days ahead to reconnoitre. This he did with conspicuous success, gaining very valuable information of the habits of the enemy, though the sector was constantly under violent shell fire.

As signalling officer during and after the attack on the 4th October, he maintained communication with great success under extreme difficulties. He had on all occasions shown great zeal and exceptional courage in the performance of his duties.

2/Lieut. DE SYMMONS HARRY LEWIS-BARNED.

As Battalion Lewis Gun Officer displayed untiring energy throughout the attack N. of the Ypres-Menin Road on 3rd October. He maintained the supply of Lewis guns in the line. On one occasion he made a valuable reconnaissance of a threatened flank, and placed and maintained Lewis guns ready to deal with a threatened counter-attack at a dangerous point.

This officer did extremely well on previous occasions and had been wounded at Vimy Ridge, where he led his platoon with great success.

No. 7032. Cpl. WILLIAM DAVID NICHOLSON.

On the morning of 4th October, during the attack N. of the Ypres-Menin Road, when his platoon' commander and platoon sergeant had become casualties, took over the platoon and led it with great gallantry, setting a splendid example. He accounted for twelve of the enemy while leading his platoon.

Later he did valuable work organising a supply of S.A.A. and water and bringing it up himself.

Eventually, as senior N.C.O. of his company, he carried out the duties of C.S.M., and finally, when his company commander was killed, took over the company and brought it out of action.

He was conspicuous for gallantry during a raid in February 1917.

No. 7550.   Sergt. FREDERICK ASHBY.

Was conspicuous for courage and good leadership before, and during, the attack N. of the Ypres-Menin Road on the 4th October.

On the 3rd October he brought up his platoon on his own initiative from support with great promptitude, and was of great assistance in beating off an enemy attack.

He was conspicuous for the excellent control of fire of his platoon.

During the attack he led his platoon with great coolness and courage in face of a heavy machine-gun fire, constantly passing up and down encouraging his men until he was wounded.   He set a splendid example throughout.

No. 7811.   C.S.M. THOMAS TAYLOR.

Throughout the fighting N. of the Ypres-Menin Road, on the 3rd-4th-5th October, showed great courage and resource.

On four occasions he passed through a heavy barrage to organise and lead up S.A.A., rations and water to the men in front, who were being attacked.

He set a splendid example and did most valuable work.

He had served with the Battalion since its landing in France and was mentioned in dispatches in 1916.

No. 5017.   Pte. EDWARD CAHILL.

During the fighting N. of the Ypres-Menin Road, on the 3rd-4th-5th October, was noted for conspicuous gallantry and devotion to duty.

On three occasions he took messages of great importance through an unprecedented barrage, and returned with the receipts showing great skill and bravery.   This man had always displayed great bravery and had done very valuable work.

No. 10358.   Cpl. FREDERICK HART.

Evinced great dash and bravery during the attack on 4th October.   After all other section commanders had become casualties and the section depleted through severe losses, he succeeded in reorganising them and establishing control. He also did excellent work in consolidation and maintaining the positions won.

No. 7718. Cpl. THOMAS CHARLES SMITH.

During the fighting N. of the Ypres-Menin Road, on the 3rd, 4th and 5th October, this N.C.O.'s section was in a trench which was being continually bombarded.

Though his section suffered severely he kept up the men's spirits by his example, placing them as far as possible in safety, while he himself remained looking out. Later during the attack he did valuable work, especially in reorganising the men and starting them consolidating.

No. 8505. L.-Sergt. BENJAMIN DAVIS.

Throughout the attack immediately N. of the Ypres-Menin Road, on the 3rd-4th-5th October, showed most conspicuous courage and devotion to duty as signalling sergeant. On four separate occasions he reset the signal lamp near Battalion Headquarters, which had been displayed by the continuous and very heavy barrage, and on three occasions he went out on the line himself, always under heavy shell fire, and mended it.

This N.C.O. came to France with the Battalion in 1914 and had never failed to carry out his important duties, regardless of personal danger. He set a splendid example to all. He was specially noted previously for his gallantry on the night of 20th-21st July 1916 in High Wood.

No. 10337. Cpl. CHARLES HARRIS.

After leading his platoon through a heavy barrage, re-organised it with the greatest coolness under heavy machine-gun fire. He collected several men and under machine-gun fire consolidated a position on a threatened flank.

Cpl. Harris had been previously noted for good work in the field.

No. 240926.   Cpl. Frederick Britton.

During the attack N. of the Ypres-Menin Road, on the 4th-5th October, was specially noted for exemplary conduct and great courage. He showed great initiative, especially during consolidation, and set a splendid example throughout the operation.

No. 655.   Acting-Cpl. Thomas Chesson.

Performed exceptionally good work during the attack N. of the Ypres-Menin Road on the 3rd-4th October. He went out by himself and on his own initiative, under heavy machine-gun fire, and regained touch, which had been temporarily lost, with the troops on the flank.

No. 1325.   Pte. J. P. Miles.

When all the company runners had become casualties, during the attack N. of the Ypres-Menin Road on the 3rd-4th-5th October, acted as a company runner and did most valuable work carrying reports and guiding up water and S.A.A. parties under heavy shell fire.

No. 8832.   L.-Cpl. George Vaughan.

As No. 1 of a Lewis-gun section during the fighting N. of the Ypres-Menin Road, on the 4th and 5th October, took charge of, and reorganised, his section when his section commander became a casualty. Later he took charge of three Lewis guns and kept them in action throughout the operation.

No. 8740.   Pte. Tom White.

Was given the very important duty of bringing up Lewis guns from Brigade H.Q. through an extremely heavy and deep barrage. This he succeeded in doing.

He was granted the Military Medal in 1916 for his splendid work as Battalion runner for two years.

No. 7545.   Pte. Edward Waghorn.
No. 24337.   Pte. Victor May.

In addition to their duties as Battalion runners, which they carried out under most trying circumstances with great zeal and bravery, these men carried out the important duty of leading up a water party through a heavy barrage and across very difficult country. They succeeded in getting every tin up, though it entailed their returning to the rear of the party to lead up stragglers and carry tins themselves. These men had been runners for a long time and had always shown conspicuous zeal and gallantry.

No. 5824. Pte. GEORGE HARRIS.
No. 21078. Pte. HENRY FISK.

In addition to their work as Battalion runners, which they performed with cheerful bravery, these two men did especial work in leading up reinforcements through a heavy barrage with great skill and bravery. They had been Battalion runners for a long time and had always done valuable work and were entirely reliable.

No. 3219. Pte. EDGAR MANNING.
No. 5142. Pte. EDWARD MEALING.

Soon after the attack, in addition to their ordinary duties as Battalion runners, which they carried out with great coolness and gallantry, carried out a valuable reconnaissance of our front line and brought back a valuable report.

They had been Battalion runners for a long time and had never failed.

No. 11229. Pte. ALFRED ARUNDALL.

Was one of a mopping-up party in the attack on the 4th October N. of Ypres-Menin Road, and showed great energy and set a splendid example, accounting for seven of the enemy almost at once.

Later, finding the sole survivor of a Lewis-gun section working his gun, he attached himself to him and did valuable work filling magazines, which were eventually emptied into a counter-attack.

No. 241799. Pte. A. MORING.

As No. 1 of a Lewis-gun section did exceptionally good work preventing the enemy from reaching our trenches on

3rd October. Later, during the attack on the 4th October, he displayed great devotion to duty and courage when all his section had become casualties, keeping his gun in action by himself and doing great execution.

No. 4767. Pte. G. B. STEWART.

Showed conspicuous courage, as company runner, when all other company runners had become casualties. He did very valuable work, and on one occasion crossed the Ypres-Menin Road to ascertain the situation of the troops on our flank. He brought back a correct report.

No. 8300. Cpl. THOMAS EDWARD TURNER.

Was a signalling corporal during the fighting on the 4th and 5th October N. of the Ypres-Menin Road. He went out before Zero for three hours on Brigade lines under a very heavy barrage and endeavoured to mend the line, which was cut by shell fire as soon as mended. On two occasions he tried to lay a line back to Brigade H.Q. under heavy shell fire.

He had served with the Battalion since it landed in 1914, and had at all times displayed extraordinary zeal and complete contempt for danger in the execution of his duty.

No. 7482. Pte. SAMUEL AUSTEN.
No. 6325. Pte. GEORGE GARRETT.
No. 179.   Pte. ALBERT SAUNDERS.
No. 4978. Pte. JOHN LIDBURY.

Worked continuously night and day collecting wounded under extremely heavy shell fire, and no amount of shelling prevented them from carrying them back to the aid post, to which they made innumerable journeys.

The diligence of their work undoubtedly saved the lives of many. They got the cases under cover quickly, and applied dressings in such an excellent manner, that in many cases no further dressing was required before sending cases back to the advanced dressing station.

Pte. Austen had been previously noted for good work on Vimy Ridge, and all these men had done splendid work in the past.

No. 11808.   L.-Cpl. REGINALD SMART.

After the objective had been gained during the attack on 4th October, and the whole of his team had been killed or wounded unaided, made very effective use of his Lewis gun in beating off a counter-attack.

He succeeded in maintaining a heavy fire on the enemy by working incessantly, during the short intervals of respite, in refilling his magazines.

No. 5003.   Pte. THOMAS FRANK JARRETT.

During the fighting N. of the Ypres-Menin Road on the 3rd-4th and 5th October, when his company had suffered many casualties and he was the only runner left, did most valuable work, keeping his company commander in touch with the flanks and B.H.Q.   Every journey he made was over ground swept by machine-gun fire or under very heavy shell fire.

He had been specially conspicuous for good work on 9th April 1917 at Vimy, and on 24th April at La Chaudiere.

No. 10199.   Pte. FRANK LEONARD PASSEY.

After the corporal and remainder of the team had become casualties, took charge of the Lewis gun and greatly helped in successfully beating off counter-attacks and maintaining positions won.

No. 6292.   Pte. EDWARD ELLEY.

As company runner made many journeys, with messages and as guide, through constant shelling and machine-gun fire.

He had been previously noted for gallant work on 9th April 1917.

No. 3184.   Pte. P. BROUGHTON.

Was conspicuous for his courage in keeping his Lewis gun in action for twenty-four hours after all the section had become casualties.   He filled his own magazines and was instrumental in repelling several counter-attacks.

No. 17935.   Pte. ARTHUR WILLIAM BAILEY.

As Battalion signaller during the fighting N. of the Ypres-Menin Road, on the 4th-5th October 1917, made frequent attempts to re-establish communication with the Brigade under very heavy shell fire.   He had done very gallant work on several previous occasions, and was regardless of danger.

No. 957.   L.-Cpl. JAMES GLEN.

During the attack on the morning of 4th October 1917, N. of the Ypres-Menin Road, showed conspicuous courage. Using his own initiative, he got to the front with the Lewis gun of his section, and with one man—all the remainder had become casualties—did great execution among the enemy counter-attacking.

No. 17142.   Pte. V. LEES.
No. 12840.   Pte. FREDERICK ASHLEY.

As assistant stretcher-bearers did most valuable work, showing always an unhesitating devotion to duty, and gallantry under continual shell fire.   They made many journeys through shelled areas, and worked night and day.

No. 9019.   Pte. EDWARD HENRY LUFF.
No. 21076.   Pte. GEORGE DOE.

As bearers did particularly good work—they set up a small post in a " pillbox " near the front line, in which they collected many wounded.   In this way they were able to relieve the pressure of evacuation from the Aid Post.   Many lives were undoubtedly saved in this way; for wounded were got under cover and kept warm until they could be evacuated. The wounds of the cases collected by them were frequently dressed during their stay at this place.   These two bearers also made frequent journeys through very heavy fire back to the Aid Post with wounded.

No. 4746. Sergt. G. BRYDON.

The very gallant conduct of this N.C.O. in assisting to repel an enemy raid, while he was carrying out a reconnaissance of the trenches to be occupied by his company before the attack N. of the Ypres-Menin Road on 4th October 1917, was brought to notice by the O.C. 9th Yorks and Lancs. Regt.

No. 498. L.-Cpl. D. NEWMAN.
No. 17746. Pte. R. W. BECKETT.

During an attack made by the enemy on the morning preceding our offensive N. of the Ypres-Menin Road, on the 4th October, which was successfully beaten off, these two men showed great courage. Had the enemy been able to secure identifications the result would have been serious.

Lieut. GEOFFREY JOEL JOEL.

Repelled two determined attacks made by the enemy upon our trenches N. of the Ypres-Menin Road on 3rd October 1917. After beating off one attack he brought up the reserve platoon of his company, borrowed a platoon from another company, and reorganised the line before the enemy delivered his second attack, which followed half an hour after the first one, and which he was equally successful in beating off.

2/Lieut. (Acting-Capt.) ROBERT BROWN.
No. 6397. Pte. JOHN LANG.
No. 7114. Pte. A. W. RUSSELL.
No. 5754. C.S.M. WILLIAM HAZELDEN.

Were all particularly noted at this period for great devotion to duty and for valuable fighting services.

No. 5345. R.S.M. ALFRED REYNOLDS.

Was conspicuous for continuous good service as C.S.M. and R.Q.M.S. and R.S.M. since October 1914. His unfailing readiness in difficult situations had been continually noted.

No. 8300. Cpl. JAMES TURNER.

As signalling corporal since August 1914, had been in every action in which the Battalion had taken part, and his services in keeping communication had been invaluable.

LIEUT. J. L. C. SUTHERLAND.

Was conspicuous for general good services and devotion to duty as Battalion signalling officer.

2/Lieut. (Acting-Capt.) H. P. WINN.

Showed great gallantry near the Ypres-Menin Road on 26th October 1917. Three times buried, and eventually being the only officer remaining with the front line of three companies, he reorganised the shattered line and beat off counter-attacks.

Lieut. DE S. H. LEWIS-BARNED.

Near the Menin Road on 26th October 1917, when all other officers had become casualties, was sent out to take command of the line. He reorganised the line successfully, both on the Battalion Front and on a portion of the 7th Division Front.

No. 4960. L.-Cpl. S. SEARS.

By his fine example and his masterly control of fire on the Menin Road, on 26th October 1917, accounted for large numbers of the enemy. He also volunteered to carry a message through a heavy enemy barrage to Battalion H.Q.

No. 10576. Pte. BARTON. ⎫ These men were conspicuous
No. 10094. Pte. WILLIAMS. ⎬ for good work and devotion
No. 17171. Pte. BRIDGE. ⎭ to duty.

2/Lieut. (Acting-Capt.) FRANK CORKE.

Made two invaluable reconnaissances of the ground, previous to the Battalion going into the line on the Menin Road on 3rd and 25th October 1917. The information obtained by him as to the habits of the enemy and his barrage areas, enabled the Battalion to go into, and come out of, the line with very few casualties, and materially assisted in the success of operations.

No. 5820.   Pte. C. COOPER.

Was conspicuous for continuous good work and devotion to duty.

2/Lieut. FRANK CORKE.

Was particularly noted for conspicuous devotion to duty and skill in reconnaissance.

No. 5084.   Cpl. (L.-Sergt.) ARTHUR LAFFLING.

Was noted for conspicuous and devoted good work during the campaign during three years.

No. 4975.   Pte. JOHN LIDBURY.

Was specially noted for general good work, particularly in actions on Menin Road in October and November 1917.

2/Lieut. (Acting-Capt.) ROBERT BROWN.

Performed continuous good service in the Field during the past three years.

Capt. (Acting-Major) WILLIAM WILBERFORCE.

Performed continuous good service.

No. 5345.   R.S.M. ALFRED REYNOLDS.

Was noted for continual good work during the past three years.

No. 21078.   Pte. HENRY R. FISK,
No. 23253.   Cpl. GEORGE GOULD,   were all noted
No. 10199.   Pte. FRANK LEONARD PASSEY,   for continuous
No. 17935.   Pte. ARTHUR WILLIAM BAILEY, good work and
No. 5142.   Pte. EDWARD MEALING,   devotion to duty.
No. 7114.   Pte. A. W. RUSSELL,

No. 5597.　Pte. J. READING.

On 22nd February 1918, the front line N.E. of Spresiano being shelled, two men were buried and had their legs taken off by the collapse of a shelled dug-out.　Pte. Reading, during the continued shelling dug out one man alive, applied first aid and put him in a place of safety, thereby undoubtedly saving this man's life.　He then returned to the dug-out and recovered the body of the second man ; severe shelling was going on all this time.

PART VII

June to July 1918

NIEPPE FOREST

No. 2073.   Sergt. HENRY JAMES HIRSHFIELD.

During the operations on the 28th, 29th and 30th June 1918, showed extraordinary courage, leading his men forward in the attack. Rushing forward, he attacked nests of the enemy, many of whom he killed. When the objective was reached he volunteered to go forward and give covering fire and to assist in destroying the bridges. This was successfully carried out despite heavy machine-gun fire. Throughout the operation he showed great gallantry and set a magnificent example to his men.

No. 7811.   C.S.M. THOMAS ROBERT TAYLOR.

During the operations on 28th, 29th and 30th June 1918, displayed the utmost dash and gallantry, himself killing many of the enemy, and by his organising abilities, general cheerfulness and complete disregard of danger greatly assisted his O.C. Company to bring his company to its final objective. When the first objective was reached he went forward and took charge of the operation of destroying the bridges, which was successfully accomplished, although under heavy fire. When all the officers of the company had become casualties he was of great assistance in reorganising the company.

No. 20134.   L.-Cpl. HENRY TAYLOR.

During the attack on 28th, 29th and 30th June 1918, when the left flank of the line was exposed, on his own initiative rushed forward with a Lewis gun and put out of action a number of the enemy. Eventually he was wounded.

No. 23271.   L.-Cpl. WILLIAM PIGGOTT.

When the objective was reached during the operations on the 28th, 29th and 30th June 1918, immediately crossed the canal, whilst our own barrage was down, and cleared the enemy trench for a distance of 300 yards.   Although four of his Lewis-gun team had become casualties, he, with the remaining man, continued to keep the gun in action, so keeping the enemy fire down.   He behaved splendidly throughout the operation.

No. 15150.   Pte. CHARLES ROBINSON.

During the operations on the 28th-30th June 1918, went forward with his N.C.O. to clear an advanced enemy trench beyond the canal, when the rest of his section had become casualties.   Later he went to the rear, through the enemy barrage and machine-gun fire, and brought up magazines to the advanced Lewis guns.

No. 4978.   Pte. JOHN LIDBURY.
No. 179.   Pte. ALBERT SAUNDERS.

As company stretcher-bearers during the operations of the 28th-30th June 1918, worked throughout the operations with complete disregard for danger and, although under heavy enemy shell and machine-gun fire, continued to dress wounds and carry wounded to the R.A.P.

No. 19387.   Pte. ALFRED GEORGE HEWITT.

During the advance on the 28th-30th June 1918, showed great courage, killing several of the enemy.   When his platoon was consolidating, he went forward into the long grass and killed a number of enemy snipers, thus enabling the platoon to consolidate without loss.

No. 31070.   Pte. ALBERT EDWARD BISHOP.

During the operations on the 28th-30th June 1918, showed great dash and courage.   When the objective had been reached he volunteered to go forward and destroy the bridges. He acted as covering party while they were being destroyed : during the whole operation he was under heavy rifle and machine-gun fire.

No. 20207.   Pte. JOHN ALFRED BROOKS.

In an attack on a strong point during the operations of the 28th-30th June 1918, was first man there. He killed several of the enemy single-handed, and showed great bravery and coolness throughout the operation.

No. 28333.   Pte. HARRY GORDON BUNKER.

After a Lewis-gun team had been knocked out during the operation on the 28th-30th June 1918, although he did not know much about the gun, took charge and gave covering fire to his platoon whilst they dug in, remaining at his post until relieved at night.

No. 8505.   L.-Sergt. BENJAMIN DAVIS.

Did invaluable work during the whole operations of the 28th-30th June 1918. He was in charge of Battalion signalling arrangements, which he carried out with exceptional judgment and fearlessness. Under the heaviest artillery and machine-gun fire throughout the day, he displayed the greatest courage, resourcefulness and devotion to duty in repairing broken lines, and inspired his men to similar efforts. It was thus, mainly through his efforts, that communications were maintained with companies during critical stages of the operations.

No. 5142.   Pte. EDWARD MEALING.

As a Battalion runner did splendid work throughout the operations on the 28th-30th June 1918, continually carrying messages to the front line through heavily shelled areas. He also took up a Lewis gun to the front line when one had been knocked out through heavy machine-gun fire. His fearlessness and devotion were magnificent.

No. 10024.   Cpl. HARRY COLLETT.

During the operations on the 28th-30th June 1918, was in charge of ten ration trucks, when he came under heavy artillery and machine-gun fire consequent to an S.O.S. signal. Regardless of danger, he displayed wonderful leadership in keeping both men and animals in hand when a stampede seemed imminent. He personally selected cover for each animal, and later led them forward again. He showed the greatest coolness and judgment under most trying conditions. He had previously displayed great resourcefulness and devotion to duty during an unbroken record of service since landing with the original Expeditionary Force.

No. 17539.   Pte. ARTHUR WILLIAM BAILEY.

As a signaller during the operations on the 28th-30th June 1918, did splendid work in repairing the lines which were continually broken by shell fire. It was through his devotion to duty, carried out under heavy fire, that communication was maintained with companies.

He had on many previous occasions done similar good work.

No. 240737.   Cpl. WILLIAM CARTER.

During the operations on the 27th, 28th and 29th June 1918, led his section forward with the utmost gallantry during the advance, and on reaching objective showed great skill and coolness during consolidation under heavy fire.

No. 5720.   Pte. WILLIAM HEATH.

During the operations on the 28th, 29th and 30th June 1918, took charge of two squads of stretcher-bearers and with these he worked continuously, carrying back wounded through heavily shelled areas. When he had finished carrying wounded he took back all the dead he could find.

No. 23127.   Sergt. GEORGE NORMAN.

During the operations on the 28th, 29th and 30th June 1918, found the German dug-outs full of machine gunners who were getting their guns ready for action. He immediately attacked these men, and by his initiative and promptness undoubtedly saved many lives. As platoon sergeant he showed great courage and coolness throughout the action.

No. 20052.   Pte. JEREMIAH WEBSTER.

Whilst under heavy shell fire, during the operations of the 28th-30th June 1918, seeing two of the enemy checking the advance of the Battalion on our left (2nd K.O.S.B.) with a machine gun, rushed forward, shot the two gunners, and captured the gun.

No. 30997.   Sergt. FREDERICK KICK.

Throughout the operations on the 28th-30th June 1918, showed great coolness and courage under fire, and did splendid bayonet work, mopping up a party of enemy machine gunners.

No. 9477.   Pte. WILLIAM PATEY.

With Sergt. Kick was responsible for mopping up a nest of enemy machine gunners. He showed great initiative by bringing his Lewis gun to bear, killing several of the enemy. His action undoubtedly saved many casualties.

No. 16014.   Cpl. FREDERICK GARROD.

During the operations on the 28th-30th June 1918, set a fine example to his Lewis-gun team, of whom he had splendid control. After the objective had been gained, he went forward under heavy fire to final objective and brought back most valuable information to his O.C. Company.

No. 16014.   L.-Sergt. FREDERICK GARROD.

Was conspicuous for great devotion to duty in subsequent operations to the above.

Lieut. ALBERT EDWARD JOHN BURDEN.

During the operations on the 28th-30th June 1918, led his platoon forward with conspicuous gallantry to the final objec-

tive. He set a fine example to his men, himself killing several
of the enemy. Later, when all the officers in his company
had become casualties, he took command of the company and
organised the consolidation with great coolness under heavy
enemy machine-gun fire. His conduct throughout the operations was magnificent.

2/Lieut. WILLIAM JOHN CHARLES OUZMAN.

During the operations on the 28th-30th June 1918, controlled
his platoon with the utmost coolness, and set a fine example
of dash and courage. On reaching the final objective, after
his Company Commander had been killed and all the other
officers had become casualties, he took command of the company which he reorganised under fire from enemy machine guns
and snipers. Later, when his trenches were being heavily
shelled, he walked about on top, regardless of danger, joking
with his men and keeping their spirits up by his cheerfulness.

2/Lieut. FRANK CORKE.

During the operations on the 28th-30th June 1918, after the
final objective had been taken, went forward through heavily
shelled areas and did a most valuable reconnaissance. Later,
when Battalion H.Q. was being heavily shelled, he set a fine
example of coolness, helping with the wounded. He showed
conspicuous courage and devotion to duty throughout the
operations.

This officer had twice previously been specially noted for
most excellent work.

Lieut. (Acting-Capt.) ROBERT BROWN.

When Battalion H.Q. was being heavily shelled, during
the operations on the 28th-30th June 1918, set a fine example
of coolness and courage, assisting the wounded, and himself
moving several wounded men to a safer part of the trench.
Later he twice went forward through heavily shelled areas to
check the Battalion dumps, at the same time bringing back
valuable information on the general situation.

2/Lieut. JOHN RESTARICK GARBUTT.

Went forward with three sections carrying ammunition and entrenching tools to the forward companies, during the operations on the 28th-30th June 1918.

He led his party through the enemy barrage with the utmost coolness, showing a fine contempt for personal danger. He arrived within three minutes of the final objective being gained, which greatly assisted the consolidation. He then led his men back through the barrage and rejoined his company in reserve.

Lieut. WILLIAM FREDERICK WHITFIELD.

During the operations on the 28th-30th June 1918, went forward with three sections carrying ammunition and entrenching tools to the forward companies. He led his party forward through the enemy barrage with great gallantry, and arrived within three minutes of the objective being gained. He remained with one of the forward companies, who had lost nearly all its officers, and was of the greatest assistance in organising the consolidation under considerable fire from enemy machine guns and snipers. When this was completed he rejoined his company in reserve.

No. 20087. L.-Cpl. FREDERICK FLINT.

During the operations on the 28th, 29th and 30th June 1918, led his section to the final objective with the utmost gallantry. himself accounting for many of the enemy with the bayonet, He set a fine example throughout the operations.

No. 31115. Pte. HERBERT STANLEY FIELD.

As No. 1 of a Lewis-gun section, during the operations on the 28th-30th June 1918, led his section forward most gallantly. On reaching the final objective he went forward with his gun, and by skilful handling, under fire from enemy machine guns and snipers, he accounted for a number of the enemy. He set a fine example throughout the operations.

No. 4263.   Pte. RICHARD ARTHUR HANSCOMBE.

During the operation of the 28th-30th June 1918, when all the company runners had become casualties, repeatedly took messages to Battalion H.Q. under heavy shell fire. His fearless conduct and fine sense of duty set a fine example to all.

No. 950.   Pte. PATRICK JACK CRONIN.

As a company signaller, during the operations of the 28th-30th June 1918, worked exceptionally hard. He continually went out under heavy shell fire to find and mend lines. By his fearless conduct and high sense of duty, he was responsible for the maintenance of communication with Battalion H.Q. throughout the operations.

No. 5782.   L.-Cpl. JOHN GABRIEL.

During the operations on the 28th-30th June 1918, was in charge of the company stretcher-bearers, and set a splendid example in organising the immediate removal of the wounded, whilst the attack was still in progress. He made repeated journeys under shell fire to the dressing station, and his marked coolness and judgment was undoubtedly the cause of the safety of many seriously wounded men.

Lieut. CHARLES EARL FALLET, U.S.R. (Attd. R.A.M.C.).

Was conspicuous for continuous good work and devotion to duty.

Capt. (Acting-Major) JACK KAY.

Was noted for continuous good work and devotion to duty.

PART VIII

August 1918

BATTLE OF BAPAUME AND GOUZEAUCOURT

No. 205707.   Sergt. ELIJAH JAMES SMITH.

Was acting C.S.M. of his company on the 24th August 1918. All officers of his company having become casualties, he took over command, chose the ground for consolidation, and re-organised and filled with renewed vigour the men of his company who had wavered when they saw their company commander fall.   He organised the company under heavy shell fire and, by his splendid example, the company successfully accomplished their share in the attack.   On the 29th of August he led his company successfully in a minor attack, securing the flank of the Battalion, and eventually brought the company out of action with the minimum of loss.   His courage and resolution, initiative and energy were of the greatest possible value.

No. 20293.   Pte. GEORGE WELDRAKE, *alias* No. 201212.   Pte. GEORGE WILSON.

Volunteered for a daylight patrol on the 24th August 1918 after the capture of Irles.   He proceeded about 400 yards in advance when he saw enemy emerging from a shell hole.   He fired on these in spite of the fact that other enemy threw hand grenades at him.   Four machine guns then opened on him at short range, but he covered the withdrawal of his spare scout. He then again went forward, firing from cover, and was instrumental in forcing the enemy to withdraw.   He killed several of the enemy, and by his accurate shooting caused the machine guns to cease fire, and the remainder of his section were, by his action, enabled to go forward and seize the position and machine guns.

No. 19151.   Sergt. CLARENCE WHITE.

On the 23rd and 24th August 1918 behaved with the utmost gallantry.   On the 23rd, seeing that two leading platoons were losing direction, he collected the company signallers and runners and led them fearlessly through the northern outskirts of the village of Irles, and thence to the high ground east-ward, which was the objective.   Having secured the right flank of his company, he then walked down the line under heavy machine-gun fire and indicated to the sections the best places for consolidation.   On the 24th, he was conspicuous when further adjustments in the line were being made, and, through the whole of a successful operation, was of the utmost assistance to his company commander.

No. 30961.   Pte. FREDERICK GARD.

On reaching the objective of his company took back a dis-position message to Battalion H.Q. through a heavy machine gun and shell barrage.   On his way back he met an armed German and took him prisoner.   On the 24th August in day-light, Pte. Gard volunteered to take another important message to B.H.Q., although he knew he was under observation.   He succeeded in getting through safely with the message and returned at once over the open, in the face of intense machine-gun fire, with a reply for his company commander.   This message was of the greatest importance, and failure to deliver it would have jeopardised the success of the operation.

No. 10247.   Sergt. ALFRED THOMAS GILBERT.

On the 23rd August commanded a platoon in the attack on Irles.   Realising the seriousness of a large gap which he noticed to exist in the attacking line, he changed his direction and led his platoon to a flank in the face of heavy machine-gun and rifle fire.   He then cleared an enemy trench, taking several prisoners and an enemy machine gun which was in position to enfilade the attacking line.   His immediate grasp of a serious situation, and his own personal courage and example, inspired his men and saved, what threatened to be, a most dangerous situation.

No. 4041.   Cpl. GEORGE WILLIAM HARRIS.

Displayed great initiative and courage in dealing with an
enemy machine-gun post which enfiladed the attacking line of
the Battalion on 23rd August 1918. He led his section to a flank,
and under cover of fire from his Lewis-gun section he rushed at
the head of the remainder of his men and took the enemy
machine gun, killing the team. The situation demanded
initiative and promptness of action, and this N.C.O., by his
own personal courage and leadership, dealt with it in a most
admirable manner.

No. 485.   Sergt. ERNEST PAGE.

Was Acting-Sergt.-Major of his company. After his company
commander was wounded and the objective was taken he
assisted in reorganising the company. Throughout the whole
operation he showed great coolness and the greatest bravery
under heavy machine-gun fire. This N.C.O. had been wounded
five times during the campaign and had always shown great
coolness and absolute contempt for danger.

No. 11467.   Pte. HAROLD SAXBY.

On 23rd August 1918 worked his way through the village
of Irles with his Lewis gun and put out of action two enemy
machine guns which were holding up the advance of his
company.

On 29th August he used his gun with the greatest effect on
the extreme flank of the Battalion. His action on that day
ensured a successful advance to the objective of the right flank
of his Battalion and the left flank of the Battalion on his right.
His action was particularly noteworthy as, at the time, his
platoon had no officer or N.C.O. and only three men remained
of the Lewis-gun team.

No. 11679.   Pte. CHARLES CHRISTOPHER NORRIS.

On the 29th August 1918, though not himself a Lewis gunner,
when the number one of a Lewis-gun section became a casualty

immediately took charge of the gun, led the section on to the objective, inflicting heavy casualties upon the enemy. He then personally superintended the consolidation of the captured ground. He set a magnificent example to all ranks.

No. 5723. Pte. JOSEPH COWELL.

On the 29th August 1918, as platoon runner, advanced with his platoon to the attack in support of another company which had lost all its officers. The platoon sergeant becoming a casualty before reaching the objective, Pte. Cowell assumed command of the platoon on the extreme right of his Battalion. He led his men forward under complete control and operated his one remaining Lewis gun most successfully in covering the advance. He established touch with the Battalion on his right and then superintended the consolidation of a line of shell holes in touch with the troops on his right and left. On the morning of the 30th August on being relieved, he brought his men out with only one further casualty through a shell-swept area. His conduct throughout was magnificent. He inspired all men to expend themselves to the utmost.

No. 23253. Cpl. (Acting-Sergt.) GEORGE GOULD.

Displayed great gallantry in bringing his platoon Lewis guns into action when the objective had been reached. He personally rushed a machine-gun position under heavy fire, and captured the gun, taking several prisoners. He displayed great gallantry and coolness throughout the whole operation, and his example was of the greatest value to all ranks.

No. 24335. Pte. THOMAS MASTERS.

As No. 1 of a Lewis-gun section throughout the actions on the 23rd and 29th August 1918, led his section with the greatest determination and success. On the 29th August he succeeded in dispersing an enemy trench-mortar team which had formed up to fire on the advancing troops. He killed several of the enemy and took the gun.

No. 20118.   Pte. ARTHUR POUNTAIN.

Throughout the whole of the attack on August 29th, under heavy machine-gun fire from ground and aeroplane, conveyed messages from the front line to Battalion H.Q. with the utmost disregard for danger.   On the Battalion being relieved during a very dark night, he volunteered to go out to search for a relieving platoon which was lost.   He succeeded in finding this platoon just as it was approaching the enemy position, and led it safely back to the relief of the platoon then in position.

No. 11236.   Pte. VICTOR HORACE MILLS.

The leaders of two sections having become casualties, took command of them and led them in such a way as to secure the left flank of his company and Battalion.   Under heavy machine-gun fire he led the men on to the objective and personally superintended its consolidation, with complete disregard of personal danger.

No. 31255.   Pte. WILLIAM LE PETIT.

A patrol which had been sent forward on the 29th August, came under heavy machine-gun fire and two men were wounded.   Pte. Petit left his position and picked up the men who were wounded and carried them back to a position of safety in spite of heavy machine-gun and rifle fire.

No. 21105.   L.-Cpl. JOHN TOLHURST.

Led his Lewis-gun section into action, and, after his No. 1 had become a casualty, acted as No. 1.   Although under heavy machine-gun fire, he took up successive positions, eventually silencing an enemy machine gun and killing the team.   His action forced the enemy to retire.   Throughout the attack he showed the greatest initiative in leading his section, although he himself was wounded.

No. 17944.   Pte. (Acting-Corpl.) JOHN OTWAY.

Took up successive positions with his Lewis gun, eventually overlooking a German strong point from which several machine

guns were causing casualties to the Battalion. Getting his gun
into position, he caused the enemy to evacuate the position,
leaving the machine gun behind. Throughout the action he
led his section with the utmost gallantry.

No. 10567. Pte. JAMES LARKING.

On the 23rd August 1918 went out single-handed and captured three enemy snipers who had been causing casualties to
his company. He also secured one machine gun, killing the
team.

No. 20688. L.-Cpl. HERBERT SINGER.

During operations on the 23rd inst. took command of his
platoon when his platoon officer and sergeant had become
casualties. Through heavy enfilade machine-gun fire he led
his platoon to the objective, which he successfully consolidated.

No. 31151. Pte. JAMES THOMAS FIELD.

On the 29th August a platoon of a relieving unit failing to
arrive, this man volunteered to go out and find the missing
platoon, in spite of intense enfilade shell and machine-gun fire.
He succeeded in finding the platoon, and guided it to its correct
position. When he found it, it was within twenty yards of
the enemy line.

No. 24106. Pte. ERNEST WILLIAM BIFFEN.

On 23rd August 1918, as platoon runner, did excellent work
throughout the attack. In the initial stages, in spite of heavy
machine-gun fire, he got through with his messages with the
least possible delay. At one time when conveying a message
to his Company Commander he found two sections which had
lost direction. He led them to selected positions, thereby
enabling his Platoon Commander to fill a gap on the flank.
Throughout the action he showed the greatest contempt for
danger and the utmost devotion to duty.

No. 31164.   Pte. HOBAN.

On the 23rd August this man rushed forward with a Lewis゛ gun and took up a position commanding a sunken road, from which enemy machine guns were causing casualties. His action caused the enemy to evacuate the position and take cover in dug-outs, where he kept them until they were made prisoners by the mopping-up party. His action saved many casualties.

No. 23271.   Pte. (Acting-Cpl.) WILLIAM PIGGOTT.

During the attack on 23rd August, in spite of heavy machine-gun fire, he took up a position with his Lewis gun commanding a sunken road. His accurate fire caused many casualties to the enemy, and caused the remainder of the machine-gun team to surrender, the machine gun being afterwards taken.

No. 242121.   Pte. BURLEY.

On 23rd August 1918, pushed forward through the village of Irles with one other man, and succeeded in capturing an enemy machine gun, its team, and a number of the enemy. He had always displayed the greatest bravery and disregard of personal danger.

No. 240022.   L.-Sergt. BENJAMIN BLACKBURN.

On 23rd August 1918, when his platoon officer had become a casualty, led his platoon with the greatest gallantry and secured the objective. He consolidated the line of his platoon under heavy enfilade machine-gun fire. His efforts during the action had the result of securing the right flank of the attack, and his securing of high ground materially assisted in the capture of Miraumont.

Lieut. (Acting-Capt.) E. J. FULCHER.

Whilst in command of a support company near Bapaume on 29th August 1918, finding that all the officers of an attacking company had become casualties, and that the attack was

wavering, pushed up a platoon of fresh troops and urged the
line up to the objective, which, by his action, was successfully
gained and consolidated. His initiative and energy restored
a very ticklish situation, and secured the flank for a further
advance which took place, and was successful mainly through
his action.

2/Lieut. A. J. PURCHASE.

All other officers of the company being casualties, took command of the company and of elements of three other Battalions
on 24th August, securing a flank. On 29th August, in command of a company, he so led his command that he attained
his objective with the loss of one man, capturing thirty prisoners
and two machine guns, and accounting for many of the enemy
by his accurate fire control and direction. He had done con-
spicuously good work.

2/Lieut. PHILLIP LEVELIS-MARKE.

As Intelligence Officer was of the utmost value to the
Battalion. When all officers of a company had become
casualties he took command and reorganised the company,
refusing to be relieved until operations were concluded. A
most gallant officer, full of zeal and energy.

Lieut. C. S. MILFORD.

In command of the left company, performed a most important
operation in the taking of Irles. His courage and resolution
secured ground 1000 yards beyond the objective, organising a
defensive flank until touch could be secured. He captured
many machine guns and prisoners. Had it not been for this
officer's resolution (the troops had marched a long way before
deploying, and advanced straight to the attack) and determination in pushing on without hesitation, this most important
operation might have been a failure. Later, when asked by
the New Zealanders to assist their flank, he went personally
to superintend the operation, and in doing so was wounded.

x

Lieut. J. W. E. DARLOW.

Whilst in command of the support company in the attack
on Irles, noticing that gaps existed both in the centre and
on the flank, at once pushed forward platoons to fill these
gaps. During the night he visited all the front companies
and assisted in the consolidation, sending back to Battalion
H.Q. most valuable information. On the 24th, when the
Division on the right was observed to be attacking, he went
forward with a patrol and cleared up a gully which would have
held up the attack, capturing a trench mortar and nine of the
enemy.

This officer displayed powers of leadership and initiative
of a high order, and his personal example was of great
encouragement to tired troops and filled them with renewed
vigour.

2/Lieut. BURT SANSOM.

On the 23rd-24th August, whilst in command of a platoon
which was ordered to cover the right flank of the Battalion in
the high ground at Irles, cleared four sunken roads and
secured the flank. He personally, with his runner, rushed
two machine-gun posts and killed or captured the teams and
guns. His platoon captured three machine guns and forty
other ranks concealed in dug-outs. Afterwards he went
forward on patrol, and captured a 5.9 gun and two anti-tank
guns and several other prisoners. His personal example,
vigour and energy greatly aided the Battalion in securing this
valuable position.

Further, after this officer succeeded to command his company on 24th August—all senior officers having become
casualties—he led his company with the greatest success
during the remainder of the operations, particularly during
the attack on 29th August. He established the closest liaison
with the Battalion on his flank, and was instrumental in securing
the capture of a machine gun, and six of the enemy who were
enfilading the unit on his flank. He displayed great initiative
and devotion to duty.

No. 7718.   Sergt. THOMAS CHARLES SMITH.

On 27th September took charge of his company when all officers and the C.S.M. had become casualties. He led forward the company in face of heavy fire until it was impossible to advance any further. He then consolidated a line of posts which was held. His personal courage and disregard of danger were most marked.

No. 7734.   L.-Cpl. ERNEST DEGAVINO.

By skilful leadership and use of ground on 27th September 1918, when taking his Lewis gun team to fill a gap in the line, got his team within forty yards of the enemy trench, opened fire and put a Bosche gun out of action.

No. 31147.   L.-Sergt. JAMES REDLEY.

When his platoon commander and other senior N.C.O.'s had become casualties on 27th September, took charge of his platoon and admirably controlled the fire of the men, causing diminution in the enemy fire.

No. 30974.   Pte. GEORGE MEAD.

As No. 1 of a Lewis-gun team, kept up covering fire whilst the remaining men of his section were digging-in on the ground gained. His first gun being blown up, he salvaged another and put it into working order, and kept it in action in spite of heavy enemy machine-gun fire.

No. 31135.   Pte. FREDERICK GODDARD.

On 27th September, as a company signaller, under heavy machine-gun and shell fire, he ran out a wire for 200 yards to the advanced post of his company. His reel of wire being blown up, he returned for more. On his return journey he picked up an N.C.O. of his company who was wounded, and carried him back for 200 yards. He went out again, in spite of very heavy fire, with a stretcher, and with the aid of another man brought in an officer who was lying badly wounded in no-man's-land.

x *

No. 454.   Pte. ALFRED BODIE.

During operations on 27th September, in spite of heavy machine-gun and shell fire, several times traversed the ground between the advanced posts and the Battalion Command Post, with important messages and very clear information as to the situation.

No. 205707.   Sergt. ELIJAH JAMES SMITH.

When all the officers of his company and the C.S.M. had become casualties on 27th September, led the company forward into the attack with great gallantry. When held up he organised consolidation on the line gained and, after two runners had been hit in endeavouring to proceed to Battalion H.Q. to report on the situation, he himself went through a very heavy barrage, making on his arrival a very clear statement as to the situation. He immediately returned to his company, of which he remained in charge until relieved. His personal example and contempt for danger were the admiration of all ranks.

No. 10247.   Sergt. ALFRED THOMAS GILBERT.

On 27th September showed exceptional gallantry and devotion to duty. When the attack of his company was held up, he went forward alone under very heavy shell and machine-gun fire, and attempted to bomb the enemy out of the trench, which was the objective.

No. 5336.   Pte. JOHN LONSDALE.

On 27th September, as stretcher-bearer, showed conspicuous gallantry and devotion to duty in bringing in wounded for many hours, under very heavy enemy fire. His devotion to duty was undoubtedly the cause of saving many men from dying of their wounds. He displayed the greatest gallantry and the utmost disregard of danger.

No. 1538.   Pte. WILLIAM JOHN JUDGE.

Whilst acting as stretcher-bearer worked incessantly under exceedingly heavy artillery and machine-gun fire, moving about in the open to attend to wounded.   His action was the means of saving many lives.

No. 23271.   Cpl. WILLIAM PIGGOTT.

On 27th September 1918, although being wounded just after leaving his trench, continued to advance.   Wounded a second time in the face, he continued to lead his men, rallying them in the face of heavy machine-gun fire.   He led his section to within 20 yards of the enemy trench.   When bombed back by the enemy, he went forward on his own throwing bombs. When it became obvious that the attack had failed, he sent his men back singly to a position from which fire could be brought to bear on the enemy trench, he himself remaining, covering the movement of his men by throwing bombs, and by his accurate rifle fire.   Having covered the movement of his men, he then attempted to rejoin them, but was again hit and died.

No. 28509.   Pte. JAMES BURTON.

On 27th September, in spite of being wounded, advanced, discharging rifle grenades to cover the advance of his section. When he had expended all those immediately available, he returned to his trench through heavy machine-gun fire and brought up a further supply, which he continued to use with great skill and determination.

No. 29663.   Pte. CHARLES JAMES COLK.

Together with Pte. Burton worked as a rifle bomber, covering a Lewis-gun post.   They bombed a strong point in which were three enemy machine guns, which they put out of action.

No. 20120.   Pte. GEORGE MASON PURDY.

When in charge of the company stretcher-bearers, on 27th September, worked continuously for thirty hours, part of the time under heavy machine-gun fire. He got in many wounded men by daylight, and moved about in the open, in spite of machine-gun fire, dressing the wounds of those whom he was unable to move.

No. 8168.   C.S.M. HOWARD THOMAS HYLANDS.

On 27th September showed the greatest gallantry in assisting to organise the line when an attack had failed and the Battalion had suffered heavy casualties. He moved about in the open in spite of heavy enemy fire, encouraged the men to hold on to the ground gained. He had always consistently shown great power of leadership and personal courage.

No. 8832.   Pte. GEORGE VAUGHAN.

Showed the greatest gallantry in leading forward his section in face of heavy machine-gun fire. When unable to advance further, he formed an isolated post, and encouraged his men to hold on although heavily shelled. He twice went back to the Battalion Command Post through heavy machine-gun fire, bringing back valuable information as to the situation, and then immediately returned to his post, where he remained until he led his men forward to the objective on the following day.

No. 9992.   L.-Cpl. WILLIAM BOOTH.

On 27th September formed an isolated post in spite of heavy machine-gun fire. He was twice buried by explosions of enemy shell, but continued to consolidate the position he had chosen. He brought back valuable information to the Battalion Command Post, at the same time bringing in a wounded officer who was lying in no-man's-land. He returned to his post, carrying a supply of ammunition.

No. 202768.   Cpl. HAROLD CHRISTOPHER.

Took command of his platoon when its commander was wounded. Later, when a post of great importance on the flank of the Battalion had been blown in by heavy shelling, on his own initiative he took a patrol forward and re-established the post and remained there until the conclusion of operations.

No. 914.   Pte. BEVAN,   ⎫ were all noted for good
Lieut. A. J. CATHCART,   ⎬ work and conspicuous de-
No. 21109.   Sergt. J. F. WADE, ⎭ votion to duty.

NOTE TO APPENDIX

OWING to the lack of surviving officers to verify acts of bravery, the number of acts recorded in this Appendix for the years 1914 and 1915 are necessarily fewer in number than those in the later stages of the War, when a record was kept at Battalion Headquarters.

The following names, however, appeared in the *London Gazette* as being mentioned in Sir John French's dispatches :

Lieut.-Col. A. MARTYN, commanding.
Major M. P. BUCKLE, D.S.O., senior Major.
Captain R. M. G. TULLOCH.
Lieut. G. B. LEGARD, Adjutant.
Sergeant-Major H. S. DOE.
Company Sergeant-Major W. PENNY.
Sergeant J. POWELL.
Sergeant J. SAWARD.
L.-Cpl. J. RYAN.
Pte. G. BIGGS.
Major P. ROBINSON.
Lieut. P. F. WILBERFORCE-BELL.
Captain H. D. BUCHANAN-DUNLOP.

INDEX

37153968R00234

Printed in Great Britain
by Amazon